POCKET
ENCYCLOPEDIA

GARDEN PLANNING

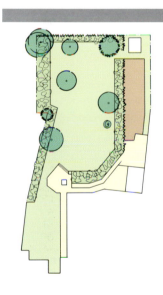

POCKET
ENCYCLOPEDIA

GARDEN
PLANNING

Contributing editor

John Brookes

DORLING KINDERSLEY
London • New York • Sydney • Moscow
www.dk.com

DK

A DORLING KINDERSLEY BOOK

www.dk.com

First published in Great Britain in 1992
by Dorling Kindersley Limited,
9 Henrietta Street, London WC2E 8PS

Designed by COOPER WILSON DESIGN,
Studio Two, The Ivories, Northampton Street,
Islington, London N1 2HY

Edited by Jane Rollason

A CIP catalogue record for this book is available
from the British Library

ISBN 0-86318-834-6

Printed in Singapore by Kyodo Printing (Co) Pte Ltd

CONTENTS

INTRODUCTION

The best gardens grow out of good design and planning. A successful garden is above all one that is appropriate – appropriate to surrounding buildings, to the landscape, whether rural or urban, and to its function, whether productive, decorative, or recreational. Gardens that are well made and individually styled usually work best both for their environment and for those who use them.

But the way you want to use your garden should determine how it evolves. Long before putting pencil to paper to draw up a plan, let alone putting spade to earth, ask yourself what you want your garden to do for you and your family.

Location is a major influence on design. The country garden, for example, is part of its surroundings in a way that a small urban plot can never be. It can contribute significantly to the look of the countryside. Creating and maintaining a country garden involves much more than just horticulture and recreation. It involves caring for a piece of the natural world – features such as old trees, ancient walls, streams, and ditches that may fall within your boundaries, but are part of a much wider network.

In an urban setting, on the other hand, a garden has a different function and is for people rather than plants and wildlife. It becomes an enjoyable and possibly stylish extension to your home rather than an interruption in the flow of the countryside.

Whatever style of garden you choose to work towards, the key to its eventual success is design – planning and styling your space to suit your way of life, the character of your home, and its surroundings.

An enchanting garden
A pleasing combination of foliage, form, and flower colour overlays a strong design pattern in this delightful and simple garden, right – the ideal formula, whatever or wherever the situation.

The evolution of garden planning

The original idea behind the garden was to provide a retreat from the overwhelming wildness of Nature. High walls and hedges enclosed ordered, formal layouts. Geometric pattern was of more interest than horticultural content. During the sixteenth and seventeenth centuries gardens began to escape their boundaries and invade the surrounding forests.

The influences of landscape painting from Italy and the romantic ideal of the life of the noble peasant fuelled a move towards more natural landscape gardening. Fashion dictated Palladian-style architecture surrounded by parkland. Streams became lakes and views were moulded by mass planting of indigenous trees. Towards the end of the eighteenth century, as foreign plant material was beginning to be brought back from the empire, the idea of decorative planting began to evolve.

Alongside the gardens of the great landowners, the cottage garden tradition continued. Here plants were grown for culinary and medicinal purposes. Planning was haphazard and the garden was made to work.

The seventeenth-century enclosed garden
Box-edged beds enclosing a limited palette of decorative garden plants arranged geometrically were used to create pattern in the small seventeenth-century garden. This formal layout, based on designs from Holland, France, and Italy, was an expression of a desire to bring Nature under control.

The eighteenth-century landscape garden
The rolling "improved" landscape of the eighteenth-century parkland garden was the antithesis of the introspective, protected seventeenth-century garden. Armies of manual labourers were brought in to re-mould slopes, shape lakes, plant out indigenous trees in carefully planned groups, and punctuate the whole with decorative classical incidents, such as temples and statuary.

The effects of industrialization

After the social upheaval of the Industrial Revolution in nineteenth-century Britain, the emerging middle class sought to copy grander gardens on a reduced scale. The gardens of middle class villa homes were the earliest suburbs. The labouring classes gardened too, though still on the cottage garden principle.

A new scientific approach to the world in the Victorian era made the botanic garden fashionable. The barriers went up again to exclude the indigenous countryside, and newly introduced exotic species were grown within, creating gardens alien to their surroundings. Rhododendrons and camellias were imported and planted widely, plants that are now considered altogether native in many parts of Britain.

Return to the rural idyll

Again the pendulum swung around the turn of the twentieth century, as the Arts and Crafts movement idealized the traditional skills and materials of the pre-industrial world. The twentieth-century garden featured shrub and perennial material more appropriate to its surroundings than the exotica of the

The nineteenth-century Victorian garden
A style called "gardenesque" epitomized the Victorian look. Exotic trees such as the monkey puzzle (Araucaria araucana) *were sited amidst spectacularly colourful and intricate arrangements of carpet bedding. The conservatory housed a further collection of exotics too tender for the winter frosts of the outdoor climate.*

Victorian garden. The enclosed garden was rustic but medieval, rather than sympathetic with the landscape of which it was a part.

Developments in America

It was not until the mid-twentieth century, however, that the form of garden layout was radically changed, starting in the sunny climate of California. The early Californian garden was of Spanish origin – a garden of shaded patios and cooling fountains based on the famed Moorish gardens of southern Spain. To this was added the swimming pool, limited planting dictated by the climate, and Japanese design influences.

The suburban plot

In the British Isles, after the Second World War, a major stimulus to design was the need to provide small, serviceable gardens for young growing families on the new housing developments of the sixties and seventies. The often mundane results, despite good planning, arose from the standardization of materials. The rise of the ubiquitous garden centre has brought about the parallel demise of specialist growers, with their expert knowledge and their more discerning range of plant material. The suburban plot is depressingly similar whatever its location.

New perspectives

At this point we should perhaps question our current garden thinking. Are we right to perpetuate the horticultural approach as a suburban ideal, with its neat, twice-weekly mown lawns? What is wrong with longer, rougher grass, with plantings of subjects more naturally suited to their surroundings? We have been conditioned to the merits of perfected artificiality and seek horticultural excellence as the only yardstick of a garden's being, when the aspiration of an average gardener's personal paradise is a much more relaxed place. Not to say that the lawn has had its day, but that we should at least consider the alternatives.

The early twentieth-century garden
By the turn of the twentieth century, garden styling had become more rural, although harking back to medieval times in its fondness for the garden as a closed room. Planting was full and flowery, and a strong sense of tradition came through the hard materials used for walls, paving, gates, and doors, all finished to an exacting level of craftsmanship. Sissinghurst in Kent and Hidcote Manor in Gloucestershire, English models for the country garden worldwide, were made in this era, when both labour and land were cheap.

· CHAPTER ONE ·

CHOOSING A GARDEN STYLE

What is "style" in a garden? An outside
space that displays a clarity of purpose
derived from an aesthetically pleasing
arrangement of shapes and patterns.
But how do you relate abstract concepts
of style to the plot of land behind your
house? After all, there are so many
practical considerations to take into
account, for example location, existing
boundaries, the style of your home, and
how you want to use the space.
The art lies in treating each element of
your garden – walls, furniture, steps, or
pergola – as part of a single design.
Always consider how one relates to
another in terms of colour, shape,
texture, and function, and in terms of your
overall plan. A piecemeal approach, with
haphazard features and ill-considered
materials, tends to have unstylish results.
The next few pages consider those factors
that will determine the most appropriate
style for your garden – its location,
climate, aspect, soil type, and function. A
visual resource of garden styles and ideas
follows, designed to provide inspiration, to
be plundered, to be adapted, to help you
choose your own unique style.

Stylish transition
*A carefully considered design elegantly realized.
Sympathetic materials extend the kitchen into an
outdoor eating area. Generous and dramatic planting
using strong form and subtle colour clothe the
transition from house to garden.*

Location

Gardens with similar layouts but in separate locations can feel completely different. An enclosed town garden, for example, will seem much smaller than the same size plot in a more rural open setting.

In town
The very fact that you have a private, outside space within a tight urban mass makes the town garden so attractive to use in the summer and to look at throughout the rest of the year, helping you to keep in touch with the natural environment. Planning here will be influenced by the proximity and feel of the surrounding buildings and by how much the garden is overlooked by neighbouring houses.

Lack of light throughout the year is among the hazards of the walled town garden, making plants reach upwards and inwards to gain the most from it. Shade might come from nearby buildings or an overhanging or tall tree in a neighbouring garden. On the other hand, the walled garden can be a sun trap and become far too hot at certain times.

Bearing these factors in mind, the design for an enclosed town garden should be simple, with the object of making an outside room furnished with permanent sculptural groupings of plants. Colourful annuals can be grouped and arranged in containers to provide contrast. You might also consider an overhead canopy, perhaps a pergola, to provide some seclusion. The character of the town garden should be quite different from that of gardens in other situations and should not be a reduced version of the country model.

In the suburbs
The larger suburban garden has greater demands made on it. It may need to accommodate the growing family. Open spaces will be used for children's play. Space will be needed for vegetables to supplement the dinner table. While the design of the town garden anticipates passive enjoyment, the suburban family garden design should provide for more active use with large terraced areas for play and entertainment. Initial planting in a suburban garden may be limited to screening for privacy, and only as the children grow up will it come to include more specialized decorative groups.

In the country
The whole outlook on rural gardening is now more relaxed, with a move towards creating a more manageable piece of land. The area of garden needing moderate maintenance may be restricted to the house surround, with alternative and less demanding treatments for the garden beyond.

In some rural settings the surrounding landscape, whether open moorland or cultivated fields, can be borrowed both to

Urban setting
A crisply styled town garden, designed as an extension of the house for the urban family to use and enjoy. Paving to echo the flooring in the kitchen, neat gravel surfacing, carefully chosen and sited evergreens, and a decorative sculptural feature – the design requirements and solutions of an urban plot.

enlarge the apparent size of your plot and to provide inspiration for the garden style. Some landscapes have such strong qualities that they cannot be denied in gardens located within them. Character might lie in ground conformation or extreme soil type which produces a particular vegetation, surrounding woodland, or visually strong local materials such as stone or slate. Any of these strong, natural characteristics has to be used within the concept of the garden. Imported, substitute forms will seem trivial.

In other areas the landscape around will have quieter charms that are equally worthwhile and attractive. Again your garden style can blend and harmonize with what surrounds it.

Rural location
This cottage garden, right, with its apparently casual planting, epitomizes relaxed rural gardening, finding just the right balance between cultivated garden and natural countryside. Self-seeded Alchemilla mollis, *cranesbills, and euphorbia merge and cascade onto old stone paving.*

Climate

Climate and weather are major influences on the character of a location. They will have moulded the vernacular building style through past centuries and walls, paths, and fences will traditionally have been made from locally available wood and stone. Indigenous herbage will have been used for hedging and infills, lending gardens a particularly local feel.

When considering what your local climate will support horticulturally, you can do no better than to look and see what is supported naturally and in agriculture, in rural and suburban situations, and of course what is growing in other gardens. The main climatic factors that influence plant growth in an area are its altitude and the intensity and length of

Hot climate garden
Desert sun and lack of rain can produce striking examples of gardens moulded by climate. Architecture and choice of plants combine characteristically in this hot climate garden, right.

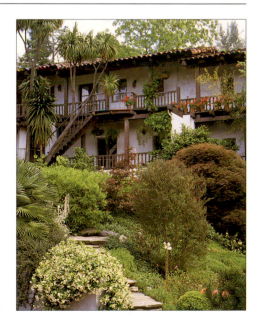

its winters. Horticultural possibilities can also be greatly affected by wind. Wind off the sea, for example, will be salt-laden up to 8km (5 miles) from the coast. The range of plants that can stand its full blast is quite small.

Climatic conditions can vary considerably from garden to garden. Trees and buildings can funnel prevailing winds and cause extensive damage, although open fences or hedges can be sited to counter the force of the wind by filtering away its strength. A solid barrier such as a wall, which in other circumstances can do so much to promote plant growth by retaining the sun's heat, in the wrong place can simply increase wind turbulence and be inappropriate as a wind break.

Cold temperate garden
*Boxwood (*Buxus *sp.) stands the coldest New England winter and is a traditional garden element, here planted with maple (*Acer *sp.), right.*

THE SUN'S PATH

Surrounding buildings or trees might inhibit the number of sunlight hours a garden receives. When the sun rides high over obstacles in the summer months, there will probably be more than enough light even if bright sunshine is limited to only part of the day. But in the winter when the sun is lower in the sky, direct sunlight might not reach the garden for months on end.

In this walled garden only the central part is guaranteed direct sunlight all year round. The low arc of the sun dramatically increases the areas of shade through the day.

☐ Winter shade
■ Summer shade

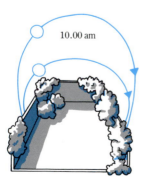

10.00 am

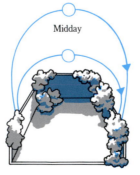

Midday

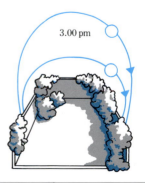

3.00 pm

FROST PATTERNS

Homes and gardens close to one another but at different heights, perhaps one on a hill and one on a valley bottom, will experience considerable differences in temperature in summer due to wind and in winter due to frost. Frost is an important factor to take account of. Cold air flows downhill like water into valley floors and basins, where it lies. If your garden happens to be in the way, any solid barrier will trap the cold. It is possible, however, to deflect the flow of cold air with carefully planned planting.

Gardens in valleys or otherwise below hills are likely to be in frost pockets, causing their micro-climates to be surprisingly cold and influencing plant choice. Spring-flowering fruit trees, for example, might not be suitable. Frost will remain in a frost pocket until dispersed by wind or sun.

Frost trap

Site and aspect

Acquiring a new garden site can be an exciting part of moving home. You may have to adapt what you have inherited from the previous owners or start from scratch with a completely new site.

Older, established gardens will have existing vegetation with which to work. Small urban areas, including basement or rooftop areas, will have surrounding walls to establish the character of the garden, and with luck a little vegetation too. A heap of builder's rubble may have attractive features beneath, which you can incorporate into your plan. Look, for example, for a change of level, distant views, or the shape of a neighbouring tree in relation to your own plot.

The aspect of a house will rarely influence your choice of home but it will have a significant effect on the type of garden that you can make. The ideal aspect in much of the northern hemisphere is open to the south-west, gaining full benefit from long summer days. A sunny, south-facing frontage gives a shady, north-facing rear garden, and while many plants will grow in the shade, your terrace will have to be a distance from the house if you want to sit in the sun. In hot climates, you might want an area of reliable shade near to the house.

There are very few aspects that present insuperable problems to garden planning, but frequently too little consideration leads to a plan which makes the garden difficult to live with. Tall planting or building in the line of the

sun's regular path, for example, can cast shadows which restrict plant growth and give the garden a cold feel. A garden on a slope may allow a good view, but if you want to work the land, you may need retaining walls to create level areas. A site which falls towards the house may produce drainage difficulties, especially in winter.

CONSIDERING ASPECT

The houses illustrated here have opposite aspects – the one with house front facing south giving a north-facing garden, and the one with house front facing north giving a south-facing garden. A rear seating area has been well positioned in each garden to catch the sun.

House front facing south

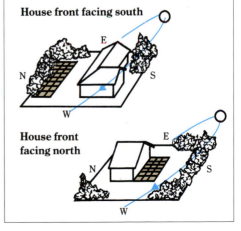

House front facing north

Soil

The look of any landscape depends on its underlying geology. Substrata of gravel, clay, or rock condition both the texture and mineral content of the surface topsoil and determine its alkalinity or acidity. The nature of the topsoil in turn supports a natural vegetation that has allowed a certain type of agriculture or forestry to develop. Traditional local building to house the people working on the land was constructed using available materials – stone or brick, flint or wood – marking out distinctive regional styles.

The type of soil which you inherit, if any at all, will thus affect the character of the garden too, for certain plants prefer an acid soil, others a more chalky or alkaline one. The consistency of the soil will either allow it to warm quickly, encouraging early spring growth, or cause it to remain cold and sticky for longer, with slower plant growth.

All too often a new site has a meagre layer of topsoil, perhaps only a dusting over clay compressed by building work. Check this out before you move to a new property – the removal of clay and its replacement with more fertile topsoil can be expensive, and only possible where there is easy access to the land for earth-moving machinery.

Soil types

Most soils will grow most plants. Only extreme soil types may cause problems. Soil condition depends on texture, and the texture in turn is determined by the size and consistency of the

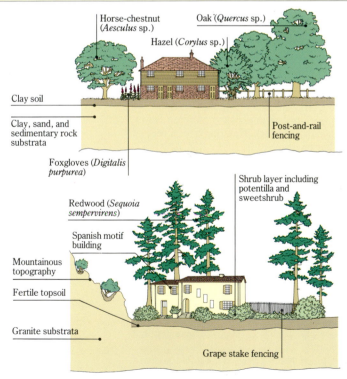

EXAMPLES OF THE INFLUENCE OF GEOLOGY

South of England
Over the clays of the weald of southern England, the indigenous vegetation includes oaks, chestnuts, and hazels. Traditional vernacular building is constructed of locally made bricks and tiles, and often has oak weatherboarding. Post-and-rail fencing is also of oak or oak and chestnut.

Horse-chestnut (*Aesculus* sp.)
Oak (*Quercus* sp.)
Hazel (*Corylus* sp.)
Clay soil
Clay, sand, and sedimentary rock substrata
Post-and-rail fencing
Foxgloves (*Digitalis purpurea*)

California, USA
The varied topography of California includes rich soils over hard, igneous rock substrata. Local building might well be in Spanish style, utilizing indigenous redwoods, especially for garden decks and grape stake fencing. Surrounding hillsides retain pockets of soil between barren slopes and rock outcrops.

Redwood (*Sequoia sempervirens*)
Shrub layer including potentilla and sweetshrub
Spanish motif building
Mountainous topography
Fertile topsoil
Granite substrata
Grape stake fencing

RECOGNIZING SOIL TYPE FROM NATURAL VEGETATION

Although soil type can be modified by the location of a site, certain types of plant are attracted to and flourish in certain types of soil. In many parts of Europe, for example, the rhododendron growing is a sure sign of an acid soil, while forms of viburnum usually indicate chalky, alkaline soils. Birch (*Betula* sp.), pine (*Pinus* sp.), gorse (*Ulex europaeus*), and broom (*Genista* sp.) usually indicate a light, shady, and often acid soil.

Plants that have seeded themselves in a garden plot, therefore, can give you a good idea of the soil type you will inherit with your plot. Willow herb or fireweed (*Epilobium* sp.), for instance, grows in a fertile, moist soil, as does the nettle. Heaths and heathers are standard vegetation on acid soils, which are usually sandy or peaty and poor. While ferns are adaptable plants and can be found growing on wet and dry soils, they mostly indicate a heavy, damp soil, suggesting clay. A sure indicator of a wet soil is the buttercup (*Ranunculus* sp.), which is often seen in low-lying garden corners and across poorly drained lawns. An alkaline, chalky soil is often the chosen home of Dog's mercury (*Mercurialis perennis*), a prolific colonizer of sunny or shady areas.

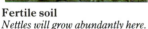

Fertile soil
Nettles will grow abundantly here.

Heavy, clay soil
Ferns are a good indicator of clay.

Poor, acid soil
Heathers thrive on poor, acid soil.

particles that make it up, and the proportion of organic matter in it. A clay soil is composed of very small, tightly packed particles and retains moisture even in warm weather. It is often a cold and sticky soil, but if it does finally dry out in hot weather, it will crack. A sandy soil is composed of much larger particles. It will drain well and warm up quickly in spring, and is therefore known as a warm soil. The line between draining well and draining too quickly is a thin one. A soil that drains too quickly will be a poor one as all the nutrients normally held in solution around each soil particle will leach away. The ideal soil from the point of view of texture is a loam, consisting of a mixture of slightly more sand than clay particles, with a high organic content.

Improving your soil

Incorporating organic manure in a clay or sandy soil will improve its condition enormously, both by improving its texture and feeding the soil. The crumb-like consistency of well-rotted manure will bind together the particles of a loose, sandy soil or divide up the fine grains of a sticky, clay one. The bacteria it contains will activate either soil type to promote plant growth. You can test the organic content of your soil by examining it closely and running a handful through your fingers. Ideally it should be of a crumbly consistency, neither too spongy and sticky nor too dusty. It should look dark in colour and smell sweet.

The pH scale

Another test of soil type is its relative acidity or alkalinity, measured on a sliding scale, known as the pH scale (see p. 20). Plants grow in soils within the range of pH4.5 to pH7.5. A measurement between pH5.7 and pH6.7 is ideal for the majority of plants.

A chalky soil has a high calcium (alkaline) content and will have a high pH reading. It can be made more acid by adding heavy dressings of organic material, such as farmyard manure or compost. When adequately manured, a chalky soil will become quite fertile. An acid, peaty soil is at the other end of the pH scale.

Unlike other soils, peat is derived from plants and is therefore organic itself. A naturally occurring peaty soil will often need to be drained. It can be made more alkaline or "sweetened" by adding lime in the form of ground limestone. A dose of 2.25kg per 9m^2 (5 lb per 10 yd^2) will raise the pH between 0.5 and 0.75 of a point. Bought peat has usually been sterilized and contains little or no food value, but it will improve soil texture. In the UK you can test the pH value of your soil by submitting a sample to your county

horticultural station for analysis. Otherwise you can use a home testing kit, many types of which are readily available on the market.

It is one thing to improve the texture and drainage characteristics of your soil and make it suitable for healthy plant growth, but it is a wasteful process to spend much time and effort trying to change the soil type of your garden in order to grow a particular range of plants that is alien to your locality. You can always use containers to hold a special soil type for plants that are not happy in your local soil.

pH SCALE AND VALUES

The pH scale measures the alkaline or acid content of soil. Soil testing kits are available fairly cheaply. They assess the pH value of your soil simply and accurately by measuring the concentration of hydrogen particles in soil suspended in distilled water.

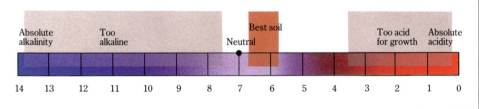

| Absolute alkalinity | | Too alkaline | | | | | Neutral | Best soil | | | | Too acid for growth | Absolute acidity |

| 14 | 13 | 12 | 11 | 10 | 9 | 8 | 7 | 6 | 5 | 4 | 3 | 2 | 1 | 0 |

Function

A key factor in working out a garden design is function. At an early stage, analyze your or your family's needs and recognize that needs evolve. If there are younger children in the family, the demands they make on the garden will change as they grow.

Necessities
Before thinking about the trees and shrubs you would like to include in your garden, consider the practical aspects of your outside living space. Think of rubbish storage and access to it, the compost heap, fuel storage, a clothes

Paved service area
Practicality demands hard surfaces around the kitchen door, but the effect can be softened by planting in containers, as right, on walls, or overhead.

drying area, and garden tools and machinery storage. All these areas will need to be serviced by hard, dry paving, preferably lit at night. Think about winter use as well as summer, and night as well as day. Some areas will need an electricity or water supply.

Kitchen produce

If you want a herb garden, it should ideally be near the kitchen. Consider carefully the size of any vegetable plot and how much time you can realistically devote to vegetable growing. Perhaps you should limit your crops to salad and soft fruit.

Design for your needs

Always remember that your own garden must be planned to satisfy you and your family, and not necessarily others. Slavish copying of another garden design may not be successful. It is up to the gardener to be his or her own designer. Looking closely at pictures and diagrams of other people's designs and ideas, like this open-air "room", below, designed mainly for eating and entertaining out of doors, can nevertheless be a wonderful source of inspiration.

The demands of play

Next consider recreational demands. Will children play in the garden, first perhaps in a sandpit, soon followed by ball games against any available wall? Planting in these areas will need to be limited for the time being. A barbecue space will be useful for summer eating and entertaining, and perhaps a further terrace for table tennis or lounging and sunbathing in the hot months of the year. The growing, prosperous family might also need a second garage space or somewhere to park a boat or caravan in the winter months.

Room to garden

If there is a gardening enthusiast in the family, think about room for gardening – a table for potting up, and perhaps a greenhouse or cold frame. As the children leave home, you might want to cultivate the land more. Gardening often remains an interest into retirement, and the level of maintenance involved can be increased or decreased according to available time and energy during this period.

National styles

Although garden styles are imported and exported around the world and very similar garden designs can be found on different continents, distinct national styles do exist and their characteristics can be identified. In America, for example, we might identify East Coast, West Coast, Southern, desert, and prairie looks. In Africa there is the tropical look and another version of the desert look, one which takes its flavour from the beaten red earth, native pots, and tough plants. The feel of any garden is closely linked to local styles of building and materials. Low, flat buildings create an open look, while tall, narrow buildings give an enclosed impression. Garden styles also reflect different ways of life and traditions. The traditional Japanese garden, for example, includes religious symbolism. As well as providing a cool retreat from the heat, the North African garden has a traditionally Islamic geometry and pattern.

Native vegetation and the quality of light affect overall impression too. Strong light from a sun high in the sky creates hard-edged, deep shadows, while a softer light throws a more warming glow.

Japanese sanctuary, left
An ordinary town garden is transformed into a serene and contemplative retreat. The ragged brick paving, bamboo fencing, and loosely laid gravel combine to create a gentle, abstract rhythm.

Functional style, below
Pattern and materials echo and complement the architecture of the house in this stylish German garden. Concrete squares boldly frame planting and pool features.

Mexican style, above
Strong architectural forms mirror strong natural ones. The cacti and succulents cast dramatic shadows on the adobe walls.

An Italian-style garden

A formal garden design in a classic Italianate style, fully integrated with the building around it. The central, water-filled courtyard is surrounded by a covered walkway, leading at one end to the reception hall.

The courtyard pattern is composed of four brick island beds, and square stepping stones symmetrically arranged around an urn-shaped fountain raised on a stone plinth. The bold, geometric island beds are filled with colour –

yellow lily-flowered tulips (*Tulipa* sp.) in the spring followed by white snapdragons (*Antirrhinum* sp.) in the summer – and edged with neatly trimmed box (*Buxus sempervirens*). With colourful planting providing a strong visual focus, the fountain fills the air with the sound of splashing water. Stepping stones link the beds to the tiled walkway, providing access for maintenance. Water lilies (*Nymphaea* sp.) grow from submerged planting boxes, their loose and floating forms contrasting with the sharply defined outlines of the island beds. Flowering evergreens, flourish beneath the walkway.

The garden plan

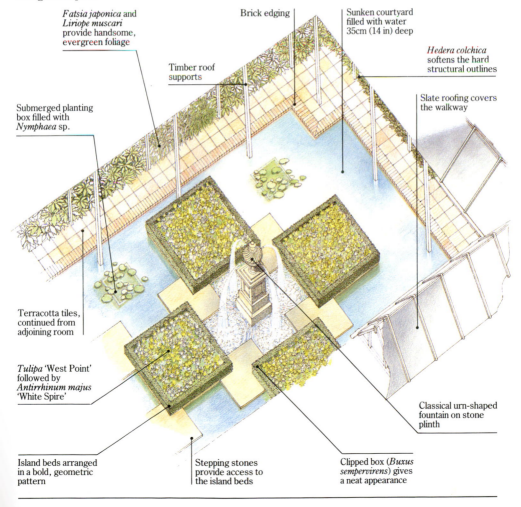

Fatsia japonica and *Liriope muscari* provide handsome, evergreen foliage

Brick edging

Sunken courtyard filled with water 35cm (14 in) deep

Hedera colchica softens the hard structural outlines

Timber roof supports

Slate roofing covers the walkway

Submerged planting box filled with *Nymphaea* sp.

Terracotta tiles, continued from adjoining room

Tulipa 'West Point' followed by *Antirrhinum majus* 'White Spire'

Classical urn-shaped fountain on stone plinth

Island beds arranged in a bold, geometric pattern

Stepping stones provide access to the island beds

Clipped box (*Buxus sempervirens*) gives a neat appearance

An American frontage

The front garden creates the first impression and provides the setting for a house. As the scene for comings and goings, it should provide a balancing, tranquil, and static appearance. The front of this handsome American house, below, features an L-shaped covered way which gives shelter from both sun and rain. Within the right angle of the covered way is a beautiful, established golden maple (*Acer japonica aureum*) and beyond it is a large cedar (*Cedrus atlantica*). The existing design of the garden consists of a long border curving around a simple, well-proportioned circular pond. The border separates house and garden, and the eye is held by the fountain.

Different approaches

The first alternative design, opposite above, binds together the disparate elements of the garden with a simple gravel surfacing. The attraction of the existing house and trees is essentially one of form, and this theme is continued with clumps of bamboo (*Arundinaria* sp.) and masses of low-growing juniper (*Juniperus sabina tamariscifolia*) complementing the pool.

Gravel is used again in the second alternative design, opposite below. Squares of gravel alternate with masses of box (*Buxus* sp.) in a more formal and architectural garden. Each square is edged with brick to match the surfacing of the entrance path. Different plants could be substituted here, depending on soil and climate. Lavender (*Lavandula* sp.), for instance, would provide a woollier look, though it should be clipped after flowering. Planting must be evergreen to maintain the pattern throughout the seasons.

Curved front garden

A front garden design, bordered by covered walks and dominated by fine trees, should essentially be a simple pattern offsetting the house beyond. A strong, serpentine line divides lawn from planting and outlines the static shape of the pool, below.

Alternative designs

Gravelled landscape

*Gravel is used as an anchor in this proposal, right. New plants complement old and include bamboo (*Arundinaria *sp.), masses of low-growing juniper (*Juniperus sabina tamariscifolia*), and a mound of azalea beneath the existing maple (*Acer japonicum aureum*). The fountain jet has become a single vertical, giving a restful effect.*

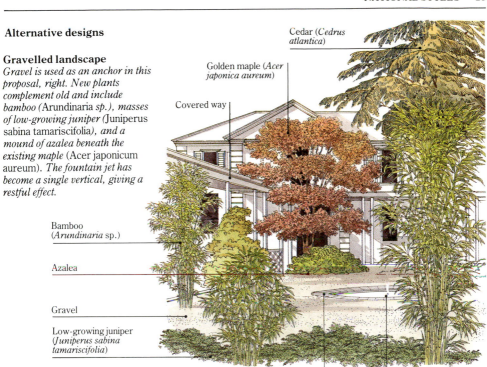

Cedar (*Cedrus atlantica*)

Golden maple (*Acer japonica aureum*)

Covered way

Bamboo (*Arundinaria* sp.)

Azalea

Gravel

Low-growing juniper (*Juniperus sabina tamariscifolia*)

Slab edging

Fountain

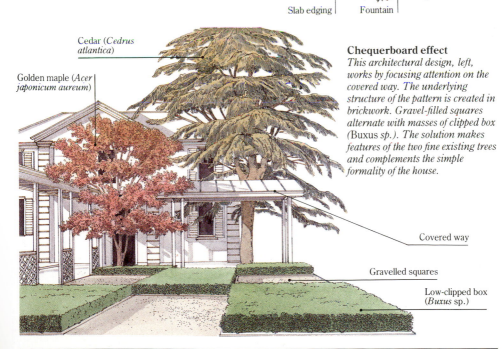

Cedar (*Cedrus atlantica*)

Golden maple (*Acer japonicum aureum*)

Chequerboard effect

*This architectural design, left, works by focusing attention on the covered way. The underlying structure of the pattern is created in brickwork. Gravel-filled squares alternate with masses of clipped box (*Buxus *sp.). The solution makes features of the two fine existing trees and complements the simple formality of the house.*

Covered way

Gravelled squares

Low-clipped box (*Buxus* sp.)

An English corner

This old English garden, with characteristically haphazard planting and paved paths, features an old barn with a corrugated iron roof. A barn like this in a garden has great potential, but is often either ignored or underplayed. One solution is to fashion the surrounding garden to fit whatever function you want the barn to perform. In the existing garden the barn is used as a retreat and as a place for storage.

In the two alternative designs opposite, the aim is to bring the barn more emphatically into the garden. In each case the strong ground pattern is based on a grid determined by the spacing of the piers of the barn. In the pool-house version, the grid itself forms the ground pattern, picked out in paving brick.

The proposal with the swimming pool uses the barn as a shelter and background. The garden loses its cottage English feel here, and takes on a much more international flavour. Barns and swimming pools belong to different eras, so careful planning is necessary to tie them in together. The barn structure has been given greater prominence by tiling the roof and adding an ornamental turret. The brick pillars and walls are echoed in the square patterning of the terrace which surrounds the pool. Planting is architectural with fastigiate cypresses, phormium with its sword-shaped leaves, and the tall flower spikes of *Kniphofia*.

The second proposal, opposite below, retains a rural, English feel, and the planting is more generous to create a sheltered corner for sitting in the sun. Cottage garden plants with gentle forms and shapes, such as a white-flowering shrub rose and a lemon-flowering potentilla, enhance this mood. The tall, lemon spikes of verbascum harmonize with the yellow-green flowers of euphorbia.

An integrated rural feature
An old barn such as this, below, can either be a handsome addition to a garden or an eyesore. In order to combine barn and garden successfully, the planting must harmonize with the structure.

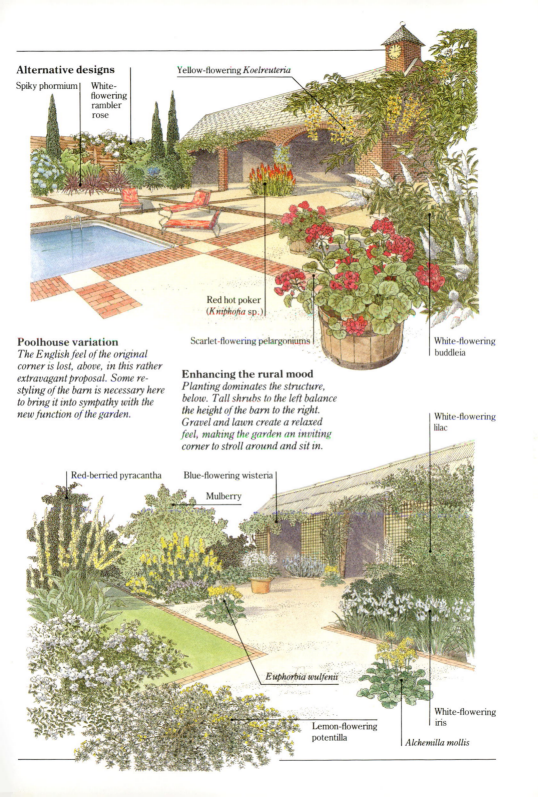

Alternative designs

Spiky phormium

White-flowering rambler rose

Yellow-flowering *Koelreuteria*

Red hot poker (*Kniphofia* sp.)

Scarlet-flowering pelargoniums

White-flowering buddleia

Poolhouse variation
The English feel of the original corner is lost, above, in this rather extravagant proposal. Some re-styling of the barn is necessary here to bring it into sympathy with the new function of the garden.

Enhancing the rural mood
Planting dominates the structure, below. Tall shrubs to the left balance the height of the barn to the right. Gravel and lawn create a relaxed feel, making the garden an inviting corner to stroll around and sit in.

White-flowering lilac

Red-berried pyracantha

Blue-flowering wisteria

Mulberry

White-flowering iris

Euphorbia wulfenii

Lemon-flowering potentilla

Alchemilla mollis

Urban gardens

T owns and cities offer a bewildering variety of structures to live in, with gardens or outside living spaces to match. The exterior architectural style of your home will probably influence your interior decoration; it may influence your choice of garden style as well. Every architectural style can be echoed in the line and form of garden layout, in the choice of materials and surfaces used, and in the style and groupings of containers and furnishings. You can adopt a purist approach and be historically accurate in every detail, or you can simply aim to bring alive the mood or essence of whatever style you have chosen.

A classic town garden

The strong structure of this small town garden anchors the eye within the site and prevents it from being overwhelmed by the towering plane tree (*Platanus* x *acerifolia*) in one corner. The garden belongs to one of a terrace of six-storey nineteenth-century houses. The tree relates in scale to these, and though it casts much of the garden in shade, it does afford some privacy from overlooking neighbouring houses.

The clean, well-defined lines of the garden layout reflect the sophisticated, modern interior design of the house. The brick used to construct the surfaces matches that of the house, linking house and garden sympathetically. In the winter months when the plane tree is bare, the geometric pattern of the garden can be clearly seen and appreciated from every level of the house. Two paved

areas allow for family lunches and entertaining in the summer months. The hard lines of the brick flooring are softened by areas of washed pea gravel. The brick flooring, set in concrete, forms a series of pads that link the house to the paved seating areas.

To make the basement dining room lighter, an area 3m (10 ft) long was dug out immediately in front of it. A brick plinth, part way down the garden, can be seen from this room. Currently home to a tub of annuals, it will eventually house a sculptural feature.

Traditional-style furniture includes a teak bench surface resting on a built-in brick seat and a freestanding teak table and chairs. With its simple lines this furniture sits happily in the classic surroundings.

Planting
Much of the garden is in deep shade with the rest getting only intermittent light, so shade-tolerant plants, such as ferns, bamboos, and ivies feature strongly.

Most of the planting is confined to the raised beds, leaving plenty of room in the middle of the garden for summer entertaining. Gravel planting, including *Alchemilla mollis* and *Iris foetidissima*, prevents this area from looking too stark. A great variety of evergreen planting, including *Choisya ternata* and *Skimmia japonica*, provides year-round interest. The bold plant groupings relate in scale to the layout and give it a unified feel.

Using pattern
An L-shaped area of planted gravel links the two seating areas, left. The combination of gravel and brick paving offers textural interest as well as pattern, and lends itself to a crisp and tidy urban feel.

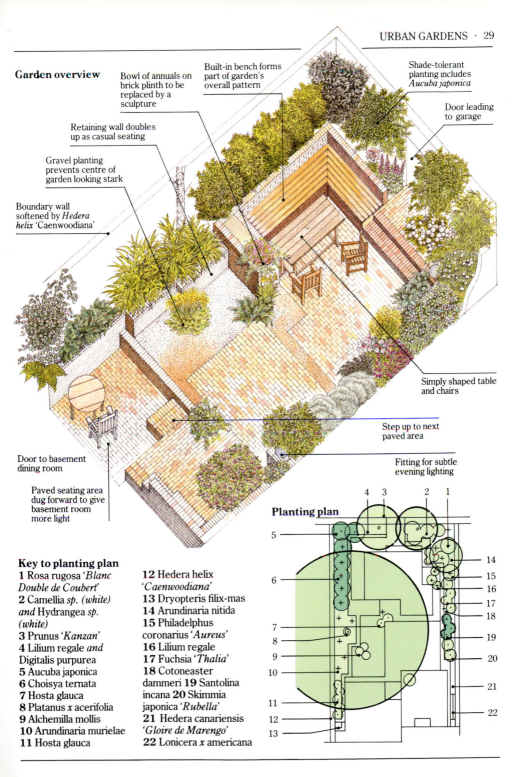

Garden overview

Bowl of annuals on brick plinth to be replaced by a sculpture

Built-in bench forms part of garden's overall pattern

Shade-tolerant planting includes *Aucuba japonica*

Retaining wall doubles up as casual seating

Door leading to garage

Gravel planting prevents centre of garden looking stark

Boundary wall softened by *Hedera helix* 'Caenwoodiana'

Simply shaped table and chairs

Door to basement dining room

Step up to next paved area

Paved seating area dug forward to give basement room more light

Fitting for subtle evening lighting

Planting plan

Key to planting plan

1 Rosa rugosa *'Blanc Double de Coubert'*
2 Camellia *sp. (white) and* Hydrangea *sp. (white)*
3 Prunus *'Kanzan'*
4 Lilium regale *and* Digitalis purpurea
5 Aucuba japonica
6 Choisya ternata
7 Hosta glauca
8 Platanus *x* acerifolia
9 Alchemilla mollis
10 Arundinaria murielae
11 Hosta glauca

12 Hedera helix *'Caenwoodiana'*
13 Dryopteris filix-mas
14 Arundinaria nitida
15 Philadelphus coronarius *'Aureus'*
16 Lilium regale
17 Fuchsia *'Thalia'*
18 Cotoneaster dammeri 19 Santolina incana 20 Skimmia japonica *'Rubella'*
21 Hedera canariensis *'Gloire de Marengo'*
22 Lonicera *x* americana

A simple town garden

The wall of the garage forms the boundary of this simple town garden, below, viewed here from the house. In the existing garden it has been made into the focal point by building a pergola and decked terrace out from it. The pool on the left has a raised stone surround. General surfacing is of granite setts. Plants include holly (*Ilex* sp.) on the right in the foreground, facing the large leaves of *Vitis coignetiae*. Bamboo (*Arundinaria* sp.) and Portuguese laurel (*Prunus lusitanica*) make up much of the remainder of the planting. A fast-growing Russian vine masks an ugly height transition with neighbouring buildings.

Different approaches

The first proposal, opposite above, uses a strong gridded pattern, harmonized with the proportions of pool and garden. The ground pattern is composed of precast concrete slabs with an infill of brick. The concrete matches the stone pool surround and the brick matches the garage construction. Most of the existing evergreen planting remains, with a low species of *Cytisus* included at the end of the pond. The Russian vine is replaced with a contorted hazel (*Corylus contorta*), with evergreen pyracantha planted behind.

In the second proposal, opposite below, the circles of grey granite sett paving draw the eye to the centre of the garden and the pond, making a strong alternative grouping. Planting to screen the garage includes *Malus floribunda* on the right, with evergreens in front. Behind the pond are grouped *Rhus typhina*, with *Viburnum plicatum* in front. Perennial planting includes iris and aster for autumn interest. At the rear of the garden, hellebores are planted in the shade, with small-leaved golden ivy that will grow up to cover the garage. Tubs of bright annuals and bulbs for early spring effect provide the finishing touch.

Virtue out of necessity

This garden terminates at the garage wall. In the existing design, below, the roof of the garage has been extended into a pergola with a decked terrace beneath. The idea works well and provides a sheltered seating area within a small simple garden.

Alternative designs

Gridded design

A strong ground pattern connects pool and garage, right. Heavy overplanting is needed here to knock back and soften the dominant design. A contorted hazel (Corylus contorta) *is planted as a feature tree beyond the pond for added winter interest.*

White-flowering pyracantha

Pampas grass (*Cortaderia selloana*)

Daylilies (*Hemerocallis* sp.)

Contorted hazel (*Corylus contorta*)

Cream-flowering broom (*Cytisus kewensis*)

Pink-flowering rushes (*Butomus* sp.)

Precast concrete slabs

Brick infill

Blue pansies (*Viola* x *wittrockiana*)

Honeysuckle (*Lonicera brownii*)

Iris sp.

Mixed hellebores

Viburnum plicatum 'Mariesii'

Rhus typhina

Moving the focus

The grey, granite sett paving swirls from the end of the pond encompass a planting of perennials, backed by Viburnum plicatum 'Mariesii' *and* Rhus typhina *to provide autumn colour, left. On the other side of the garden the view of the garage is baffled by a flanking* Malus floribunda, *with a grouping of tubs beneath for annual colour.*

Crab apple (*Malus floribunda*)

Skimmia japonica 'Rubella'

Busy lizzies (*Impatiens* cvs.)

Blue-flowering asters

Granite setts

Cream-flowering *Aruncus sylvester*

A family garden

The concept for this garden design, right, grew out of the needs of the family. The garden was no more than a border-edged rectangle of worn grass at the time the dining room extension was built to the back of their nineteenth-century house. They wanted a paved area for eating out of doors, a hard surface for a bench outside their studio/workshop at the end of the garden, a small sandpit, and a soft area where the children could play. As all these elements were worked in together, the design began to evolve as a series of small rooms, each room having its own character and function.

The regularity of the original rectangular site was loosened by turning the rooms on to a diagonal axis. The zig-zag shapes created in the process are accentuated by brick edging. The large raised bed helps rationalize the slope of the garden from right to left (looking out from the house). Slight changes of level through the garden increase the ground pattern interest. A shallow step leads from the

Secluded urban retreat
Dense planting at ground level, up walls, and overhead creates a feeling of privacy and lush growth in this urban garden, above.

terrace nearest the house down to the lawn. From the lawn another step leads up to the paved area near the workshop.

Much of the charm of this garden lies in its lived-in look, provided by the collection of bric-à-brac dotted around the garden – chimney pots filled with plants, old terracotta pots and cream pots, stone jars, and pebbles and boulders brought back from favourite holiday haunts (not too many, however – let us keep our coastlines intact).

Planting
The garden backs on to neighbouring gardens on two sides and is overlooked by a row of tall town houses on the third. The luscious planting aims to provide privacy and includes several climbers. Different varieties of climbing ivy clothe the two side walls and the trellis that gives them extra height. Scented honeysuckle (*Lonicera periclymenum*) covers the end wall.

Evergreens including *Euonymus fortunei* provide a bold sculptural backdrop to a mass of colourful annuals and perennials, such as pink and white astilbes, purple loosestrife, and yellow creeping buttercups. Hydrangeas and assorted ferns grow happily in the shadiest corners. A variety of herbs, geraniums, and small-leaved ivies grow in clusters of pots around the garden.

GRAVEL OR GRASS?

Gravel would usually be a better surfacing choice than grass in a garden this size, below. Small areas of grass can look rather depressing, particularly in winter, when they become dull and covered in muddy wormcasts. Gravel is not a safe or pleasant medium for children to play on, however, and grass makes sense for the young family. Here a small, brick-edged lawn fits neatly between the paved areas, rather like a Persian carpet on a tiled floor.

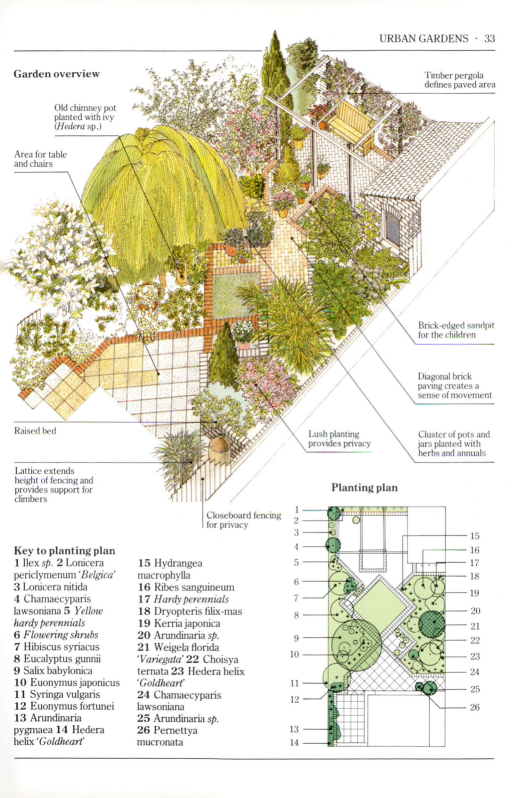

Garden overview

Timber pergola
defines paved area

Old chimney pot
planted with ivy
(*Hedera* sp.)

Area for table
and chairs

Brick-edged sandpit
for the children

Diagonal brick
paving creates a
sense of movement

Raised bed

Lush planting
provides privacy

Cluster of pots and
jars planted with
herbs and annuals

Lattice extends
height of fencing and
provides support for
climbers

Closeboard fencing
for privacy

Planting plan

Key to planting plan
1 Ilex *sp.* **2** Lonicera
periclymenum '*Belgica*'
3 Lonicera nitida
4 Chamaecyparis
lawsoniana **5** *Yellow
hardy perennials*
6 *Flowering shrubs*
7 Hibiscus syriacus
8 Eucalyptus gunnii
9 Salix babylonica
10 Euonymus japonicus
11 Syringa vulgaris
12 Euonymus fortunei
13 Arundinaria
pygmaea **14** Hedera
helix '*Goldheart*'

15 Hydrangea
macrophylla
16 Ribes sanguineum
17 *Hardy perennials*
18 Dryopteris filix-mas
19 Kerria japonica
20 Arundinaria *sp.*
21 Weigela florida
'*Variegata*' **22** Choisya
ternata **23** Hedera helix
'*Goldheart*'
24 Chamaecyparis
lawsoniana
25 Arundinaria *sp.*
26 Pernettya
mucronata

Suburban style

As they grow, families move out from city centres to give themselves more space. Suburban gardens often have considerable and conflicting demands made on them: perhaps a kitchen garden is needed to supplement the table, an open space for children's play, and a terrace for entertaining outside. Planting might be limited while children are young and take over more of the garden as they grow up and play less outside. The greater size of the suburban garden provides considerable scope for planning and ideas.

A suburban garden

Suburban gardens can be rather predictable, perhaps with a central lawn and border planting, and one or two nondescript features. The original garden on which these two designs, below and opposite above, are based was largely lawned, but did have an informal pool to one side. Interesting planting included a bamboo clump, a *Clematis montana* scrambling over the lattice fence, and mounds of Japanese azalea around the edge of the pool.

Different approaches
The first design, below, is more formal and provides additional interest at the terrace end of the garden – a piece of sculpture stands above descending levels of water. The concept is crisp, with the strong forms of the pools and sculpture softened by bold planting. The bamboo clump remains but is backed by a mass of yellow-flowering *Ligularia* sp., beyond which is a group of the horizontally layered foliage of *Viburnum plicatum* 'Mariesii'. Low junipers (*Juniperus sabina tamariscifolia*) reach down to the water beneath the sculpture, backed by autumn-flowering *Anemone japonica alba*. Paving continues beyond a formal, clipped hedge to provide a balance to the sculpture and to complete the progression.

The second proposal, opposite above, makes more of a feature of the terrace that ends the garden, extending it back towards the house in an abstract design of interlocking squares at different levels. These are tied together by a small, circular pool, with *Sagittaria* sp. providing strong foliage planting within it. Planting in this design is subordinate to the structural concept.

Alternative designs

Formal approach
Water is used formally here, right, with the flow allowed to descend at intervals and provide foreground interest to the concrete sculpture. The top paved terrace acts as a counterbalance. Planting complements the sculpture, and bamboo is included for its bold leaf shapes.

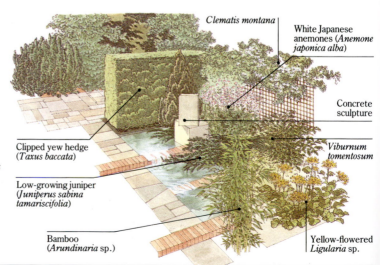

Clipped yew hedge (*Taxus baccata*)

Low-growing juniper (*Juniperus sabina tamariscifolia*)

Bamboo (*Arundinaria* sp.)

Clematis montana

White Japanese anemones (*Anemone japonica alba*)

Concrete sculpture

Viburnum tomentosum

Yellow-flowered *Ligularia* sp.

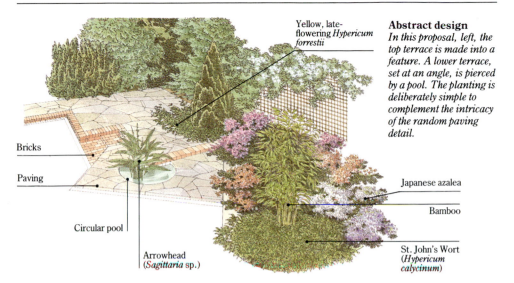

Yellow, late-flowering *Hypericum forrestii*

Bricks

Paving

Circular pool

Arrowhead (*Sagittaria* sp.)

Japanese azalea

Bamboo

St. John's Wort (*Hypericum calycinum*)

Abstract design
In this proposal, left, the top terrace is made into a feature. A lower terrace, set at an angle, is pierced by a pool. The planting is deliberately simple to complement the intricacy of the random paving detail.

SMALL SUBURBAN PLOT

This small garden belongs to one of a terrace of single-storey houses, designed so that the wall of one house becomes the garden wall of another. A planting area is retained against this wall with U-shaped precast concrete blocks. An adjoining row of blocks forms a permanent garden bench, furnished in the summer with cushions. The paved area is bursting with plants, culminating in a single millstone fountain feature set among boulders. The boulders are laid in a concrete saucer so that the overflowing water is retained and pumped back up through the centre of the millstone. Pergola beams successfully divide the garden and frame a view to the small area beyond. Mixed paving materials of a coarse aggregate concrete block interlaced with a pattern of granite setts make the area appear deceptively large. Planting is full and areas of planting interlocking with paving give movement to the garden, again making it seem larger.

Key to planting plan
1 Miscanthus sinensis 2 Picea abies 3 Ligularia stenocephala 4 Kniphofia *sp.* 5 Arundinaria nitida

Rural style

Understanding the essence of a style is the key to interpreting it in your own space. The classic cottage garden, for example, has a homely rural image of roses rambling around a door and relaxed country planting. Many gardeners try to recreate this style and fail, ending up with an incoherent and patchy effect. The apparent disorder of country gardens is in fact controlled; because, whether in Devon or on Long Island, it is contained within a strong underlying framework. The colour of walls, paintwork, and roofing, the texture of brick, clay, or stone, echoing and harmonizing with local colours and materials, make up the strong structural elements, which are then overlaid with soft, gentle masses of plant material.

A cottage-style garden

Now a relaxed country cottage-style garden, this site, below right, started out with an area of random paving outside the back door, leading up to an area of rough grass that had been used as a dumping ground during alterations to the house.

The owner's requirements included an open area for furniture and potting up plants, and a design that would contain and steady a mass of soft, billowing, country-style planting without dominating it, and that would blend in well with the surroundings.

A loose and relaxed style of planting needs a structure that combines hard materials and strong skeleton plants to prevent it from becoming a muddle. By contrast, in a small garden where the emphasis is on activities other than gardening, the primary function of plants is to soften the strong, hard lines of the structural elements.

The randomly paved area adjacent to the house was kept to provide an open area and to counterbalance the spectacular array of plants planned for the rest of the garden. The grass was taken up and replaced with a combination of gravel, stone, and brick. Brick was used to build a gentle step up from the paved terrace adjacent to the house, to edge the beds, and to make a few simple divisions within the rest of the site. A coating of pale, washed gravel was rolled into a 5cm (2 in) layer of unwashed binding gravel, to provide a textural contrast with the plants grown in it. Old paving slabs and brick, complementing the colour of the gravel and the house, were laid at various points throughout the gravelled area to make a path and give easy access to the plants. The patterns of the paving contrast with the loosely structured style of the planting.

Country-style planting
The abundant planting is typical of the country garden. Caring for a variety of plants is time consuming, and this style of planting is only for the keen, year-round gardener.

A harmonious effect is achieved in this garden by planting in drifts – several plants of the same type grouped together. Dotting single plants about the garden creates a restless, incoherent appearance. Particular

Visual links
Gravel, paving, and planting, right, all serve to link this country home to its pleasant, cottage-style garden.

care was taken here in the combination of colours. The greens, greys, and golds of the foliage act as a foil to the flower colour.

Structure and interest during the winter months are provided by evergreen shrubs such as *Mahonia japonica* and the almost evergreen *Viburnum* x *burkwoodii*. Their dark green foliage contrasts with the grey of plants such as *Senecio* 'Sunshine', *Hebe pinguifolia* 'Pagei', the purple-bronze leaves of *Ajuga reptans* 'Burgundy Glow', and the beautiful red winter stems of Dogwood (*Cornus alba*).

Planting plan

Key to planting plan

1 Mahonia japonica
2 Philadelphus coronarius **3** Rosa *'Comte de Chambord'*
4 Dianthus *sp.*
5 Ceanothus thyrsiflorus *'Repens'*
6 Anaphalis vulgaris *mass* **7** Viburnum x burkwoodii
8 Rosa *'Pearl Drift'*
9 Dianthus *sp.*
10 Aquilegia vulgaris *mass* **11** Cornus alba

12 Crypotomeria japonica **13** Lavandula angustifolia **14** Melissa officinalis *'Aurea'*
15 Senecio *'Sunshine'*
16 Alchemilla mollis
17 Agapanthus x *'Headbourne hybrids'*
18 Alchemilla mollis
19 *Perennials growing through gravel*
20 Nepeta x faassenii
21 Hebe pinguifolia *'Pagei'*

Garden overview

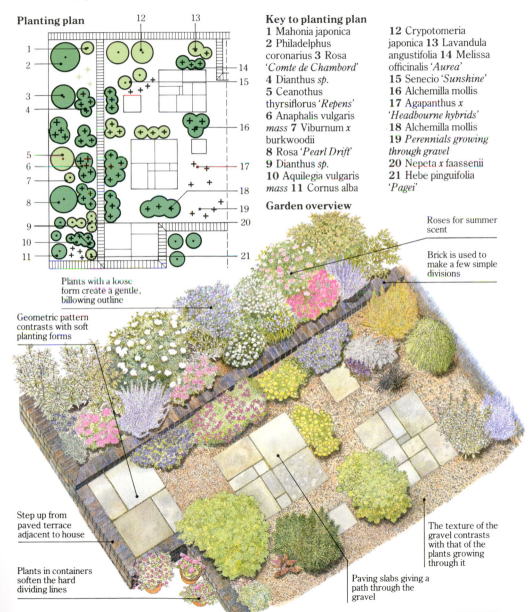

Roses for summer scent

Brick is used to make a few simple divisions

Plants with a loose form create a gentle, billowing outline

Geometric pattern contrasts with soft planting forms

Step up from paved terrace adjacent to house

Plants in containers soften the hard dividing lines

The texture of the gravel contrasts with that of the plants growing through it

Paving slabs giving a path through the gravel

ANATOMY OF A COUNTRY GARDEN

Faced with an overgrown or unstructured country plot, it can be useful to divide the plot in your mind's eye into three zones, as shown below. Every garden has its unique features that need special treatment, of course, but this approach provides a useful starting point.

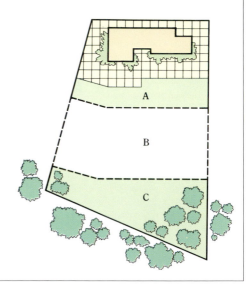

Zone A   Area adjacent to building
This is the area reserved for any formal treatment you wish to include in your garden. The plan here will be conceived to follow the form of the house, using materials sympathetic to the structure. Planting may be bold in form and colour, but always in tune with the building.

Zone B   Transitional area
Here your style can progress from domestic to landscape in a way dictated by topography, climate, and scale. This area may be used for recreation with planting to suit, but tempered by progression towards wilder planting as it approaches Zone C.

Zone C   Boundary area
The aim in the boundary area is to develop planting that is in complete sympathy with the countryside beyond, so that the boundary line itself goes unnoticed. If you need a physical boundary, it should be as unobtrusive as possible, following the local style.

A traditional rural garden

This old garden, right, has a charm that one would hesitate to disturb. The dominant old apple tree, complete with rambler rose, provides character and focus. In this situation the gardener wanting to re-design should accept the mature planting and concentrate on the planting at ground level. A modern layout would be discordant here.

Different approaches
Far better to extend the traditional charm of the garden by turning it into an ecological area. The first proposal, opposite top, uses grasses and berrying shrubs to attract birds and flowering perennials to encourage butterflies. The pool will support water life and the grasses will offer protection to small creatures.

Alternatively, the garden could be revitalized to enhance its old world feel as in the second proposal, opposite centre. The apple tree becomes more of a feature with a

Undisturbed country charm
There is a fine line between maturity and neglect. Discreet care is exercised here, above.

bench seat around it. Perennial planting includes traditional species of phlox, aster, lupin, delphinium, together with low-growing herbs, such as sage, rosemary, and rue.

Alternative designs

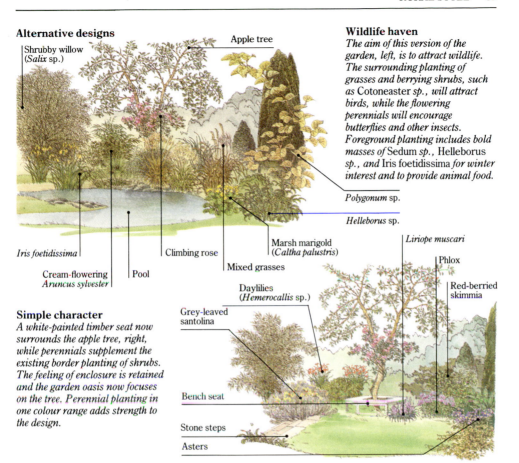

Shrubby willow
(*Salix* sp.)

Apple tree

Iris foetidissima

Cream-flowering
Aruncus sylvester

Pool

Climbing rose

Mixed grasses

Marsh marigold
(*Caltha palustris*)

Wildlife haven

The aim of this version of the garden, left, is to attract wildlife. The surrounding planting of grasses and berrying shrubs, such as Cotoneaster *sp., will attract birds, while the flowering perennials will encourage butterflies and other insects. Foreground planting includes bold masses of* Sedum *sp.,* Helleborus *sp., and* Iris foetidissima *for winter interest and to provide animal food.*

Polygonum sp.

Helleborus sp.

Simple character

A white-painted timber seat now surrounds the apple tree, right, while perennials supplement the existing border planting of shrubs. The feeling of enclosure is retained and the garden oasis now focuses on the tree. Perennial planting in one colour range adds strength to the design.

Liriope muscari

Phlox

Red-berried
skimmia

Daylilies
(*Hemerocallis* sp.)

Grey-leaved
santolina

Bench seat

Stone steps

Asters

MODERN COTTAGE GARDEN

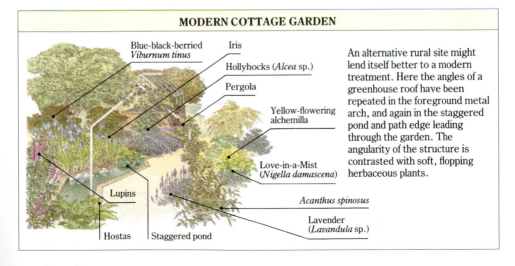

Blue-black-berried
Viburnum tinus

Iris

Hollyhocks (*Alcea* sp.)

Pergola

Yellow-flowering
alchemilla

Love-in-a-Mist
(*Nigella damascena*)

Lupins

Hostas

Staggered pond

Acanthus spinosus

Lavender
(*Lavandula* sp.)

An alternative rural site might lend itself better to a modern treatment. Here the angles of a greenhouse roof have been repeated in the foreground metal arch, and again in the staggered pond and path edge leading through the garden. The angularity of the structure is contrasted with soft, flopping herbaceous plants.

A woodland garden

The cultivated section and wild areas seen from this existing woodland garden, below, are clearly defined by the strong line of the hedge that divides the two. Natural woodland acts as a backcloth for the plant forms within the artificially created garden, producing a sense of seclusion and contrast.

Different approaches

When a boundary line must be defined in some way, a less open solution is needed. In the first proposal, opposite above, silver birches have been established nearer the garden to link the natural woodland with the cultivated area, even though the boundary hedge remains. Additional planting of wild grasses to the right repeats the original foreground planting, but otherwise the distant garden planting has been removed to allow woodland and garden to blend. The foreground raised bed has been timber-clad and planted with alpines. The far boundary is a single wire that allows a view to the woodland.

In the second proposal, opposite below, the garden is made completely open to the woodland beyond by removing the distant garden planting. The effect is to make features of the silver birches (*Betula* sp.) and the trunks of the oak trees (*Quercus* sp.). The shape of the lawn is softened, with cultivated grass disappearing into the shadow of the woodland and an outpost of wild flowers, including foxgloves (*Digitalis* sp.) on the right. In the spring, *Narcissus* and crocuses and later bluebells will flower in the areas of rough grass.

Definite divide

The existing garden, below, is deliberately separated from its woodland setting by the small raised bed, the rectangular shape of the lawn, and the shapes, forms, and flower colours of the plants chosen. The cultivated garden appears to be a protected, exotic area.

Alternative designs

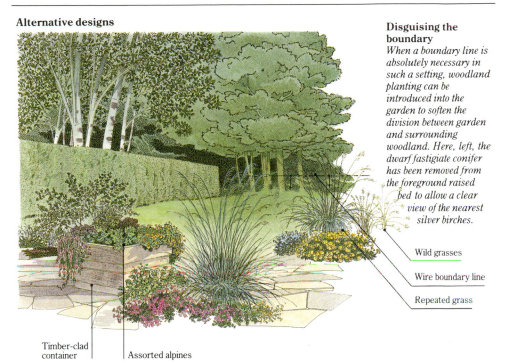

Disguising the boundary

When a boundary line is absolutely necessary in such a setting, woodland planting can be introduced into the garden to soften the division between garden and surrounding woodland. Here, left, the dwarf fastigiate conifer has been removed from the foreground raised bed to allow a clear view of the nearest silver birches.

Wild grasses

Wire boundary line

Repeated grass

Timber-clad container

Assorted alpines

Silver birches (*Betula* sp.)

Areas of rough grass

Removing the boundary

Here the boundary hedge has been removed, right, to open the view to the woodland and to allow the garden to flow naturally into tree shadow. The foreground grasses and the raised bed, a feature of the cultivated garden, have been removed to make way for plant forms that extend the woodland feel right up to the house.

Sedums

Alchemilla mollis

Pinks (*Dianthus* sp.)

Mimulus sp.

Foxgloves

Feature gardens

A single feature in a garden can provide an anchor to an overall design. Water, for example, is a powerful visual element, and a pool or pond can determine both garden style and planting. A dramatic view beyond the fence or hedge may be impossible to compete with, so the garden is moulded to enhance and complement the view instead. Or you might want to concentrate on a particular type of planting, such as herbs, vegetables, herbaceous perennials, or grasses, and let the garden take its character from that.

A water garden

This pool, the bridge, and all the smaller components of this group work together as one sculptural unit to provide a visually pleasing whole throughout the year.

The pool is a rectangle, crossed by a timber bridge at right angles to it. The bridge structure is made of softwood horizontals laid across metal braces. Because it has no handrails, the bridge needs to be wide enough for a pedestrian to feel safe crossing. One edge of the pool is let into a bricked terrace, laid in a basketweave pattern with a contrasting brick-on-edge surround.

The key plants in this design are foreground fescue grass (*Festuca ovina glauca*) with the sword-like leaves of *Phormium tenax* beyond. The far side of the pond is decorated with a sumach tree (*Rhus typhina*), while the distant jar is highlighted against a bamboo.

In design terms the plan is quite formal, but subtle touches such as the counterpoise of the urns and the well-considered plant groupings make it appear pleasantly informal.

Tranquil scene
In this exquisite water garden, below, line, pattern, texture, and colour combine and contrast, flowing one into the other, to delight the eye and create a haven of peace throughout the year.

Planting plan

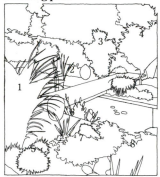

Key to planting plan
1 Miscanthus sinensis
2 Typha maxima *(in the water)*
3 Arundinaria *sp.* 4 Rhus typhina
5 Festuca ovina glauca
6 Phormium tenax 7 *Annual
nasturtiums (*Tropaeolum *sp.)*
8 Bergenia beesiana

A shaded water garden

Two raised areas of water make a visual centre for this shaded town garden, which backs on to the rear wall of a neighbouring dwelling.

The layout is an abstract pattern of interlocking rectangular shapes in brick, though with the addition of a change in level. The plan culminates in a terracotta bust, offset by the painted wall behind.

The raised pools make an attractive feature. The edges of the pools also provide casual seating. Planting in such a location is difficult because of shade and dripping rainwater from the overhanging trees, but ferns and mosses do well in these conditions. The positioning and form of the foreground shrub, a cotoneaster, offset the shape of the pools. The only hard material used is brick.

Quiet backwater
The simple subtlety of this water garden, below, works so well because the carefully conceived modern plan is executed in traditional materials.

Planting plan

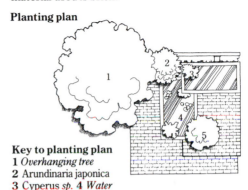

Key to planting plan
1 *Overhanging tree*
2 Arundinaria japonica
3 Cyperus *sp.* 4 *Water*
5 Cotoneaster *sp.*

A garden with a view

The garden with an imposing view has its own set of design problems, some of them highlighted here, below and opposite. In this situation where the view is dominating, the gardener has to decide on the balance between the attraction of the foreground garden planting and that of the countryside beyond. The balance can be altered by revealing more or less of the view and by altering the strength of the composition of the cultivated area of garden in relation to the whole.

A pool has been chosen as the link between garden and country beyond, with dramatic results. The far banking of the pool forms an invisible boundary. A small sculpture of a hawk, an indigenous bird, placed centrally on the far edge of the pool provides a further link between garden and country. Its reflection draws the eye down into the cultivated area and along to the mass of vibrant red tulips.

Different approaches

In the first proposal, opposite above, the foreground detail has been cleared so that the far bank line has much of the feel of the hills beyond. The realistic bird sculpture is now set higher and to one side so that it counterpoises the view against complementary but not intrusive planting.

The second alternative, opposite below, reduces the width of the view. Larger planting on the left has been designed to create a feeling of the country encroaching into the garden. Planting here is of garden forms of indigenous genera, such as shrub roses. In the left foreground, the stag's horn sumach (*Rhus typhina*) is a good compromise between rural and "domestic" plants.

Natural detailing

Water can make an attractive transition between cultivated garden and borrowed landscape. Below, the detailing of the pond is natural, with boulders used to make an informal surround.

Exposing the view

Foreground details have been cleared to open the garden to the view, right, with the bird sculpture placed to one side to balance it. Planting remains as in the original.

Existing white-flowering *Amelanchier* sp.

Bird sculpture

Existing summer-flowering *Butomus* sp.

Alternative designs

Reducing the view

Below, the view has been closed off from the left, drawing the eye to the other side. Planting has been allowed to intrude into the garden and frame a simple fountain. As well as Rhus typhina, *subjects include* Helleborus *sp. and* Amelanchier *sp.*

Cleared foreground

Random paving edge

Marsh marigold (*Caltha palustris*)

Rhus typhina

Additional *Amelanchier* sp.

Burble fountain

Cotoneaster *salicifolius floccosus*

Rosa rugosa alba

A deck garden

Well-constructed decking, or areas of wooden planking, provides a pleasing and sympathetic garden surface. It is widely used in regions where timber is plentiful, in parts of the United States, for example, and where the climate is extreme, with cold, snowy winters and long, dry summers. In places like the British Isles, where there are moist winters and often wet summers, decking is less appropriate because wet timber can be slippery and unattractive.

This deck garden, right, is constructed in timber and furnished with plants. The design works from above as well as ground level. Particularly in towns, gardens need a strong ground plan and plants with large leaves that allow the underlying design to show through.

The sunny area of the garden is decked to form both a terrace and a surround to the main feature, the pond, and to provide a junction between house and garden. A low bench seat, backed by a herb bed, is built on to the deck (out of the picture). To the sides there is planting contained by stained wood retaining walls to match the decking.

A detail of interest is the concealment of the pool edge by the decked terrace. The pool container itself could simply be of fibreglass.

Decking in the water garden
Decking provides a sympathetic foil to the sheet surface of still water, and to luscious water plants, above.

Decking can be combined with a restrained selection of plant forms and leaf shapes in a disciplined way to achieve a quiet calm in either a busy urban quarter or a rural backwater.

A rockery garden

Before planting a rockery garden, think carefully about the natural form you are copying. An alpine bluff has characteristics that the gardener should note. An exposed rock face will produce a crumble of rock particles, or scree, at its base in which only hardy, tufted plants can find a home. Larger, less hardy plants can only survive in the areas sheltered by the rock formation away from the exposed face. Any fastigiate plant must be sited in a sheltered spot, but a well-positioned vertically growing plant will relieve the otherwise horizontal forms that go to make a rockery garden. In each of the two designs opposite for rockery gardens, a specific weathering process has been simulated.

Different approaches
In the first proposal, opposite above, water forms part of the composition, with "worn" rock faces looking in towards the pool. A still sheet of water will reflect a rocky landscape and provide an area of calm that will balance the drama of rock and plants.

Plants used are mostly ground-hugging and shaped by their site, with *Saxifraga* sp. and *Sempervivum* sp. included to simulate the hardy primary growth of exposed sites.

In the second design, opposite below, rock faces down the length of the slope have supposedly been exposed by weathering from the right. The rock group is split by a gravel path. Low-growing plants, including alpines and alyssum, are used as in the first design, with a fastigiate juniper providing a vertical counterbalance to the strong horizontals.

Alternative designs

Introducing water
This alternative, right, includes a modest waterfall and pool. The centrally placed fastigiate conifer echoes the vertical line of the waterfall. The pool is made to look completely natural with no visible surround. Planting follows the plan for the original rockery, with the addition of a horizontal-growing juniper and low, poolside planting of sedums and primulas.

Lemon-flowering daylilies (*Hemerocallis* sp.)

Weathered effect
Here, right, the rockery feature has been re-shaped so that the rocks are revealed down the length of the slope. The vertical line of a fastigiate juniper to one side of the group balances the visual weight of the rocks below it. Low-growing plants clad the planting areas.

Fastigiate juniper

Japanese azalea

Cryptomeria japonica spiralis

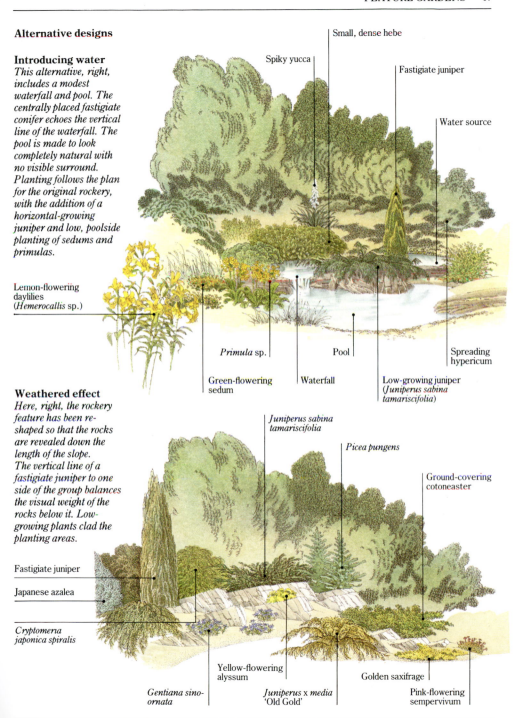

Small, dense hebe

Spiky yucca

Fastigiate juniper

Water source

Primula sp.

Pool

Spreading hypericum

Green-flowering sedum

Waterfall

Low-growing juniper (*Juniperus sabina tamariscifolia*)

Juniperus sabina tamariscifolia

Picea pungens

Ground-covering cotoneaster

Yellow-flowering alyssum

Golden saxifrage

Gentiana sino-ornata

Juniperus x *media* 'Old Gold'

Pink-flowering sempervivum

A herb garden

A typical English garden, right, perhaps fifty or more years old, where the different elements of the garden are kept separate – lawns and flowers near the house, the greenhouse screening off the vegetables and herbs beyond. With the luxuriant foliage of mature trees and shrubs marking the divisions, such a garden can hardly be improved upon. Adequate dry paving to link the working areas of the garden to the kitchen entrance, however, is an essential design feature.

The alternative proposal, below, shows how the garden could be transformed into a herb garden, retaining the greenhouse. A lattice plan of brickwork is infilled with further brick panels, alternating with brushed concrete. A raised brick pond is a focal point in the concept. The beds are filled with herbs that are free to spread over the paving, while the foreground barrel contains chives (*Allium schoenoprasum*) for a variation in plant forms. This layout makes the garden a lovely, scented place to stroll through in summer, alive with bees, while providing an attractive, enclosed area in winter filled with evergreen herbs.

The existing design
A view of a traditional English garden of the inter-war period, above, with lawn and flower planting immediately to the rear of the house, and the greenhouse marking the transition from recreational garden to working garden, with produce beyond.

Paving over the garden
Below, the plot has been made into a paved herb garden, with beds within a squared brickwork pattern, interspersed with brushed concrete. A good proportion of evergreen shrubs, such as sage, rosemary, bay, hyssop, and marjoram, are included for year-round form and interest.

A paved herb garden

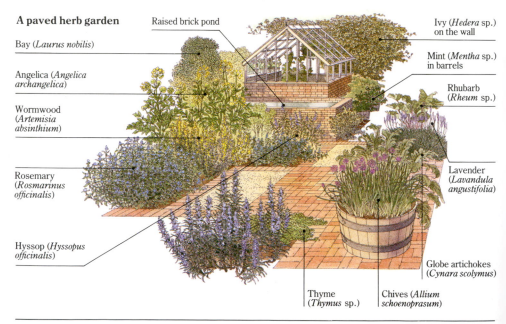

Raised brick pond

Bay (*Laurus nobilis*)

Angelica (*Angelica archangelica*)

Wormwood (*Artemisia absinthium*)

Rosemary (*Rosmarinus officinalis*)

Hyssop (*Hyssopus officinalis*)

Ivy (*Hedera* sp.) on the wall

Mint (*Mentha* sp.) in barrels

Rhubarb (*Rheum* sp.)

Lavender (*Lavandula angustifolia*)

Globe artichokes (*Cynara scolymus*)

Thyme (*Thymus* sp.)

Chives (*Allium schoenoprasum*)

A vegetable garden

Vegetable and herb gardens are demanding but very rewarding if your interest lies in using plants to produce food, spices, essences, or medications. Well-planned sections of gardens, or whole gardens devoted to vegetables or herbs can be just as beautiful as a decorative flower garden.

This garden plot, below, is approximately 10m (32 ft) square and as well as vegetables includes a herb bed (raised for easy cutting), a compost area, a workbench, and a potting shed, all arranged to be both practical and attractive. Two further vegetable areas would allow greater flexibility of cultivation and a wider range of vegetables, but with careful planning you can manage perfectly well in a limited space such as this.

In the far corner is the covered potting area and store. This roofed area can be used for sowing into seed trays and potting. Tools can also be stored here – clean and oil them after use to protect them against damp.

The summer crop bed to the left includes climbing beans and salad vegetables, such as lettuce, radish, miniature tomatoes, and ridge cucumbers. The winter crop bed in the foreground includes leeks, Brussels sprouts, cabbage, beet, and beetroot. Through summer one of the low hedges can be replaced with parsley. The summer and winter planting areas should be alternated each year so that no crop grows in the same ground in consecutive seasons. This will greatly reduce the possibility of soil-borne diseases. The raised herb bed to the right is in a sunny, sheltered spot. Suitable herbs include chives and French tarragon.

Design framework
The foreground cultivation area of this vegetable garden, below, is surrounded by a low, clipped hedge of santolina, rosemary, and box, an arrangement that would also look good in a small town garden. Paths, edging, and raised beds are all constructed in the same brick. Softwood fencing has been used to support a clear corrugated vinyl roof, with additional metal vertical supports.

A vegetable garden plan

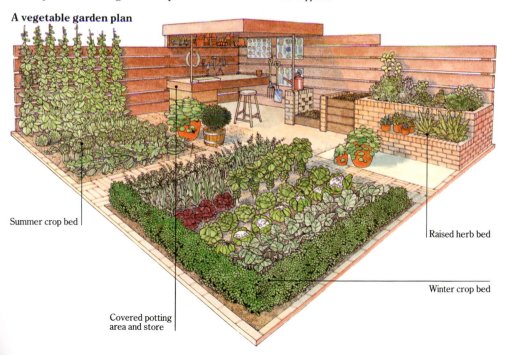

Summer crop bed

Raised herb bed

Winter crop bed

Covered potting area and store

Garden shapes

The shape of your garden plot will affect the overall design as well as the underlying pattern. Gardens often come in difficult shapes – too long, too thin, too steep – and the planning process may involve trying to re-shape or disguise. Perhaps creating swirling curves within a severe square or planting billowy masses of plants to soften sharp edges. Alternatively, imposing pattern where there is none, disguising shape where it is awkward, or, in a vertical dimension, linking different levels of a garden.

A long, thin garden

The long, thin garden site is a difficult shape to design satisfactorily. Some gardeners try to reproduce a larger garden layout on a reduced scale. The result is often small, unrelated patches of interest within too confined an area.

The long, thin urban garden shown below is located in Milan. The pattern of the garden has been turned at an angle of 45 degrees to the house, creating something quite unusual out of a potentially dull plot. There are many interesting corners made out of abstract patterns of wood and water, centred on pieces of metal sculpture. The whole is designed to be viewed from the house as well as from ground level. The designer has used only two materials – timber and cobbles – in the construction, adding strength to the layout. Railway sleepers are used to form retaining walls, a bridge, and a bench seat, and to screen a rubbish area by the far boundary.

Much of the planting is evergreen for year-round interest, with bold clumps of foliage working with the ground pattern – fatsias, camellias, bergenias, rhododendrons, and *Hedera colchica* 'Dentata Aurea' have all been incorporated with ferns (which are not evergreen) in the shaded corners.

Key to planting plan
1 Parthenocissus tricuspidata *'Veitchii'*
2 Iris pseudacorus
3 Ilex *sp., rhododendron, and* Hedera colchica 'Dentata Aurea'
4 *Large pear tree*

A rectangular garden

An extensive range of plants can be grown in a small, walled garden, particularly if it catches the sun. Much can be achieved in a rectangular garden of limited size.

The existing garden on which the two designs below were based was divided into terrace and lawn, with a closely planted rosebed marking the division. While the design tended to make the garden feel smaller, it successfully broke up the rectangle, and luxuriant planting created a feeling of seclusion.

Different approaches

These two designs are seen from the viewpoint of an upper-storey window. In the first design, below, the space is opened up to provide a broader view of the planting from the vantage point of the terrace or the ground floor of the house. The ground pattern is turned at 45 degrees to the house, creating a meander in the design. The main part of the garden is considerably widened. A piece of sculpture dramatically brings the eye to the end of the garden, which is otherwise almost lost to view.

The second proposal, bottom, offers a more formal and traditional design, with the grass area echoing the overall shape of the garden. The view is stopped at the end of the garden by a painted metal pergola. A timber bench constructed around the base of the tree to the right provides an arresting feature. Paved edging to the beds allows foreground herbaceous material, such as the bushy lavender (*Lavandula* sp.), to overflow.

Alternative designs

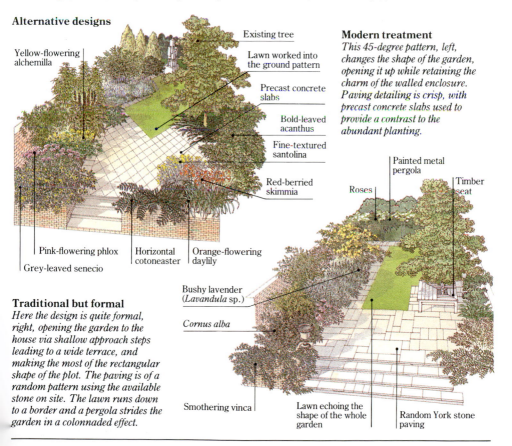

Yellow-flowering alchemilla

Existing tree

Lawn worked into the ground pattern

Precast concrete slabs

Bold-leaved acanthus

Fine-textured santolina

Red-berried skimmia

Pink-flowering phlox

Grey-leaved senecio

Horizontal cotoneaster

Orange-flowering daylily

Modern treatment
This 45-degree pattern, left, changes the shape of the garden, opening it up while retaining the charm of the walled enclosure. Paving detailing is crisp, with precast concrete slabs used to provide a contrast to the abundant planting.

Painted metal pergola

Timber seat

Roses

Bushy lavender (*Lavandula* sp.)

Cornus alba

Traditional but formal
Here the design is quite formal, right, opening the garden to the house via shallow approach steps leading to a wide terrace, and making the most of the rectangular shape of the plot. The paving is of a random pattern using the available stone on site. The lawn runs down to a border and a pergola strides the garden in a colonnaded effect.

Smothering vinca

Lawn echoing the shape of the whole garden

Random York stone paving

A terraced garden

When this modern house, opposite above and below, was built, the area around it was excavated to create a garden space and to provide light for the lower rooms. A flat paved area was included next to the house and the sides of the dug-out area banked steeply away, needing terracing and retaining. The original idea was to plant with ericaceous species, using conifers to punctuate different levels.

Different approaches

The first design, opposite above, aims to bridge the visual gap, and provide a plant scheme that matches the excitement of the house. Italian cypresses (*Cupressus sempervirens*) lend height to the planting. Bolder areas of growth, with open areas of gravel, are in harmony with the modern style of the angular concrete and glass building.

The second proposal, opposite below, is simpler. Colourful, small plants are generously massed, alternating with open spaces.

DESIGN IMPLICATIONS OF TERRACE PLANNING

A common fault when planning changes of level is failing to achieve a balance of scale between the areas of the levels. Close to the house, terraces ought to relate to the area and shape of the house plan and should be generous enough to make a visual balance with it. Often they are too small and can never look anything but niggardly and out of proportion.

Interconnecting terraces can produce layouts of great interest and dynamism, leading the eye to the top or bottom of the terraced levels and towards views or prime features within the site. As with all garden design, get the pattern and shape of the layout right before considering the detail of, for example, surfacing materials. Surfaces to choose from include turf (rough or mown grass), ground cover plants such as hypericum and spurge, cobbles, and even larger fragments of rock. Decorative features, such as pots or architectural plants, can be positioned at various points to punctuate your plan.

In this example, below, the house nestles beneath a rock face. The layout makes dramatic use of the upward-sloping site, including a grand flight of steps up to the highest point of the garden, and retaining walls shaped to match.

Dynamic terracing plan

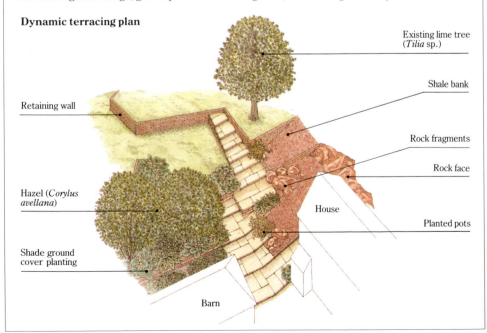

Existing lime tree (*Tilia* sp.)

Shale bank

Retaining wall

Rock fragments

Rock face

Hazel (*Corylus avellana*)

House

Planted pots

Shade ground cover planting

Barn

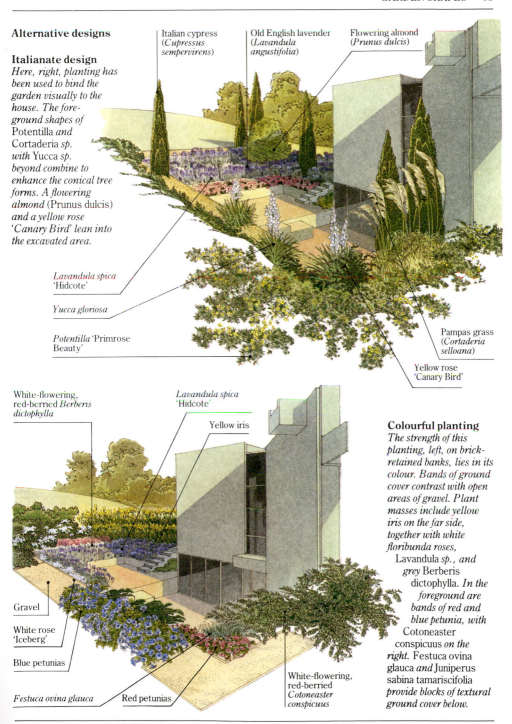

Alternative designs

Italianate design
Here, right, planting has been used to bind the garden visually to the house. The foreground shapes of Potentilla *and* Cortaderia sp. *with* Yucca sp. *beyond combine to enhance the conical tree forms. A flowering almond* (Prunus dulcis) *and a yellow rose 'Canary Bird' lean into the excavated area.*

Italian cypress (*Cupressus sempervirens*)

Old English lavender (*Lavandula angustifolia*)

Flowering almond (*Prunus dulcis*)

Lavandula spica 'Hidcote'

Yucca gloriosa

Potentilla 'Primrose Beauty'

Pampas grass (*Cortaderia selloana*)

Yellow rose 'Canary Bird'

White-flowering, red-berried *Berberis dictophylla*

Lavandula spica 'Hidcote'

Yellow iris

Colourful planting
The strength of this planting, left, on brick-retained banks, lies in its colour. Bands of ground cover contrast with open areas of gravel. Plant masses include yellow iris on the far side, together with white floribunda roses, Lavandula sp., *and grey* Berberis dictophylla. *In the foreground are bands of red and blue petunia, with* Cotoneaster conspicuus *on the right.* Festuca ovina glauca *and* Juniperus sabina tamariscifolia *provide blocks of textural ground cover below.*

Gravel

White rose 'Iceberg'

Blue petunias

Festuca ovina glauca

Red petunias

White-flowering, red-berried *Cotoneaster conspicuus*

A two-tier garden

This two-tier garden, opposite, lies at the back of a turn-of-the-century town house. Originally a rusty metal stairway led from a narrow balcony to a shabby grassed area below. Because there was no visual link between the two they were viewed quite separately. The design brief was to unify the two levels, making the whole area appear more spacious, and to create a stylish pocket of calm within a busy urban environment.

Styling the new structures
The old metal balcony and stairway were replaced and widened. Timber was chosen for the new structure to forge a visual and textural link with the door and window surrounds. The higher end section of the balcony railing screens the upper tier from passers-by in the alleyway that runs alongside the house. The sage green paintwork echoes the Art nouveau flavour of the interior design and the patterning of the cross bars successfully blends with the architectural style of the house.

The original garden had an area of grass at ground level. The design called for a hard surface to unify this area with the structure of the house, and a mellow stone was chosen to blend with the soft green paintwork.

A hop (*Humulus lupulus*) climbing up the balcony provides an additional visual link between the two tiers and, along with other plants and an existing tree, gives the garden an air of freshness. The overall effect is of a calm and simple retreat, with restful colours used in both planting and structural materials.

Vertical garden
A two-tier space with balcony and stairway provides the perfect site for vertical plants. A variety of climbers have transformed this small entrance area, left, into a lush vertical garden. Ivy (Hedera *sp.*) *forms the evergreen base, and is contrasted with the grey rosettes of* Echeveria *sp. To the side is jasmine* (Trachelospermum jasminoides) *and around the door a fruiting vine* (Vitis *sp.*).

Garden overview

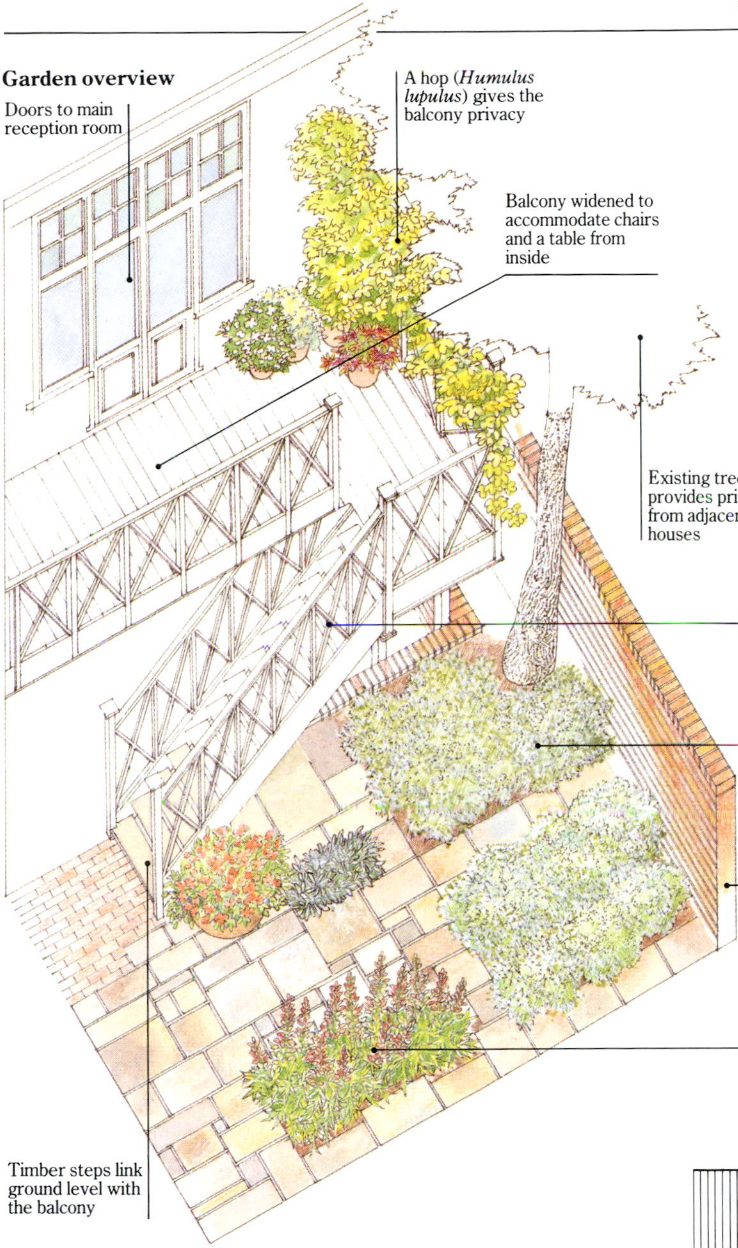

Doors to main reception room

A hop (*Humulus lupulus*) gives the balcony privacy

Balcony widened to accommodate chairs and a table from inside

Stylish design

Planting is restrained but effective, left. Containers provide bright splashes of colour. Herbs at ground level fill the air with aromatic freshness. The balcony will act as an outdoor extension to the reception room and the paved terrace to the basement games room. The overall effect is of a calm and simple retreat.

Existing tree provides privacy from adjacent houses

Balcony cross bars echo the architectural style of the house

Herbs with aromatic foliage give the garden an air of freshness

Existing brick boundary wall matched in brick of new edging and paving

Dramatic form of bear's breeches (*Acanthus spinosus*)

Planting plan

Timber steps link ground level with the balcony

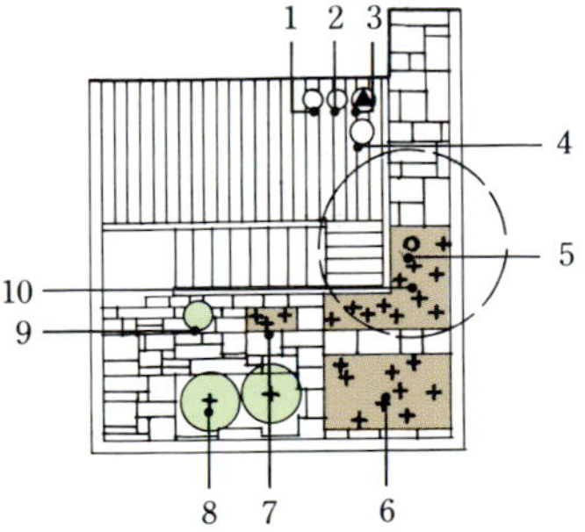

Key to planting plan

1 Olearia *sp.*
2 Thymus *x* citriodorus
3 Humulus lupulus
4 Pieris formosa forrestii
5 Robinia pseudoacacia
6 Thymus *x* citriodorus, Myrrhus odorata *and* Chrysanthemum parthenium *massed*
7 Salvia officinalis
8 Acanthus spinosus
9 Impatiens *sp.*
10 Origanum vulgare *and* Nepeta *sp. massed*

Small space gardens

The word *garden* often conjures up images of lawns, herbaceous borders, soil and secateurs, mulches and manures, and sometimes people try to cram all of these into the tiniest space. But a small space needs a different approach. First break free of preconceptions about what it should and should not contain. Next consider all the design elements and techniques that can be combined to produce a stimulating effect – sculpture, water, minimal planting, lighting at night, or dense, jungly planting. Design and planning are particularly crucial in a small space, because there is literally no room for error.

A courtyard garden

This modern atrium-type house, opposite, has a central courtyard overlooked by all its rooms. Although the walls are glass, the courtyard receives little light. A limited range of plants would do well here. Good choices might be ferns, Japanese anemones, and *Forsythia* sp. Planting could be in gravel for easy care.

An enclosure like this is an exciting prospect for the garden designer. Plants need to look good from all sides and throughout the year. The conditions here are quite different from those of more usual exposed sites. The courtyard has a micro-climate, with still air warmed by heat from the house. If this environment also received the sun, it would support very exotic planting. A temporary roof in the winter would give extra protection.

INCREASING APPARENT SIZE IN A SMALL GARDEN

A good first step is to extend the feel of the garden inside your home. Divisions between inside and out can be blurred by placing tubs of plants on a small paved area in the garden and on the floor of an adjoining room. The same effect can be created by using the same or similar tones of colour on inside and outside walls.

It is a common misconception that an abundance of small objects suits a small space. In fact the reverse is true. Clutter in a tiny, enclosed space can feel distinctly claustrophobic. As in interior design, the fewer the number of objects and the simpler the range of colours, patterns, and surfaces in a small space, the larger it will appear.

Limit the number of objects and structures in your garden and scale them up rather than down. Stick to a simple range of materials and try to match them to existing structures, such as boundary fencing or the walls of your home. Build in features wherever possible and choose plants carefully, grouping them in bold masses.

An Italian courtyard
Shade is needed as much as sun in this enclosed courtyard in a warm climate, right. The tiles provide a cool surface underfoot and the simple furniture doesn't distract the eye from the concept.

Different approaches

One proposal, bottom right, treats the enclosure as an outside playroom for young children. Supervision is easy from the adjoining kitchen, and the tiled kitchen unit is extended on the garden side of the glass wall, providing a stand for container plants and a small table where children can sit. The sandpit could later be turned into a pond. The paved area could be slightly sunken to provide casual seating around the edge and to protect the glazing from wheeled toys.

A romantic alternative transforms the area in the other design, below left. The whole enclosure becomes a reflective sheet of water, throwing light into the house. The pool is lined with the same tiles as the kitchen and the water flows through individual tiles raised up on integral pillars.

A bed of white *Iris laevigata* provides the central feature. A few brightly coloured koi carp, a mass of simple fountain jets, or underwater lights for night-time will all help to bring the courtyard to life.

Alternative designs

Visual set-piece
This romantic design, left, reflects light through the windows of the surrounding rooms. The pool is lined with tiles to match those in the kitchen and further brightened by colourful koi carp. Iris laevigata provides the central feature, with water weed planted around its base to keep the water clean. A proposal like this is best implemented at the same time as the house is being built, because excavated material will need to be carried through the house to the site.

| Tiles | White-flowering *Iris laevigata* | Tiles raised on pillars | Koi carp |

Tiled standing for pot plants

| Purpose-built children's furniture | Tiles | Sandpit |

Activity centre
Here the courtyard becomes an extension to the house, right, providing a play area for young children. Supervision is possible from the house. The built-in furniture matches the kitchen units. Potted plants are practical in a children's area – they can be moved around as necessary and removed altogether if they are in danger of getting damaged. The Vitis coignetiae in the corner provides plenty of greenery without taking up too much valuable play space.

Balconies

A balcony, however small, can be transformed into a valuable visual and spatial extension of the living area it adjoins, providing enjoyment all year round. Even a windy or dusty balcony can be a pleasant place to tend a few plants or sit and entertain in the summer.

Styling a balcony

Create a visual bond between balcony and interior – the same flooring, the same colour scheme, the same furniture, plants grouped around the doorway. Artificial lighting, from either inside or out, will enable you to use the balcony into summer evenings and to make it a year-round view in its own right after dark.

Shade and shelter

Awnings, a large umbrella, or roller blinds can be used to provide shade. Plants can be useful here too, remembering that the shade they cast cannot be rolled in when the sun has moved round. Shrubs, like box (*Buxus* sp.), or climbers, like ivy (*Hedera* sp.), can be trained up trelliswork, fencing, or railings, and will give shelter from the wind and a measure of privacy, as well as obscuring unwanted views. If you have a lot of plants, try to fit a water point nearby to make watering easier. Otherwise you may find yourself making endless trips up and down stairs with a watering can. Any scheme that involves structural changes may need permission and professional advice, for example about the weight capacity of the balcony.

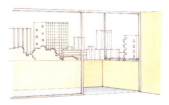

City skyline, above
A small city balcony is transformed, right and below, into a stylish outside living area, against a dramatic urban backdrop. The balcony space is surrounded by a low boundary wall, separated from a neighbouring balcony by a glass panel, and divided from the living area by sliding glass doors.

Tropical mood, above
Strong, tropical pattern and colour are used inside and out, bringing light and life to the balcony. Matching awning and roller blinds, picking up the colour of the interior wall, give privacy and shade when needed. Tropical detail is furnished by the Kentia palm (Howea belmoreana), the slatted linen curtain, ceiling fan, and wickerwork chairs.

Sculptural chic, left
A yew hedge (Taxus baccata) is sited in this alternative to give shade and privacy, and clipped box (Buxus sp.) provides year-round sculptural interest with minimal upkeep. Pots of bulbs and annuals bring a splash of seasonal colour.

Roof spaces

For town and city dwellers, rooftops are particularly valuable areas that can often be transformed into congenial places for sitting, sunbathing, entertaining, or eating out of doors, even under the stars.

Creating a rooftop room

Try to create a room-like atmosphere so that you feel you are sitting in a roof garden rather than perched on top of a building – the enormity of the sky overhead and a view stretching into the distance can otherwise be overwhelming. Walls can be painted, the original roofing material replaced or covered with weatherproof flooring or lightweight paving, artificial lighting can be installed, and comfortable and relaxing furniture introduced.

Planting can then be used to add a refreshing touch of greenery and colour that will soften the stark lines of surrounding buildings. Because roofs are exposed to the elements, permanent planting must be resilient or given shelter from strong winds.

A convenient water supply and regular maintenance are vital for rooftop gardening – the wind has a dehydrating, foliage-burning effect, and container-grown plants have a limited moisture reserve.

Consult the owner of your property and/or a structural engineer before using a roof or making any structural changes to it. Heavy elements are best sited over or close to direct structural support, which is usually at the edges of the roof space.

Informal room

A bright and informal rooftop area, above. The area in front of the disused chimney stack has been turned into a jazzy bar. Timber tiles are laid over bitumen flooring, and used for a raised sun deck.

Formal garden

The same space, below, with a more formal design, based on squares and rectangles, picked up in the timber beams, trellising, raised beds, and pools, echoing the pattern of the skyscrapers beyond.

Windows

Windows make an excellent focus for decoration with paint, trelliswork, plants, and containers. Planning and thoughtful planting are important in a window setting, just as in any garden design.

Window decoration

First look at the colour of the window frame, its surround, and the interior colour scheme. Decide whether you want the window to look most striking from inside or from outside, and focus the arrangement accordingly.

If you have no windowsill or your window opens outwards, hang a windowbox beneath or pots beneath and around. Alternatively, climbers can be grown from ground level and trained around a window. If your window is at street level and you want a measure of privacy, plants in windowboxes or grown up from the ground can be used to screen the room from people passing by.

Make sure all plant containers are properly secured on sills and walls, with no danger of falling onto the pavement below. Also try to water at a time when nobody is passing underneath and likely to be dripped on. Bring moveable pots inside for watering.

Using climbers, left
Trellis attached to the exterior wall around the window supports yellow climbing roses. The trelliswork has been carefully chosen to extend the pattern of the windowframe.

Fragrant planting, right
Herbs grow in a windowbox that hangs below an outward-opening window. On warm summer evenings with the window open, rich fragrances drift in to the dining room.

Mediterranean style, left
A collection of terracotta pots filled with begonias and basil makes a colourful contrast with the dark blue window and pale blue walls.

Hanging basket, below
A refreshing glimpse of greenery from inside a high-rise flat.

Basement gardens

The outside area left to basement homes is often little more than a small space wedged between street level and front door, or a small sunken back yard. Towered over by adjacent walls, basement gardens tend to be gloomy and damp. Despite these unpromising characteristics, there are many ways of making them both stylish and usable.

Improving conditions
Basement areas are often damp. Repairing or installing a damp-proof course in surrounding walls will ensure garden drainage and moisture never infiltrates inside. Surface water should be channelled into a storm water system if possible. A basement area that has been excavated to a level where there is nothing but impervious subsoil must have adequate drainage for gardening. Before planting, the subsoil should be excavated to a depth of 1m (3¼ ft) and filled with a layer of loose hardcore, followed by a layer of compost.

Structural changes
Basement areas can be transformed by building in a series of slightly raised "pads". Two or three arranged in an overlapping pattern will create a sense of movement to prevent the eye wandering up surrounding walls and out of the site. Gentle changes of level can also be used to great effect in areas between street level and the basement entrance.

Colour can bring interest and brighten up a shady area. Paint the walls, use *trompe l'oeil*, experiment with mirrors to make the area appear larger.

Visual anchors
Including a feature to anchor the eye within the site will prevent it from being dominated by surrounding buildings. Whether you choose a piece of furniture, a plant, or a sculpture, keep it large in relation to the size of the space. Scale features up rather than down, and stick to one or two striking objects rather than a clutter of smaller ones. Tiny, delicate features will look insignificant and will not hold the eye.

Single-colour planting
A basement yard can be dramatically brought to life by a vibrant, single-colour planting scheme, perhaps light tones of gold and silver. Foliage shape and texture could be used in the same way. Be wary of what you plant alongside a high wall – tall plants will lean inwards to reach the light. For some suggestions for shade-loving plants, see pp. 153–4.

A BASEMENT DESIGN

A transformation
The dark basement area below is transformed into an inviting and airy space, right. The original steep flight of steps is replaced with a series of gentle changes in level, making a gradual transition to street level. Storage is often a problem in small gardens, and is built into the design here. It acts as a visual pivot for the level changes, and provides the area near the house with a measure of privacy. The built-in cupboard houses the dustbins.

The existing space
A dark basement, right, poses a design problem. It consists of a dingy, sunken area reached by steep steps from street level. The paved area is surrounded by walls.

Inside-outside garden

An inside-outside design creates visual integration between the inside of the house and the garden throughout the year. The link can be effective from the depths of winter, when floodlit snow, for example, can look spectacular from the comfort of a warm sitting room, to mid-summer, when open doors and windows make the garden an extension of the home, for eating, play, and entertaining. Some designs take the feeling of internal decoration outside to balconies or patios, while others bring the style of the garden indoors.

The link between in and out can be enforced by flooring materials extended outside, well-placed indoor plants, and furnished terraces. Matched colours can strengthen the bond and increase the apparent size of the outside area. While an open door allows the easiest movement between inside and out, views through windows provide similar opportunities for integrating garden and home.

CREATING A LINK

When a glass wall separates room and garden as in this house, right, you have a special opportunity to get maximum use out of the garden. In summer the two are physically linked through the open doors. The sense of space remains through winter if the garden is well co-ordinated with the room in terms of colour, pattern, and any permanent furnishings, and itself provides strong visual interest. Garden lighting will continue the effect after dark.

Existing living/garden room, right
This relaxing room has a large expanse of glass, with doors giving access to a paved terrace used for casual meals outside and family living in summer.

Paved garden, below
The first alternative proposes a fully paved garden ideal for entertaining. The concrete slab ground patterning runs from outside, across the threshold, and into the room, linking inside and outside seating areas. Brick paving and matching coloured walls emphasize the link. Tiled flooring is practical in a room giving onto the garden.

Visual effect, below
In the second proposal, the outside space is designed with visual effect in mind rather than as a living area. The composition is abstract, using broad masses of a single plant, contrasted with clipped trees in square tubs. A mural depicting abstract geometric shapes draws the eye to the far wall beyond a ground design of lawn and paving.

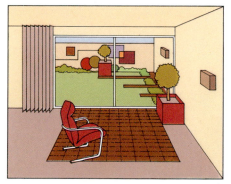

The outside dining and seating area, right, is a good example of how in and out can be successfully linked. Brick paving leads out from the house to the terrace, and brick steps complete the transition from house to garden. The covered section of the terrace, which provides shelter from blazing sun or inclement weather, is actually part of the house structure and is defined by painted white beams. Planting in containers and a herb bed to the side of the covered area soften the effect of large areas of brick and bring the garden closer to the house.

Relaxed outside dining
White painted woodwork and furniture define this attractive terraced area, right. A fine spot for relaxed eating and enjoying a view of the garden.

INTEGRATING STYLE IN A SMALL SPACE

The views through the glass doors show two small outside spaces that have been styled to continue the mood of the interiors they adjoin. Establishing a strong and stylish link between inside and outside is an effective way of using space. Planting is minimal, maintenance will be limited, and these areas are very much outside "rooms" rather than gardens.

Italian romance
This scene, above, has an air of classically inspired sophistication. The soft ochre of the walls inside and the fence outside create a gentle backdrop to the strong pattern of the black and white chequered flooring. A dramatic swagged curtain gives an aura of grandeur to the scene, echoed by the round stone table and the classical bust on the wall. The simple white chairs are as suitable for use inside as outside. Their moss green upholstery links the eye with the elegant cypress that conceals the drainpipe. The overall effect is very striking.

Mondrian-style space
The bold patterns, simple shapes, and bright primary colours of a Mondrian rug are the starting point for the design of this garden, above. Buttercup yellow flooring establishes the link and the colours of the rug provide inspiration for the red table and slatted blinds, the dark blue curtains and chairs, and the pale blue of the wall outside. A functioning drainpipe has been disguised between two false pipes to create an unusual sculptural feature. A container-grown fern sited on the pipes balances the yuccas to the right.

CHAPTER TWO

PLANNING YOUR GARDEN

While the prospect of designing a garden
from scratch may seem daunting, if you
take a measured approach, the pieces will
fall into place. Planning a garden is the
same as planning a room in the house – it
combines practicalities with aesthetics.
If you break the planning process down
into its component stages, the mystery of
"design" evaporates: assessment of site
and requirements, measuring up, drawing
to scale, evolving a pattern within the
context of the style you have chosen, and
finally translating the pattern into areas of
structure and planting. Spend time at each
step to consider all possibilities and to
think through the implications of your plan
at all times of the year. Think of the
garden after heavy rainfall, after drought,
under snow, in hot sun, on a windy day,
and at each season of the year.
A good design, successfully realized, will
bring you enormous pleasure, whether
you are working in the garden, relaxing in
it, or watching it mature over the years.
Careful planning and thought at this stage
will help you get that design right.

Integrating the elements
*Good planning is particularly crucial if you want to
combine several features, as in this garden, left. The
pond, the pergola, the circular lawn, contrasting hard
surfaces, and a wealth of planting were all carefully
designed and integrated on paper before a stone was
laid or a shrub planted.*

Size and shape

Once you have decided on a garden style, the first step towards producing a design is getting some hard facts down on paper. With pencil and plain or graph paper, you can begin to measure up your site.

Start with the house. Most houses are built to a regular plan with angles at 90 degrees. Measure up the dimensions of the building, working around it from face to face, taking running measurements to the windows and doors as you go, as shown in the example survey, opposite. This should produce an accurate outline.

If you live in an older house with odd corners and ancillary buildings, you might find it easier to search out the deeds, which will include a detailed outline drawing.

Next, carefully draw up the house measurements to a working scale – at least 1/100 and preferably 1/50 for a smaller garden. Allow enough space to add the garden boundary around your house outline.

Now measure the garden. Measure lines or offsets at 90 degrees from the house to the boundaries of your outside space. If necessary, mark these offsets on the site with string so that you can move along them and take further offsets, again at 90 degrees, to any existing features within striking distance. Work around the lengths of the perimeter of the site, noting the measurements as you go.

If any elements of the garden are left "floating" on your layout and cannot be located by taking 90-degree offsets, take measurements to them from any two points already noted. You can then locate the precise position of these elements using a process known as triangulation, see opposite.

Now measure the size and relative positions of smaller features, including details such as the girth of tree trunks and the span of any overhanging foliage. Note any internal walls or fences, any steps and manhole covers. Be as accurate as possible.

Measure and plot any changes of level. First mark the positions of the top and bottom of the level change. If the change of level is considerable, you may need the help of a surveyor, who will quickly give you some spot levels to key points in the garden relating back to a datum or zeropoint, usually coinciding with a threshold into the house. For smaller changes of level, you can take your own measurements by a system known as boning, see below. This system is simple and accurate, and the only equipment you need is a metre pole, a plank, and a spirit level.

Mark the direction of north accurately on your survey – this will determine the ultimate orientation of the garden pattern. It is all too easy to forget the scale of the survey, so note that down too.

MEASURING GRADIENTS

Boning, or judging gradient by eye, is a useful technique for surveying a simple slope. You need a pole exactly one metre long, a plank, and a spirit level. Nestle one end of the plank into the ground at the top of the slope. Prop the plank horizontal using the metre pole, sliding it along under the plank as necessary and using the spirit level. The slope falls a metre over the distance from the anchored end of the plank to where it meets the metre stick. Measure this distance. If you cannot reach the bottom of the slope in one go, repeat the process, moving the end of the plank down to the mark of the first metre stick. Add the vertical measurements and then the horizontal ones to find the overall gradient.

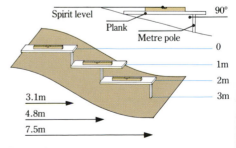

Example measurement
This example produces a gradient of 1 in 2.5, a fairly steep slope in gardening terms.

MAKING AN OUTLINE SURVEY

A simple survey, like the one shown below, shows all the relevant details of an existing plot, providing you with a basis for a new design.

To make your own survey you will need a tape measure, skewers, ruler, set square, pair of compasses, pencils, and squared paper. Make a rough sketch of the area on which you can record measurements out in the garden. Next, measure from your house to the boundary, either getting someone to hold the end of the measure for you or securing it to the ground with a skewer. Having filled in as many measurements as you can, you are ready to draw up the survey.

If your garden is irregularly shaped and difficult to measure, you will need to use the triangulation method described below. This method is also useful for determining the position of features such as trees or ponds, which may not be within easy reach of a 90° offset.

Using scale
This plan has been drawn up to a scale where one unit of measurement represents a hundred units in the garden. Use a larger scale if possible, say, 1/50, which will help you to draw up your plan accurately and with plenty of detail.

The completed survey

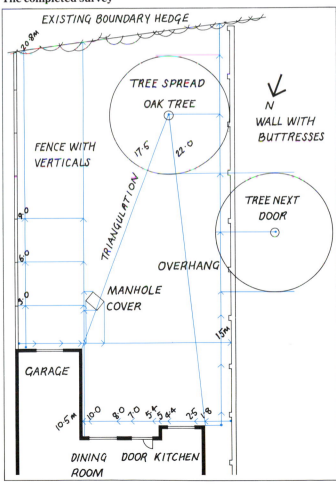

Triangulation
This technique will help you determine the position of features within your garden. Start by finding two fixed points from which to measure everything – the corners of your house are ideal. Measure the house, then measure the distance to each main feature (such as an existing tree) or each boundary, first from one house corner, then the other (see above). To transfer these measurements to your plan, set your compasses to the measurements required in the scale and make two intersecting arcs (see left).

Line and pattern

The underlying framework of any garden, whether formally or naturally styled, is made up of pattern. The lines may be blurred by rambling plants or accentuated by clipped hedges and shrubs, but the pattern provides the essential character of the design.

The lines which you draw on your plan will eventually mark the edges of the contrasting areas of the layout, the paths and service areas, the lawns and planting areas. Lines can be cleverly used to create optical illusions. Lines which run away from the viewer, for example, will make a site appear longer – even

more so if they deliberately converge, perhaps by making a path narrower as it gets further away. Lines running horizontally across the view will give added breadth to a site.

Good design depends on choosing the right pattern for the right job. Some patterns create a static feel, while others appear to have movement in them, as the examples below show. A garden with room for a focal point within its boundaries and a garden with a view will both accept a pattern with movement in it. Lines in the pattern should lead the viewer to the view or the object. Conversely, if there is

CHOOSING A PATTERN

There are endless permutations of pattern, most of which can be adapted for garden planning. The ones suggested here are drawn on a square grid. Making a guiding grid like this is part of the planning process (see *Evolving a framework*, pp. 76–7). The more static designs will tend to hold the eye on focal points within the garden, while the more dynamic patterns will lead the eye around the space. Static patterns evoke a feeling of calm and tranquillity, while dynamic patterns help to create drama and excitement.

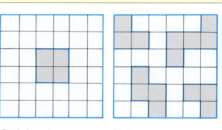

Static formal

Abstract

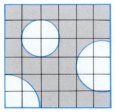

Dynamic

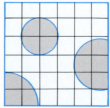

Static abstract

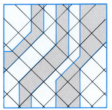

Dynamic diagonals

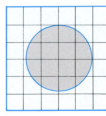

Static formal

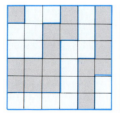

Positive abstract

Negative abstract

Dynamic curves

Abstract curves and squares

SIMPLE CIRCULAR DESIGN

The basic concept
Two overlapping circles form the basis of a simple and effective pattern, below left. The paper plan shows clearly the proportions of what will be the
pool and brick circle in relation to the bay window of the house. At this stage they can be adjusted as necessary until the design fits the available space. The next stage is to rework the plan in 3-D.

The paper plan

The plan in 3-D

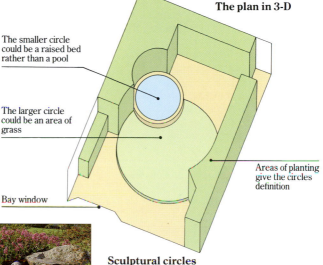

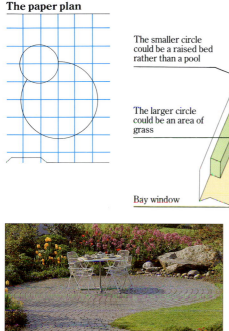

The smaller circle could be a raised bed rather than a pool

The larger circle could be an area of grass

Areas of planting give the circles definition

Bay window

Sculptural circles
Bringing the areas of planting into the third dimension and raising the smaller circle gives the pattern a sculptural form, above. This is a useful exercise in helping you to visualize the finished garden.

From plan to reality
The two main circles make a simple and pleasing geometric pattern. The pool adds depth to the design and the circular theme is echoed by the round table, left.

no focal point or ultimate goal for the viewer, a static pattern is more suitable. A small walled garden with no outside interest, for example, needs a patterned layout which will hold the eye within the site.

The house and surrounding buildings will influence the pattern you choose. A modern, abstracted design might suit a twentieth-century semi-detached house, while a symmetrical, formal plan might better suit an eighteenth-century house. Crisp outlines go with glass and steel, while a relaxed structure suits the country cottage.

Don't get bogged down in choosing surface materials or plants at this stage. Think in terms of large areas and elements, rose beds rather than individual species of rose, terraces rather than brick circles or granite sett squares.

The basic patterns shown opposite illustrate a few ideas drawn up on an idealized square plot. No decisions have yet been made about what the lines enclose, but each pattern creates a different feel and will make a different garden. Look for a pattern that will support your overall style and will accommodate the various elements you want to include.

3-D shape and texture

Once you have decided on a ground pattern in line form, the next stage is to take the design into the third dimension. The ultimate shape of the plan will emerge as heights and spans of walls, changes of level, trees, and shrubs, whether planned or existing, are combined with the two-dimensional line plan.

What makes one plot a pleasant place to be and another not, are the shapes and proportions of the plant masses that hold and surround the various parts of the garden. These shapes and proportions can either work with or against the other three-dimensional structure on the site – your home.

Whether they balance or not becomes more apparent as the garden matures and the fully grown trees and shrubs are in front of you. And here lies one of the most difficult aspects of garden design – trying to imagine the planted areas as they will be in years to come, while planting twigs in the earth now. Even the great landscape artists of eighteenth-century English parks experienced this problem. They could re-shape the landscape by making lakes and

COMPOSING ON A SMALL SCALE

Give the same attention to every grouping of elements in your garden, however small the scale. Simple compositions that juxtapose interesting shapes and textures, like this one, below, create points of interest. Here plants of different shape and texture are contrasted with a smoothly rounded concrete ball.

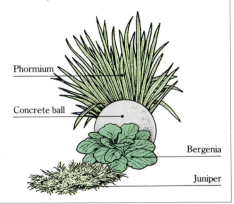

Phormium

Concrete ball

Bergenia

Juniper

THE GARDEN IN THREE DIMENSIONS

The overall shape of the garden is created by three-dimensional effects. Space can be moulded by the siting and subsequent growth of trees, shrubs, and smaller plants. The two examples, below, show how two different layouts on the same site can produce very different effects.

In the more formal layout, below, foliage is grouped to hold the eye, the masses of trees and shrubs balancing each other.

In the informal layout, bottom, foliage is grouped to lead the eye around a central mass and suggests hidden extensions to the garden. In both gardens foliage (mass) balances the open area (void).

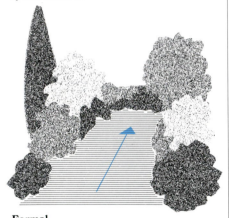

Formal

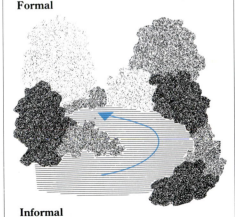

Informal

shifting vast areas of earth, but they had to plant out their rolling parkland with tiny trees which we see now in their maturity, more than two hundred years later.

Each planting area will be made up of groupings. As well as considering the shape of each mature plant and its leaves and stems, look at the texture and quality of light that it reflects or diffuses. Compare, for example, a rhododendron leaf, which is flat and dull, with a camellia leaf, which is bright and shiny. Multiply the different effects by the number of leaves on an average bush and the total adds up to a considerable contrast. If your planting plan includes deciduous species, take account of the tracery shapes and texture of their bare branches and shoots in winter and early spring. Other elements which help mould garden shape are walls, fences, raised beds, even built-in barbecues in a small area. The materials used will affect the feel of the garden considerably too, reflecting or absorbing the light, or giving a hard or a soft finish.

Balancing shape and texture
The bold and simple plan of this urban garden, below, holds the eye. The garden presents a green picture from the various levels of the house that it serves. The firm shape of the design is softened but not obliterated by foliage forms.

Using colour

Bright splashes of colour, which every seed catalogue would have you use, are quickly come and gone. Most plants actually flower for no more than one month in the year, and many for considerably less. Your primary concern should be subtle colour – the hues and tones of the permanent foliage which last the year through. The foliage colours of both deciduous and evergreen shrubs and trees are remarkably varied, from the dark green of some conifers and yew (*Taxus baccata*), which seem almost black on the skyline in winter, to the light grey-green of whitebeams.

The "walls" of the garden should be a background mass of understated colour. If this colour is too strong, it can distract from and disrupt any herbaceous or annual colour planted in front of it.

Natural colour
The colours of flowers indigenous to northern Europe are fairly low key – cream, lemon, white, green. Soft spring colours give way

to pale early summer ones, which intensify through the summer months, until the mellow tones of autumn appear. Wild flowers also tend to paler colours, moving with the seasons through pinks, pale blues, then yellows and golds. Harder, hotter flower colours originate in sunny climates, where their intensity is enhanced by the strength of the sun's rays. Be guided by nature and beware of bizarre hybridized colours. Unnatural, strident colours are difficult to blend in, and tend to dominate the scene.

The effect of light
Light affects the quality of colour, so that the same colour can look very different at different times of day. Pale colours look pleasantly soft in gentle morning and evening light, but can appear washed out in a strong noon-day sun. Colours strong enough to cope with a high noon sun, on the other hand, can look too garish in the morning and evening. The many shades of green in a country setting will look different throughout the day. Early morning, bright, dew-covered green becomes hazy blue-green in high sunlight, and changes again in soft evening light.

Controlling colour
Colour contributes to the overall feel and style of a garden and should be used sensitively. Herbaceous and annual colour can be carefully chosen to complement and continue the effect of foliage shrubs. Bright yellows and oranges, for example, are stimulating and ideal in conjunction with a lively area. Softer colours, such as blues and pinks, with a touch of purple or white, will produce a tranquil, calming effect. Bright, stimulating colours and softer, recessive ones can be successfully grown alongside each other, but not mixed indiscriminately to produce a pepper-and-salt look. Locate the strongest colours in the foreground planting, and allow the colours to become paler with distance. A brilliant patch of colour in the middle of a distant view is bound to be a visual disruption, as well as having a foreshortening effect.

THE COLOUR WHEEL

Colour in the garden needs to be used with care. Differentiating between hue (a pure colour) and tone (a shade of hue) helps in understanding colour. The relationship of hues can be shown simply on the colour wheel, below left. The wheel has a warm half (magenta, red, and yellow) and a cool half (green, cyan, and blue). Hues next to each other on the wheel generally harmonize, while those opposite each other contrast.

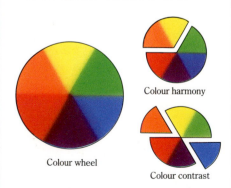

Colour harmony

Colour wheel

Colour contrast

Think about mood and how you can use colour to create and enhance it. As you compose groupings of plants, consider colour as much as shape and texture. Grade colours carefully before planting, imagining them in full bloom against the backdrop of existing vegetation. Avoid the tasteless discord that the average conifer selection tends to produce – metallic blues and dark greens, contrasted with silver and gold.

Colour in a small space
It is particularly important that colours work well together in a small space, where every garden element, from walls and paving to furniture and planting, will be close together and viewed as a whole. Quite possibly the garden will also be seen in conjunction with the colours inside your home. Create a colour scheme for your outside space as you would a room inside, co-ordinating each part of it and blending in any later additions.

Striking contrasts
The colour impact of this border, below, is breathtaking. Pinks and blues predominate, with grey in the selection of herbaceous plants and touches of lemon and white to enliven the whole. The border relies entirely on colour for its success. It has little form, with no bold foliage to subdue the colour contrasts.

Views out

Most garden owners with a dramatic rural, coastal, or even urban view beyond their boundary will want to make the most of it. But there is more to the job than simply removing any solid barriers that intervene. There are two important considerations: first, the prevailing weather direction, often the reason that the barrier was erected originally, and second, the scale of the view compared with the scale of the garden. A small "tamed" area of land can look very insignificant set beside a backdrop of rolling, impressive countryside, unless you create a controlled visual transition between the two.

INTEGRATING A VIEW

The general aim of integrating a view into a garden layout is to camouflage the actual boundary line, and to allow the feel of the countryside to run into your property.

Simply making a hole in an existing hedge or wall is not always the solution. You will need to plan planting inside the perimeter, in front of the remaining stretches of hedge or wall, to bring the view through the hole that has been created, and to strengthen the visual link by counterbalancing any feature outside with a feature inside.

If there is no existing solid barrier, an effective way to integrate the view is to plan hedging closer to the viewpoint. Then align the piece of your land beyond the new barrier with the outside world, possibly treating it in a "natural" way with orchard, rough grass, and wild flowers.

These two illustrations, below, show options for different boundary treatments based on one inviting view, with an existing willow-leaf pear (*Pyrus salicifolia*) centrally placed. The two versions are different in plan and style.

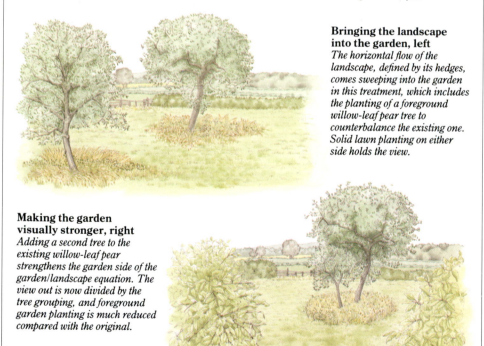

Bringing the landscape into the garden, left
The horizontal flow of the landscape, defined by its hedges, comes sweeping into the garden in this treatment, which includes the planting of a foreground willow-leaf pear tree to counterbalance the existing one. Solid lawn planting on either side holds the view.

Making the garden visually stronger, right
Adding a second tree to the existing willow-leaf pear strengthens the garden side of the garden/landscape equation. The view out is now divided by the tree grouping, and foreground garden planting is much reduced compared with the original.

A panoramic view can be too much for the eye to encompass, and too expansive for day-to-day appreciation. Seeing just a part of a fine view, framed by vegetation, can make the transition from wild landscape to cultivated plot more digestible.

Considering a frame

Any framing of a view with vegetation or structure need not necessarily be on or close to the boundary of the garden. Framing with planting nearer the viewpoint gives greater control of the way you see the view, as shown in the diagrams, right. It also avoids the common fault of evolving a garden design pattern that relates primarily to the boundary and reinforces a feeling of enclosure. If, for example, your garden happens to be L-shaped, it is a mistake to base your garden layout on a series of concentric L-shapes that converge on the house, adjoining it at awkward angles. It is much better to relate your pattern and planting to the house – after all, it is from this point that you use the garden most, not only physically, but visually as well.

Balancing scale

Controlling a view is also the way to regulate the transition of scale between garden and landscape. There is a balance to be achieved. Framing and reducing the view will prevent the cultivated garden appearing too trivial by comparison. Any formal elements, whether symmetrical or asymmetrical – walling, paving, hedging – should be kept close to the house or outbuildings, and should echo their lines. There is no place for formal elements near the boundary if you are trying to open up a view. Here the garden lines, shaping, and planting should be as sympathetic to the landscape as possible, strengthening the transition from inside the garden to the view beyond.

The space between the area close to the house and the boundary area – the transitional area – is best treated in a loose manner, and the style of planting planned to progress from the more sophisticated or exotic near the structure (where it will be more sheltered) to a wilder look as the garden approaches the natural landscape beyond (see *Anatomy of a country garden*, p. 38).

SHAPING A VIEW

Opening up a panorama totally is in most cases too demanding visually and makes the site too exposed physically. Planting and structures in the garden can be used to shape the view, while at the same time giving protection. Secondary areas of interest can be created within the planting formations, near the viewpoint.

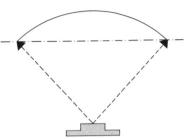

Exposed with a panoramic view

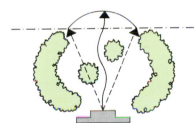

View held and masked

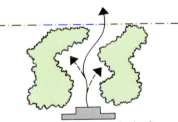

Serpentine planting to restrict the view

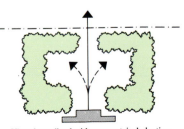

View formalized with symmetrical planting

Evolving a framework

Furnished with an outline survey of your garden (see p. 67), the next stage in working towards your own garden pattern is to evolve a framework. The most useful framework is a grid of intersecting equally spaced lines. The spacing of the lines of this grid, known as modulation, will usually be determined by either the structure of the house or the surrounding boundaries. Study these structures closely and establish which points to relate the scale of your grid to.

Relating the grid to the house

You might find that the external structure of your house suggests a strong, regular division of space. Look at the house wall facing on to the garden. If it has a formal design, for example, there will be a recognizable rhythm to the measurements between doors and windows. These intervals might suggest the spacing of your grid. Modern houses are often built of prefabricated units which similarly will suggest the spacing. Some houses, however, have weaker, asymetrical designs, and here it will be better to look to the boundaries for the scale of the grid. You may have at least one straight boundary to anchor the grid.

Relating the grid to the boundary

Walls and fences are usually constructed in a regular pattern with vertical supports at regular intervals, in concrete, wood, or brick, infilled with wood or brick. This can provide an ideal starting point with the post or pier interval as the spacing for the grid. If you have a wall with no visible supports, measure its length and divide it equally into an appropriate number of sections.

MAKING AND USING A GRID

The garden frontage of this house, below, has some intrinsic interest, particularly in the projecting wing. More dominant, however, is a boundary wall with piers spaced at regular 1.8m (6 ft) intervals, and these have provided the spacing for the guiding grid of a garden plan. The grid lines also coincide with the important features of the garden elevation of the house, making this grid particularly successful. The beginnings of a pattern have been drawn on to the grid, circles and squares being included with equal confidence. It is unlikely that all the existing features of your garden will fit a grid exactly, but it is important to establish a discipline for your plan that will encompass most elements of the layout and that will show them all in scale.

Emerging patterns
When you have drawn the basic grid, use a tracing paper overlay to try out different patterns.

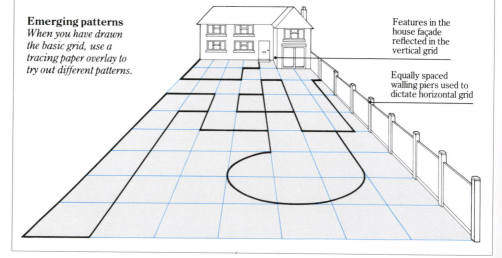

Features in the house façade reflected in the vertical grid

Equally spaced walling piers used to dictate horizontal grid

Lay a separate piece of tracing paper over your original survey and, ensuring that you are working to the same scale, extend lines across the site starting from your reference points and at 90 degrees to them. Using the same interval which separates each of these lines, overlay another set at 90 degrees to the first set, creating a grid of squares.

The squared grid can now be used as a guide for positioning elements and creating patterns in your garden. Any pattern which you evolve within these guidelines will have a scale relationship either to the building or to the boundary. If you then reinforce this relationship by constructing your garden in materials which match those of the house or boundary, house and garden will inevitably be strongly linked and your design will support a variety of treatments when it comes to infilling the pattern. After the discipline of producing such an accurate plan, you can now experiment freely with interpretations of your chosen style, being as bold as you please.

When you come to draw the pattern that will form the basis of your garden plan, use the grid as a guide wherever possible, coinciding right angles with the intersections of the grid lines and using the spacing of the grid as radii for any circles you include. At the same time don't be restricted by the grid – be flexible so that you can create a bold and positive plan. You can divide the squares of the grid in equal proportions, or even turn them through 45 degrees to accommodate specific features.

INTERLOCKING CIRCLES

The pattern of this walled garden, right, is a series of interlocking circles, inspired by the projecting bay window of the adjacent house. as shown in the diagram, below. The raised circle is edged in brick and surfaced in gravel with random planting and rock grouping.

The pattern

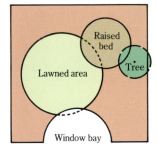

The bare bones
This diagram, above, shows the design in its most basic form. Trying out simple ideas on tracing overlays can produce sparks of inspiration.

Finalizing the plan

You now have a grid (see pp. 76–7) overlaying your outline survey (see pp. 66–7). Next prepare to mark the areas that you have allocated for particular functions – the terrace to catch the sun, the kitchen garden sited conveniently near to the house, an accessible but screened area for rubbish bins, and so on. Various factors will influence what goes where, including convenience, service paths, and safety precautions for children. Other essential considerations at this stage are climatic influences, such as prevailing winds (see pp. 15–16), aspect and the sun's path across the garden (see p. 17), views to enhance (see pp. 74–5), and eyesores to disguise and screen.

The positioning of these areas may in itself suggest an overall pattern for the garden, or at least the run of the designated hard surfacing. If no shape emerges, look back to the patterns on p. 68 and try evolving different schemes based on them.

The shape of the plot may indicate the sort of pattern that would work. A box-like garden surrounded by walls, for example, will probably need a hard, straight-edged pattern which reflects the character of the site. You can later soften the whole with bold planting to achieve a balanced overall design. Curves generally need more space than straight edges. Too large a circle within a square, for example, leaves corners that are both hard to build and later become awkward to infill.

Any garden design must work as a balanced whole, with no leftover corners and with positive balancing negative. The finished design should be clean and open, buildable, and ultimately workable. Stay within the discipline of the grid to achieve a crisp plan. Fit angles in at 90 degrees. Fit circles in so that they run cleanly into each other and connect with the line of the house or boundary. You might decide to turn the grid through 45 degrees and plan on the slant from house and boundary, or you might subdivide the squares of the grid in halves, thirds, or quarters to accommodate a particular shape. However you manipulate it, your guiding grid will provide an underlying

strength to the plan. Your plan will be positive, with bold sweeps to curves. There will be no weak, wiggling lines in the pattern. When the grid is removed and you draw up your final plan, the pattern will stand as a shape in its own right, broadly encompassing differing functions and areas of activity.

Using a grid to help your design will work for any size of garden and for any style. Try to visualize the garden in a sort of patchwork pattern, with areas of cultivation, of lawn, and of paving, rather than inhibiting yourself with a rigid layout of paths that leave awkward plots. The garden should be dominated by areas of attraction which are served by hard surfacing.

The final plan

Visualizing the plan
The success of your final plan will depend on imagining the three-dimensional results, although you will probably not go to the lengths of drawing up such a detailed plan as this, above. Always plan bold masses, resolving the detail of colour and texture as you come to create the garden in reality. This is a stage you will see develop only after much preliminary work.

STAGES OF THE PLAN

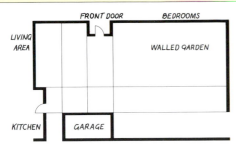

Stage 1 The guiding grid

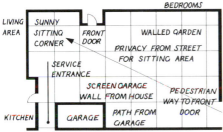

Stage 2 Adding detail

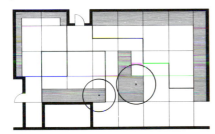

Stage 3 Evolving a pattern

An enclosed courtyard is used here to demonstrate the planning process. The living/dining area and kitchen windows look onto the garden area from the north, the front door and bedroom windows from the east wall, with the garage and boundary with the neighbouring garden opposite. The brief is to screen the garage wall from the house, provide privacy from overlooking buildings, and include an outside eating area, a grassed area, and some decorative features, such as a pool and plant groupings.

Stage 1 shows how a guiding grid can be evolved from the position and size of the garage, and the front and kitchen doorways. Stage 2 shows the grid extended to cover the whole area with notes added on site conditions and potential features. Lines coinciding with or bearing a relationship to this grid, will ensure that the features of the garden will eventually bear a strong relationship to the house and garage. Stage 3 involves the choice of pattern and areas to be planted, surfaced, or otherwise given some sort of feature. As the finished plan emerges, decisions such as what type of paving to use and whether there should be changes of level have to be made. Planting will need further planning (see Chapter Four, *Plants and planting*, pp. 136ff.). Stage 4 shows the finished two-dimensional plan, and the feel of the garden begins to emerge. Stage 5 is a sketched projection of how the actual garden will look. This is a very useful exercise, which will help you to bring the garden to life in your mind's eye and anticipate any problems that are not apparent in the two-dimensional versions. Even at this late stage you should be prepared to change anything that doesn't work.

Stage 5 The projection

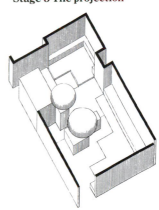

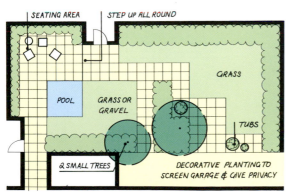

Stage 4 The completed 2-D plan

Winter replanning

The garden in winter has its own very special charms. There is satisfaction in the "put to bed" look of early winter, with leaves finally raked, bonfires burned, and manure spread. Shapes are strong in the garden at this time of year – shapes of lawns and paths, and the strong forms of evergreens that come into their own as their deciduous neighbours are reduced to their skeletal forms. There is the black look of yew (*Taxus baccata*) and if the winter is mild, the green of early hellebores with the pale yellow of winter jasmine seen against them. There is less drama, but there are the subtle and perhaps more precious pleasures of the earliest snowdrops and aconites. Winter is an ideal time for replanning, when you can see the line and pattern of your garden most sharply while it rests stark and clear from the blur of vegetation. It is also pleasant to be creative in those dead days of the season when there are no pressing garden chores demanding your attention.

If your garden is well established, you might now look to details of the layout that were not successful during seasons past. You might contemplate introducing two or three steps into a gentle slope, for example, to change the emphasis of the layout, or replacing a small area of lawn near the house with consolidated gravel for a more relaxed look.

The two gardens featured here required new layouts that solved a number of problems. In both cases you can see the original survey side-by-side with the replanned layout.

CASE ONE

The survey
This garden, below, had been developed strongly at its edges and centred on nothing. New building to the left of the site as we look at it required screening, and a vegetable plot had become too large to manage. An area of grass close to the house presented mowing problems and was difficult to keep looking good.

The revised plan
The new plan, below, includes thick screen planting to hide the new building, and re-directs the garden towards a view. The patch of grass close to the house is now consolidated gravel with random planting, which is much easier to maintain throughout the year, and the vegetable patch is reduced to a more manageable size.

The existing site

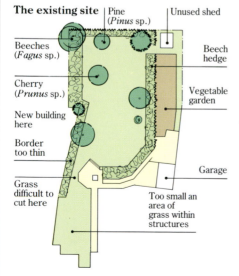

Pine (*Pinus* sp.)
Unused shed
Beeches (*Fagus* sp.)
Beech hedge
Cherry (*Prunus* sp.)
Vegetable garden
New building here
Border too thin
Garage
Grass difficult to cut here
Too small an area of grass within structures

The replanned site

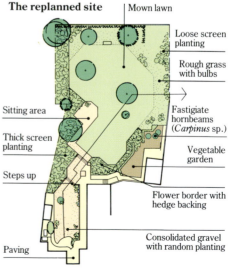

Mown lawn
Loose screen planting
Rough grass with bulbs
Sitting area
Fastigiate hornbeams (*Carpinus* sp.)
Thick screen planting
Vegetable garden
Steps up
Flower border with hedge backing
Consolidated gravel with random planting
Paving

CASE TWO

The survey

This large garden, right, had its prime views blocked by hedging, a mixed border, and an unnatural mound made from the spoil created by a pond excavation. The pond was separated from the main bulk of the garden and the house surrounds needed rationalizing.

The existing site

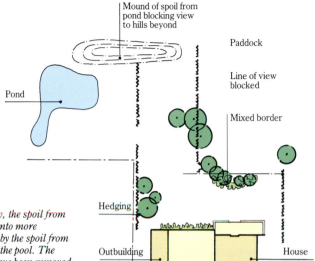

Mound of spoil from pond blocking view to hills beyond

Paddock

Line of view blocked

Mixed border

Pond

Hedging

Outbuilding

House

The revised plan

In the proposed new garden, below, the spoil from the pond excavation is contoured into more naturalistic shapes, and added to by the spoil from a certain amount of re-shaping of the pool. The central hedge and mixed border have been removed to open up the required views.

The replanned site

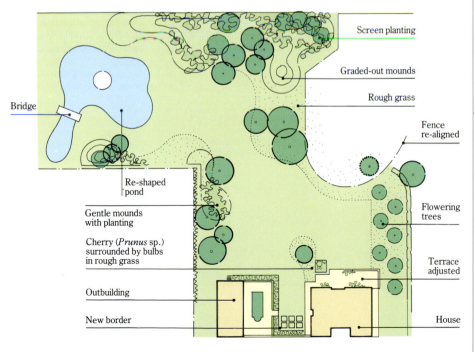

Screen planting

Graded-out mounds

Rough grass

Fence re-aligned

Bridge

Flowering trees

Re-shaped pond

Gentle mounds with planting

Cherry (*Prunus* sp.) surrounded by bulbs in rough grass

Terrace adjusted

Outbuilding

New border

House

Case study: A plan in action

The plans and photographs on the next four pages show the transformation of a small, run-down garden into an inviting and congenial outside room. This garden lies at the rear of a nineteenth-century terraced house in a busy town near London.

The brief
The new owners of the house wanted to get maximum use from their garden space – to enjoy meals in the open air, to use the area for small gatherings as well as larger parties, and, most importantly, to create an environment in which their two small children could play safely in view of the house. They wanted it to be a practical and attractive family garden, which would look good all year round.

The existing garden
The original arrangement of the garden was unsatisfactory on all fronts. There was a harsh division between two areas, neither of which invited use – a sunken paved area which was damp and shady, and an area of scruffy grass dominated by the boundary walls.

Opening out the space
The view from the kitchen/dining area was restricted by the retaining walls to a dismal view of the sunken area, so that the rest of the garden was wasted in visual terms. The view from the reception room on the ground floor and the upper floors was uninspiring. The main thrust of the new design was to open out the whole area. The original grass area was

From this . . ., left
The existing garden was divided into two equally uninviting areas, seen here from an upper storey window of the house. Both areas were dominated by walls, with a sharp change in level between the two, so that small children could not be left in the garden unsupervised. Planting was minimal and uninspired, and the whole plot had an uncared-for, neglected feel.

. . . to this, right
The original dingy plot is now scarcely recognizable under the new design, which makes every part of the garden a pleasure to use. It feels roomy, light, and inviting for play and eating out. The whole space has been successfully opened out and looks good from the house as well as from ground level.

Tackling the structure
The dramatic effect that design had on the poorly planned original garden, far left, is evident even at this early stage, left. The retaining walls of the old paved area were lowered and access to and a view of the rest of the garden were allowed by building a low flight of steps.

lowered by excavating considerable quantities of soil. It was then linked to the sunken paved area by a series of gentle changes of level. Better use could now be made of the space available and the whole garden became visible from the basement. It also made the new grassed area a lot safer for the children to play on, for the large drop between this level and the original sunken area was greatly reduced. The hard structures of the garden created a framework for the areas of planting. The planting features mainly bushy shrubs and perennials that shoot up flower colour on tall stems, with climbers to clothe the new fencing.

The new garden
The stepped levels create a sculptural effect and the angular arrangement of the retaining walls, which can also be used as seating, are echoed in the shape of the built-in brick bench which defines the eating area and saves the clutter of too many freestanding chairs. The geometric shape of the grass play area is integrated in the overall pattern. Honey-coloured brick matching the house brick was used to build the new walls, the steps, and the bench seat. Soft-coloured stone slabs were chosen for the paving, to tone in with the mellow brick of the house.

Designer's impression, below
This rough sketch shows how the final planting will soften the angular structures.

The plan, below
The geometric pattern of the new paving and brick structures with its stepped, interlocking squares can be seen here, in relation to the areas of planting.

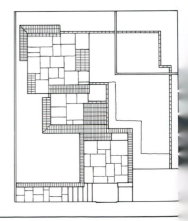

OPENING OUT THE VIEW

The most pressing problem with the existing site is the sharp change in level. The new design addresses this by creating different levels, defined in paving and brick, linked by gently sloping series of steps, that open out the view, and make the garden attractive to walk in.

Before, above
Looking across the garden from this angle, the eye is inevitably drawn down into the dank paved area that dominates the view.

The new structure, above right
The design begins to take shape with the opening up of the paved area, allowing the eye to take in the whole garden.

Six months later, right
The recently planted foreground material begins to fill out. As it matures it will grow into scale with the hard materials.

The finished product
A view of the new garden from the seating area on the rear terrace, right. It is difficult to imagine this as the unattractive, uninviting space it once was. Design was the key to this successful transformation – a plan was evolved which was structured to suit the needs of the owners and to complement the character of their home and its surroundings.

· CHAPTER THREE ·

CREATING THE GARDEN STRUCTURE

Once you have a clear idea of the pattern and form of your future garden, you can set to work outside. Creating the garden structure is about building the framework in hard materials, such as walling and paving, fencing and decking. Permanent structures, such as pergolas and storage spaces, also need to go in at this stage. Plants come later.

Now is the time to decide what materials to use. Consider what is available locally, what is appropriate to your area and site, and cost. Stone is good for paving or walling in a traditional setting. Brick or granite sett will suit both traditional and modern settings. Concrete is a universal material and not to be despised. Timber may be another option.

The pattern you now have on paper, albeit a working drawing, is still only two-dimensional. Incorporating wall and step heights, depths of ponds and so on, makes the plan three-dimensional. It is the different levels, the feeling of enclosure given by planting, and also the areas of void contrasted with the mass and height of solids, that make a garden such a pleasant place to be in.

Achieving a balance
The carefully planned structure of this garden, left, works with planting to create a perfect balance of hard and soft materials. The different types of surfacing define separate areas within the garden.

Marking out

You will probably have to clear your site before you can start marking out the new design on it. If you are starting from scratch in a new garden, it may be builder's rubble that has to go. Older gardens may need unsuitable planting removed or wildly overgrown areas cleared. Always think hard before removing a major feature, such as a tree, an area of paving, or a line of hedge. Perhaps it can be incorporated in the new design. Trees can be thinned and branches removed or braced to make a new shape – work best done by a qualified tree surgeon. Overgrown hedges can

be cut back. Also think hard before leaving a major feature. It will be more difficult to remove an old shed or greenhouse after the garden has been created, particularly if the rubble has to come through the house.

Clear all weeds from the site. You can use a herbicide (being sure to keep children and pets away when newly applied) or burn them off, as long as there is no danger to boundaries, neighbouring properties, or trees.

Now is the time to test your plan by translating it into reality with white string and pegs. If you have kept to a grid system, it will

Stage 1   The plan so far

Your garden plan will be looking something like this, right. You will have resolved the positions of surfaces, boundaries, features, and areas for planting. As yet there will be no detail about materials to be used, although you will probably have a fairly detailed mental image of the finished garden by now.

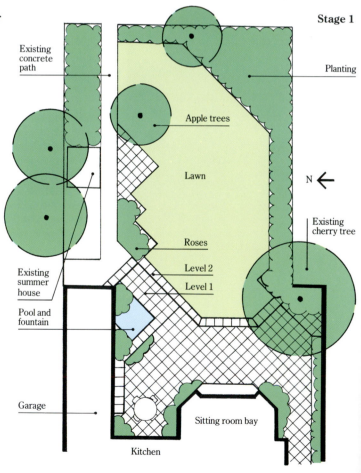

Stage 1

Existing concrete path

Planting

Apple trees

Lawn

N

Existing cherry tree

Roses

Level 2

Level 1

Existing summer house

Pool and fountain

Garage

Sitting room bay

Kitchen

be easy to line up the shapes of the plan with the buildings which provided the reference points, and existing features should fit neatly into place as anticipated.

First peg out the straight runs. Next tackle the circles, which will be easy to deduce if you have worked to a scale plan, with a piece of string attached to a central peg. Secure the peg and scrape out arcs in the earth with a nail or stick at the end of the piece of string. Peg these lines out too.

Once you have described all your patterns with pegs, join them with string. This will enable you to read the overall layout when you stand back from the garden. Look at the pattern from several vantage points – from an upstairs window, from ground level, from outside the site. Walk the pathways you have outlined, making sure there is room for a wheelbarrow or mower, and that you can easily get round corners. If there is an access path to the front door, it should have a comparatively straight way down the middle, even if the outline twists, for otherwise visitors will cut unnecessary corners. If you have marked out a sun terrace, estimate the course of the sun in summer and ensure that there is no unexpected area of cast shadow. If your plan includes a drive, there should be enough width for people to get out of a car on either side and, if possible, to turn the car. Check that your planning ideas are practical as well as visually satisfying from all angles.

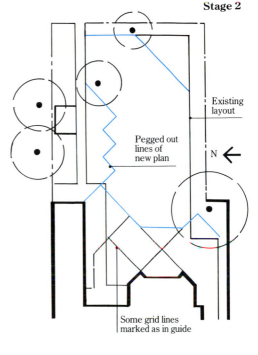

Stage 2

Existing layout

Pegged out lines of new plan

N ←

Some grid lines marked as in guide

Stage 2   Pegging out
Having evolved your plan on paper, peg out the outlines on the ground using stakes or pegs and white string, as above. If you have worked to scale from an accurate outline survey, your measurements will translate to the real garden. Adjust outlines as you go to delete any awkward corners that are created.

Stage 3   Assessing the layout
Before you start digging or building, go indoors and study the pegged-out pattern from all the windows that look on to the garden, imagining steps and changes of level where necessary, as right. You might see aspects of the plan that require slight modification to take account of all the different views from the house. The view from an upper storey can provide the mind's eye with a clear impression of the future garden.

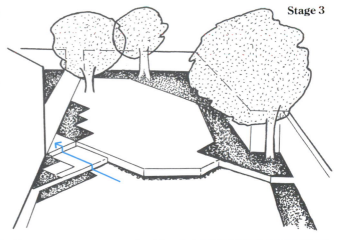

Stage 3

Building in services

One of the first jobs as you begin to create the structure of your new garden is planning how water gets in and out of the soil. And if you need an electricity supply in the garden away from the house, this is the time to plan the circuit and lay the cables. Call on expert advice if you are at all unsure about the technicalities of what you are doing.

Drainage

Few small gardens need a full drainage system. If drainage is necessary, it will be obvious – the affected area will be wet underfoot for long periods. The site may be on low-lying ground that is dry in summer but wet in winter as the water table rises. The natural vegetation will indicate this – rushy grasses and little else.

By far the most likely cause of dampness, especially in a new garden, is a layer of clay dumped during excavations or building work and covered with a thin layer of topsoil. The clay quickly becomes an impervious layer that prevents drainage. All you need to do is break this layer and the water will disperse.

Dig an inspection hole, a metre (yard) square and a metre (yard) deep, if you are in any doubt. You will be able to see the soil profile and how deep the topsoil layer is. You will also be able to see how quickly water drains away after a period of rain.

If the site is on natural clay, you have no alternative but to import fertile topsoil. A soil with a proportion of clay, however, may have become consolidated by the weight of heavy machinery. It may be possible to break up the clay deposits in this case and greatly improve the soil simply by cultivating the surface.

If your site does need draining, you will have to install an underground system with pipes of either clay or flexible plastic. These are laid to a pattern, with feeder runs to the main outlet pipe running to a neighbouring ditch or to the surface water drainage system of the house. Never connect a garden drainage system to the mains drainage system. In the United Kingdom, this is illegal.

Most drainage problems are small scale and affect a small area which has standing water on it after rain. The solution may be a simple pipe

A drainage pattern

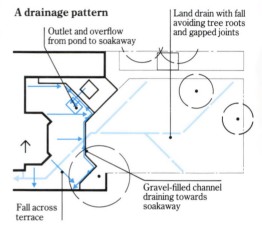

Outlet and overflow from pond to soakaway

Land drain with fall avoiding tree roots and gapped joints

Gravel-filled channel draining towards soakaway

Fall across terrace

Planning drainage
This drainage pattern, above, has minor runs to a main channel. The system runs from the top of the plan to an outlet that joins the surface water drainage system of the house at the bottom. The pattern is simple to eliminate any possible points of blockage. Terrace surfaces drain to a soakaway.

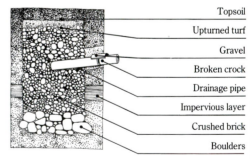

Topsoil
Upturned turf
Gravel
Broken crock
Drainage pipe
Impervious layer
Crushed brick
Boulders

Soakaway
A well-sited soakaway, like the one shown above, might be all the extra drainage required. This example penetrates any impervious layers in the soil and so allows any water draining in to pass down quickly through the layers of gravel and crushed brick to soil that is less likely to become saturated.

run to a soakaway (see p. 90). A soakaway is a hole a metre (yard) square and at least a metre (yard) deep, which is filled with rubble. It will act as a reservoir to hold drainage water, allowing it to disperse gradually. It should be sited under an area that will later be planted and at a distance from the house. It may only last five years, depending on soil type.

Irrigation

A variety of methods can be used for watering. Watering cans and hoses are obvious ones. A perforated hose laid across a planted area or over pots on a balcony or roof terrace will produce a gentle trickle of water. Or there is the water arm, which will sweep water to and fro across an area.

A more sophisticated alternative is a grid system of pipes sunk just below ground surface at an early stage of the garden construction. Water is pushed up through nozzles at regular intervals, the coverage from one nozzle reaching that of the next so that the whole area is soaked equally. The nozzles sink down when the water is turned off so that they are flush with the ground and will not impede a mower. Timers are available to switch the system on and off automatically.

Electricity

Cables for outside lighting and other powered equipment, such as fountains, swimming pool filtration plants, greenhouse heating, electric tools in the workshop, electric mowers, and security equipment, need to be laid at an early stage of the garden plan. They should either be located along the bottom of a wall or contained within protective piping and buried deeply, beyond the reach of gardening tools.

Cables need full external-type insulation. Outlet sockets should be fitted with screw caps and sited at least 1.2m (4 ft) above the ground, out of the reach of small children.

When planning cables and lighting points to entrance paths, include points for low lights at any changes of level and avoid leaving dark corners in areas you are likely to use at night.

It is worthwhile investing some time and money achieving really effective lighting. As well as allowing you to enjoy the garden from inside on cold evenings, bright lighting will help deter burglars.

Lighting fitments are available in various shapes and sizes. It is imperative that any fittings you use in the garden are purpose-made for outside use. Lighting effects will vary according to the design, ranging from spotlighting to more general floodlighting.

A watering system

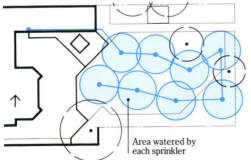

Area watered by each sprinkler

Irrigation system
A full watering system like this, above, is rarely necessary in northern Europe. The system flows from a connection to the house mains supply to eight sprinkler heads positioned so that their combined effect will soak the garden.

An electrical circuit

Garage

Wall light

Power to submersible pump

Floodlight into apple tree

Spotlight into cherry tree

Garden electrical circuit
This simple garden circuit, above, which is connected to the garage supply, feeds a pump and lighting. Ensure that all cables are sensibly sited, for example along the bottom of a wall, or buried deep in the ground beyond the reach of gardening tools.

Changes of level

Many gardens are made up of inter-connected areas of different levels. These areas need to be in proportion to each other and to the house and other buildings, and should make a visually satisfying collage effect of interlocking shapes. There are three basic ways of manipulating changes of level to advantage. You either follow natural lines, making sure that any new slope or bank is contoured in a realistic way, or you use the artifice of terracing, where flat areas are connected by flights of steps, banks, or ramps, or you create a more abrupt and dramatic change with a retaining wall.

Steps linking changes of level can become a feature as well as a necessity and, if planned generously, become a series of landings to encourage leisurely walks through the garden. The landings lend themselves to decoration with planted pots and provide viewpoints. The form of the steps should be dictated by the garden layout. Steps designed within traditional, formal layouts tend to be central within the plan and comprise one grand flight. For a more casual effect, steps may be staggered or may turn on a landing. Ramps or banks are a simpler and sometimes necessary alternative to steps, particularly where heavy machinery is used to maintain the garden or for wheelchair access. Banks are easier to construct than steps, but their location and materials need equally careful planning. For example if you want to use a loose material such as gravel, shingle, or wood bark, the gradient of the ramp must be kept to a minimum or its surface will be washed away. A combination of shallow ramps with intermediate landings may be the solution. Moulded banks are an excellent way of hiding unwanted rubble or surplus spoil from building operations or excavations for a pool.

Where space is limited, retaining walls may be the solution to the difficulties of a sloping site. A retaining wall will provide a strong, structural change of level and will hold the earth back.

However you decide to change levels, the major practical consideration is how to stabilize the soil on the banks to stop loose soil washing downhill in heavy rain. Pegged turf will stabilize a bank immediately, but the gradient should be gentle in section so that the mowing machine can operate. Planting or decorative ground cover will also stabilize a bank, but make sure you use bold masses of individual types so as not to disrupt the flow of the ground shaping.

Gently rolling effect
Ground shaping has been used in this garden, right, to encompass a swimming pool and give it shelter. The material used to make the mounds was probably the excavation from the pool.

BANKS AND STEPS

Various ways of shaping your site are shown here, below. The effect might be chiselled (1) or rolling (2). An undulating landscape (4) needs space unless you fake half of the roll with a retaining wall (3). To create ground interest with a slight change of level, excavate a shallow step on the cut-and-fill principle (5). Always remove and set aside topsoil before starting land shaping so that it can be raked over the new shaping and provide the new planting surface.

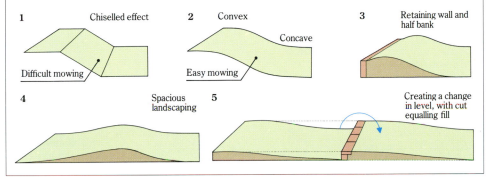

1   Chiselled effect

Difficult mowing

2   Convex

Concave

Easy mowing

3   Retaining wall and half bank

4

Spacious landscaping

5

Creating a change in level, with cut equalling fill

A gradient of 30 degrees to the horizontal is considered a reasonable gradient for a cylinder mowing machine. A gradient of 45 degrees is manageable with a hover type of mower and is just practicable as a planted bank once the subjects are established. A bank like this can be planted through a coarse netting pegged into the earth to retain the earth until the roots have established themselves.

Importing earth to create garden banks can be an expensive business. Shrubs require a minimum depth of 450mm (18 in) topsoil, although grass can make do with as little as 75mm (3 in). Don't lose the topsoil you already have. Always clear the topsoil to one side before building a bank or mound, then rake it back over. If the soil underneath is not consolidated enough, it will be liable to shrinkage. Consolidated builder's rubble can provide such an excellent drainage system that the topsoil over a mound will drain and become impoverished more quickly than other areas of the garden. Surplus rainwater may tend to collect in puddles at the bottom of your banks, unless you include a drain run or soakaway (see p. 90).

Steps

Steps constructed in tune with the garden can be an interesting and useful feature, as well as a vantage point and temporary perch. They must be gentle, low, and wide in order to be gracious and inviting. Plan your flight of steps as a means of getting from level A to level B, but not necessarily by the shortest route. Consider steps as part of the patchwork of elements that make up the garden pattern.

The materials you choose for constructing the steps will dictate their form to some extent, as will materials used for adjacent terracing, retaining walls, or other structures.

Steps built in the same or a similar material as surrounding structures will blend in well and become a pleasing part of the structural pattern of a garden or building.

There are flat gardens that can be considerably improved by constructing the occasional step right across the site. Full width steps should articulate the garden plan, providing ground interest and encouraging the eye to remain within the site.

Gardens constructed on different levels with steps between them will present problems for wheelbarrows and mowers. If possible include a ramped route for wheels if the area is large enough or perhaps a ramp alongside each flight of steps if the slope is not too steep.

CONSTRUCTION OF STEPS

Step construction is similar to building retaining walls (see p. 97). Each step riser – the vertical component – is a miniature retaining wall. Pay particular attention to the treads – the horizontal components. Each tread must be well set in concrete, with allowance for water runoff to left and right so that rainwater doesn't collect. Allowing the edges of the treads to meet with the edges of the risers at right angles creates a crisp, architectural effect. Allowing the treads to overhang the risers creates a shadow line along the riser, making the tread appear to float.

The height of each riser should be approximately 150mm (6 in), with the treads no less than 375mm (15 in) deep. Calculate the number of steps you need by first measuring the change of level across the slope (see p. 66) and dividing it by the riser height. You may need to cut into the bank or build it up at top or bottom to make the slope fit the steps.

Soakaway detail

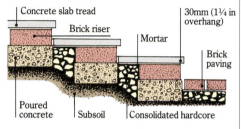

Brick and concrete, above
This flight of steps has precast concrete treads mortared to brick risers over consolidated hardcore and poured concrete.

Steps between levels, above
A single shallow step or several shallow steps can be used to make a gentle change in level. Steep steps should be avoided wherever possible. Include a soakaway for drainage in the design.

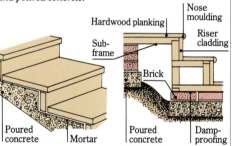

Flight of concrete steps, above
This flight of steps has precast concrete treads and concrete risers.

Decking, above
Timber steps with concrete foundations can be used to link two areas of decking.

Many small gardens are in locations which can only be reached by steps, and for some people the flight of steps *is* the garden. Pots and containers are a simple and effective way of decorating steps and of integrating soft planting with hard structure. Painting steps or adjacent walls in a colour that tones well with surrounding structures can give a dowdy flight a new lease of life. A handrail can be a stylish and practical addition to service steps, and good lighting will make them safer at night.

Planting on either side of a flight of steps can influence its character considerably. A straight flight can be made to appear curved or staggered from side to side, by letting plants encroach on to the side edges of the steps in a planned fashion. Strong, architectural plants can soften starkness or give a lift to purely functional steps.

Safety considerations are important in step construction. Treads which are too smooth or will wear quickly to an unstable surface are dangerous. Treads set absolutely level will not allow rainwater to drain quickly and they become a hazard in icy weather when standing water will freeze. Stone and timber become very slippery after rain and frost, whereas textured materials like old stock brick, or a smooth material like concrete, infilled with a rougher material such as stone, will give a firmer foothold. It is better not to introduce plant material into the pattern of service steps because it can make them unsafe to negotiate at night and slippery when wet.

Informal stepped path, above
Roughly cut stone steps lead down through a naturally styled bed planted with heathers, simulating a rocky, exposed hillside. Uneven steps like this need to be well laid and stable.

Cantilevered treads
When space is limited, steps can be tucked into a corner, as here, far right. The structure is of stained softwood, supported on a central timber rib let into the wall beneath a landing. Alternatively, treads may be cantilevered from a wall as in the diagram, right.

Treads let into a wall

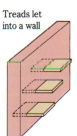

USING DIFFERENT MATERIALS

Most types of paving material are also suitable for steps, and it makes sense to connect paths and terraces at the top or bottom of steps with the same material in between. The general rule is, the gentler the flight of good wide treads, the more pleasant the steps. At the same time, however, the materials you use will often determine the dimensions of the steps.

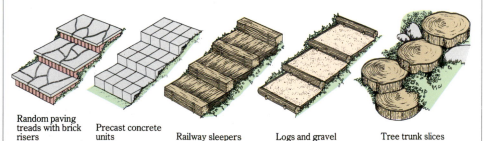

Random paving treads with brick risers

Precast concrete units

Railway sleepers

Logs and gravel

Tree trunk slices

Retaining walls

The construction of a retaining wall more than 750mm (30 in) high should not be undertaken lightly, particularly if the earth that the wall will hold back is heavy and needs draining. Any retaining structure will have to fight against the full, wet weight of earth behind it, as it acts as a barrier to the natural drainage flow downhill. Provision for drainage is essential if your structure is to be sound and lasting. Seek expert advice if you are unsure about the project, especially where the slope to be altered is steep.

You may not need to build a retaining wall at all if you grade out the bank in a series of cut-and-fill exercises (see p. 93), which you then turf and plant to retain. If you do decide to use retaining structures to support a particularly steep bank, you can again adopt a graded approach, choosing a series of small walls rather than a single, higher wall.

Choosing materials

The strongest type of retaining wall is one of concrete poured *in situ*, reinforced with metal rods or welded wire mesh – a specialist engineering job. Hollow concrete blocks, which have been reinforced with metal rods and filled with poured concrete will also make a solid retaining wall. As a smaller element, brick has less strength, and should not be built more than one metre (yard) high unless as a fascia for a reinforced concrete backing.

Natural stone that has been cut on one side, or roughly dressed, makes a good, solid retaining wall, particularly if it is built "on the batter" (sloped into the earth which it is to retain). A dry stone wall with provision for planting alpines and trailing perennials within its structure gives a charming rustic effect.

Retained lawn
Stepped retaining walls in stone, with planting between each, retain this lawn area, below. Across the wall is a random run of steps.

Railway line sleepers or logs set vertically into the ground can act as retaining material. Planks can be used horizontally, but with this method the vertical supports for the planks must be tied back into the bank with, for example, metal rods set into buried concrete and bolted to the supports. Depending on its imperviousness, however, wood will rot comparatively quickly, and will need to be replaced after a few years.

CONSTRUCTION OF A RETAINING WALL

A retaining wall must be strong enough to hold the weight of wet earth behind it. The higher the wall, the stronger it has to be. As a general rule, larger construction elements produce stronger walls. Water build-up behind the wall must be allowed to escape through weep holes at the base. An infill of ash or clinker behind the wall will direct water to the drainage area and the weep holes. These can take the form of a gap in the jointing, or a drain pipe set through the wall, angled downwards to a flush finish on the face of the wall 150mm (6 in) above ground level. A land drain at the base of the retaining wall may be required to take surplus drain-off. Whether the wall is damp-proofed or not will depend on its location and the type of wall, and whether you want plants in it or only over it. It is not possible to damp-proof a wall partially filled with earth and plants. A brick or concrete retaining wall will obviously last longer if it does not absorb water from the earth which it retains. To achieve this put a waterproof layer (of which there are many proprietary varieties available) between the wall and the earth behind.

Concrete block
A solid concrete block wall built on a concrete foundation, with a paving stone coping along the top is shown here, below. Weep holes are vertical unmortared joints. An edge of brick or concrete strip at the base of the wall makes mowing easier. Planting directly behind the coping can then be allowed to overhang the top of the wall, softening the sharp edge and blending the new walling with the rest of the garden.

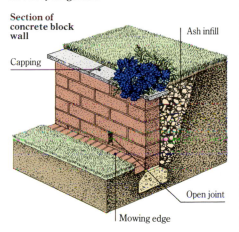

Section of concrete block wall

Capping

Ash infill

Open joint

Mowing edge

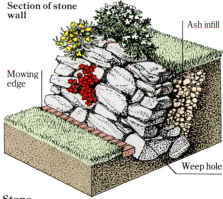

Section of stone wall

Mowing edge

Ash infill

Weep hole

Stone
This random stone wall, has been built "on the batter" (angled back into the bank it retains) for added strength. A stone wall can be laid dry, with only earth between the stones. In this way, moss and ferns are encouraged to grow in the wall.

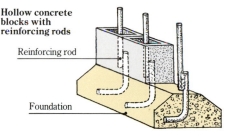

Hollow concrete blocks with reinforcing rods

Reinforcing rod

Foundation

Hollow concrete blocks
Hollow concrete blocks can be used to construct a stronger wall, pierced by reinforcement rods, as above. The hollows are finally filled with wet concrete before capping. The capping can be flush with the walling blocks or overhanging.

Boundaries

B oundaries can delineate the perimeter of a garden and provide decorative screens and divisions within it. As with all garden features, the most appropriate type of boundary and the degree of enclosure which is needed must depend on location.

Gardens tend to have regular shapes, and particularly gardens of newer properties. A common mistake is to surround the site with some standard form of structure that only emphasizes the regularity. The simplest way to relieve this monotony and to break the confines of a boundary visually is to vary the material of which it is made. Use brick or stone adjacent to the house or terrace, and perhaps timber for the rest, or build a boundary of the same material throughout but vary the height to work with your overall pattern. More interesting still is to allow the line of the boundary to break into the site itself as part of the design so that the layout appears to flow round corners, making the garden appear larger. Allow climbers to scramble up and over boundaries wherever possible.

Your choice of boundary construction should also take account of security and privacy, and the need to keep your children and dogs in, or other people's out.

Fencing

While fencing can serve the same function as a wall, it need not be so massive in construction or solid in form, and will probably be considerably cheaper. Fencing used as a boundary demarcation can give a glimpse of the world beyond and increase the feeling of space in the garden. Different types of fencing can be used within the garden to screen unsightly structures, provide shelter against the elements for both people and plants, create secluded areas, frame interesting glimpses or features, or as a decorative support for climbing or trailing plants.

Strict attention should be paid to the siting of a fence which is set up along the line of demarcation between two properties to ensure that no encroachment is made on either side. It is usual practice to face the best side of the fence outwards from your site with the supports on the inside.

A fence is no stronger than its weakest part. A well-detailed fence, carefully constructed with no weaknesses, will be more resilient and last longer. Consider the types of infill and support, how to fix the supports in the ground, and ways to protect timber fences against rot with cappings and gravel boards. Take a careful look at all the options before deciding which system best suits your plan.

Deciding on materials

Different types of wood have different lifespans. The principal European woods used for fencing are oak (English and European), larch, western red cedar, and sweet chestnut, although other woods may be used when suitable, such as Douglas fir, Scots pine, ash, elm, or beech. Redwood or cedar are used in the United States.

Bark must be stripped from timber to prevent premature decaying of the wood, and the exposed grain either treated with a preservative or sealed and painted. Creosoted wood cannot be painted. Plants will not grow against it for a season. Newly applied creosote gives off fumes which burn vegetation. Exposed metal components liable to rust should be galvanized, zinc-coated, or painted. Use screws rather than nails for fixings for a longer lasting finish.

Fencing is available in a wide variety of materials as well as wood, as the survey on pp. 99–100 shows. Bamboo, wrought or cast iron, wire, and plastic are all options which may suit your garden design. Other more unusual materials include panels of sheet fibreglass, which can be incorporated within a timber frame and used to make light and decorative fencing panels. Varying degrees of opacity and a variety of coloured finishes are available. Corrugated iron, sheet perspex, and railway sleepers can all be used as fencing elements.

TYPES OF FENCING

Bamboo
Bamboo makes an ideal screening panel, and provides a particularly good backdrop for growing bamboos or other architectural plants. Bamboo panels are made up by lashing the stems, or culms, to cross members of a heavier wood with wire or heavy cord. Rolls of split bamboo can be attached with wire to any openwork fencing, like chain link, to provide instant privacy or shelter. Such fencing will have a limited lifespan.

Closeboard
A good type of fencing for privacy and shelter. It is available in prefabricated panels, but is usually constructed on site. It is built of overlapping, feather-edged timber, between stout timber or concrete posts not more than 2.8m (9 ft) apart, nailed to two or three horizontal arris rails which slot into mortises cut into the posts.

Hurdling
Traditional woven sheep hurdles of willow or hazel, bound between stout cleft posts, look excellent for five years or so, until they begin to rot. Panels up to 1.8m (6 ft) high are available in some areas. Hurdling is useful for sheltering new plantations from the wind.

Iron railings
Low wrought or cast-iron railings have been used for a more sophisticated rural look since the eighteenth century, particularly in England and Ireland. Painted black, they become invisible from a distance, because the horizontals are so thin. In towns and cities throughout Europe, iron railings made up of vertical bars and often finished with a spike or dart provide substantial see-through barriers for houses and gardens, which are both attractive and secure.

Picket or palisade
Picket fencing is a see-through, decorative version of closeboard fencing and can suit both urban and cottage-style gardens. To achieve a crisp, New England look, picket fencing can be painted white. It needs annual maintenance to prevent it from looking shabby.

Pioneer style
Some excellent zig-zag, pioneer-type timber stock fences were used in the United States before the advent of barbed wire. They consist of pairs of posts with each pair at 45 degrees to the next pair. The horizontal timbers are slotted between the pairs.

Plastic fencing
Various types of plastic fencing system are available, imitating painted post and rail, post and chain, or picket fencing. They need little maintenance but are too lightweight for general use.

Bamboo lengths can be bound to make a solid or openwork screen

Closeboard fencing is made of feather-edged verticals nailed to horizontal rails

Black iron chain, above, is suitable for post and chain fencing

Painted picket fencing makes a decorative boundary

TYPES OF FENCING

Post and rail
Post and rail describes the simplest way of fencing with wood, or wood and metal, with one, two, or three horizontal rails, between regularly spaced vertical posts. There are a number of different construction methods. If the rails are nailed to the posts, the verticals should be about 1.8m (6 ft) apart. If the rails are mortised into the posts, spacing between verticals can be up to 2.8m (9 ft).

Ranch style
Also known as baffle fencing, ranch fencing is made up of horizontal boards, spaced at regular intervals and secured to posts set not more than 2.8m (9 ft) apart.

Board on board fencing is a variation of the ranch style fence, where the horizontals are secured alternately to each side of the verticals, providing a fence which looks equally good on both sides. Ranch style boarding can also be attached vertically to arris rails to produce a completely different effect.

Sheet fibreglass
Panels of sheet fibreglass, available in varying degrees of opacity and different coloured finishes, can be incorporated in timber frames, within the fence verticals. Sheet perspex can also be used in this way.

Stock and rabbit-proof fencing
If you live in the country, you may have problems with animals getting in or out of fences. Timber fences need a wire netting or chain link backup to make them stock and rabbit-proof. Bury the bottom edge of the wire 150mm (6 in) deep.

Wire fencing
Line wire, wire mesh, and chain link (sometimes plastic coated) are all used for fencing. The wire or chain is strained between concrete, metal, or timber verticals, with the end post taking most of the strain. This type of fencing is manufactured by the roll, and the distance between posts is not predetermined. As boundary fencing it provides

little privacy but can be a worthwhile security measure if well constructed. Wire mesh is a good support for light climbing plants.

Timber trellis for decorating or extending walls

Wooden trellis
European trelliswork is relatively simple, diamond or square patterned in softwood, made in panels up to 1.8m (6 ft) square. Folding trellis needs to be set within a rigid frame to give it stability. Much of this prefabricated material is lightweight and rots quickly, if the plants climbing up it do not pull it down first. The American market offers a wider range of trelliswork, including French provincial, Spanish, and Chinese styles, often suitable for overhead shading as well as see-through fencing.

Woven panel
Various weaves and sizes of prefabricated wooden slat fence panel are available. Lifespan depends on quality of wood. The best woods to use are oak and cedar which need little maintenance. Softwoods require regular treatment with a preservative. Use stout concrete or timber posts to support the fence panels and timber string cappings and gravel board to counter rot.

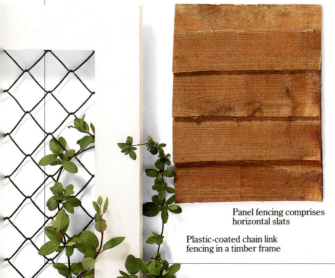

Panel fencing comprises horizontal slats

Plastic-coated chain link fencing in a timber frame

CONSTRUCTING FENCE POSTS

Sound verticals are essential to strong fencing. If you are using timber posts, bear in mind that they will rot relatively quickly, even more so if set directly in earth rather than concrete. If possible, fix the post at ground level to a metal plate or proprietary metal fixing, and then set that into concrete. Alternatively, bolt the post to a concrete spur set in concrete. If you must set the timber directly into earth or concrete, prevent the timber decaying as long as possible.

Treat it first with preservative. Place a large stone at the bottom of each post hole to preserve the timber end grain, and backfill with earth or wet concrete if the soil is light and sandy, keeping the post absolutely vertical.

Heavy frost can cause the concrete to crack and the earth to heave. To minimize damage, dig the post holes 300mm (12 in) below the depth that frost can penetrate in your area, and shovel in a little gravel for drainage.

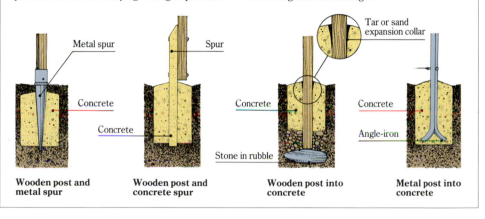

Wooden post and metal spur

Wooden post and concrete spur

Wooden post into concrete

Metal post into concrete

Hedges

It is a sad fact that many of the plants used to create a traditional type of hedge are slow growing, and many people are not prepared to wait and resort instead to cypresses (*Cupressocyparis leylandii*). The visual effect of this straggling conifer in maturity has a devastating effect on the countryside.

Country hedging
The fastest growing of the more traditional country hedging plants include hawthorn (*Crataegus* sp.), blackthorn (*Prunus spinosa*), and field maple (*Acer campestre*). None of these are evergreen. Holly (*Ilex* sp.) makes an excellent and impenetrable evergreen hedge. Gorse (*Ulex europaeus*) can also be used.

Garden hedging
Plants used for garden hedging fall into three categories: those with loose form, needing little restraining and including genera such as

Berberis, *Escallonia*, and *Pyracantha*; species that need pruning, such as laurel (*Prunus laurocerasus*); and hedges needing considerable attention that have to be kept tight and compact with clipping, such as *Buxus*, *Carpinus*, *Cupressocyparis leylandii*, *Fagus*, *Ilex*, *Ligustrum*, and *Taxus baccata*.

The type of hedge you choose will be influenced by location, site character, and what you want the hedge to do. Location will dictate species to some extent, and particularly the amount of annual snowfall. Heavy snow can crush a clipped hedge under its weight unless the snow is regularly shaken off.

A common mistake is to plant the components of a hedge too close together in an attempt to achieve a thick screen quickly. If the hedge is then neither watered nor fed, individual plants within the hedge will die down as the hedge reaches maturity. Plant at recommended distances and be patient. Remember when selecting species that quick growers do not stop growing quickly when they have reached the height you want.

Laying a hedge
Deciduous hedges, interspersed with the occasional evergreen, will grow thickly if they are laid as shown, right, by cutting half through main woody stems and intertwining and staking their bent-over tops.

Hedge in winter

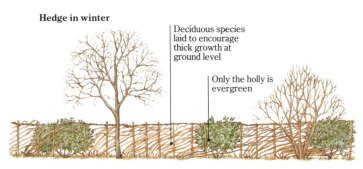

Deciduous species laid to encourage thick growth at ground level

Only the holly is evergreen

Hedge in summer

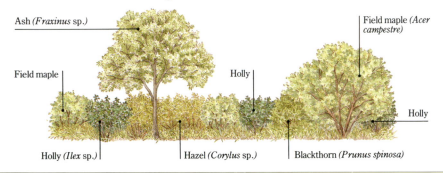

Ash *(Fraxinus* sp.)

Field maple *(Acer campestre)*

Field maple

Holly

Holly

Holly *(Ilex* sp.)

Hazel *(Corylus* sp.)

Blackthorn *(Prunus spinosa)*

HEDGE DESIGNS

Hedging plants offer great scope for three-dimensional design. This terrace, below centre, is planted with hedging subjects that are ideal for formal clipping, in a design containing contrasts of form, colour, and texture. The planting formation for a boundary hedge, below far left, should be combined with the planting distances shown in the table below right.

Planting formation

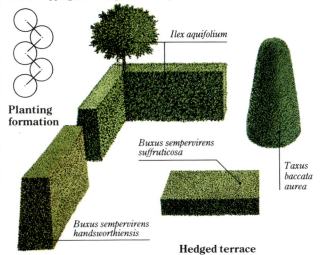

Ilex aquifolium

Buxus sempervirens suffruticosa

Taxus baccata aurea

Buxus sempervirens handsworthiensis

Hedged terrace

Planting distances

Plant spacing	(mm/in)
Buxus sempervirens handsworthiensis	450/18
Carpinus betulus	450/18
Cupressocyparis leylandii	750/30
Fagus sylvatica	475/19
Ilex aquifolium	500/20
Ligustrum sp.	450/18
Lonicera nitida	275/11
Prunus laurocerasus	700/28
Taxus baccata	500/20
Berberis thunbergii	300/12
Buxus sempervirens suffruticosa	300/12
Lavandula spica	300/12
Santolina chamaecyparissus	250/10

Walling

The walled garden for growing fruit and vegetables, as a nursery garden, and as a place of seclusion, has medieval origins. The high, brick-built walls of such enclosures still exist in many traditional country gardens.

The expense of building a wall in a new plan can be high, but the design value of walls for linking buildings visually with elements of the garden, moulding space, and strengthening character, is immense.

It is difficult to justify removing an old wall in the country – they are nearly always an immense visual asset, even in an almost ruined state. No garden element creates privacy in quite the same way, nor provides a better foil to foliage. In small town gardens, however, walls can create an uncomfortable, closed in feeling. The higher the boundary walls, the stronger the inclination to look up and out of the well they create. One way of counteracting this is to build a strong visual feature in scale with the wall.

Walling in stone

Almost any kind of stone can be used for wall construction – granite, limestone, slate, or sandstone. The two main types of walling are ashlar and rubble walling. Rubble walling can be further subdivided into random rubble, uncut stone laid coursed or uncoursed, squared rubble, roughly dressed stone, laid regularly or irregularly coursed or uncoursed, and miscellaneous rubble, using traditional materials and construction methods.

Random rubble is the most common method. The stones are not cut, but are placed within the wall to ensure adequate distribution of pressure over a maximum area, with no continuous vertical joints. Header stones are used every square metre (yard) or so to stabilize the wall, and should ideally run right through the wall. Whether this wall is coursed or uncoursed, all joints should be well filled and flushed with mortar. A decorative variation can be achieved by filling some of the joints with soil and planting them with alpines. Stone walls have traditional cappings in various areas, such as a course of slate.

Traditional stone wall
No mortar has been used to joint the miscellaneous rubble of this wall, above, just patience to ensure vertical joints do not coincide.

WALL STRENGTH

Below are some ways of building a strong and stable wall without the need for piers or supports. The overlap design simply steps the line of the wall forwards and backwards by the thickness of a brick. Overlaps should be at intervals of not more than 2.5m (8 ft), and the wall should be no more than 1.8m (6 ft) high. Zig-zag and serpentine or crinkle-crankle walls will also support themselves, taking their strength from their deviations, although they require more space.

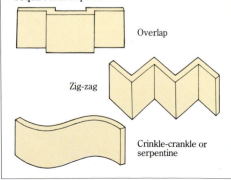

Overlap

Zig-zag

Crinkle-crankle or serpentine

Walling in brick

Brick is the most commonly used walling material. Three types are suitable for external use. Commons, made for general purpose building, are the cheapest, have no finish, and are particularly subject to weathering. Facings, used where appearance is of prime importance, have either a hand finish or a wire-cut weather resistant finish on the side facings only. And engineering bricks, which are the hardest and most impervious.

Bricks laid horizontally in the direction of the wall are known as stretchers, those laid end-on across the direction of the wall are known as headers. The arrangement of bricks within a wall is known as the bond.

Brick bonding

Four standard types of brickwork bonding, shown below, are generally used in wall construction. Bonds have marginally differing strengths, so the bond will to some extent be determined by the thickness of the wall. For a one brick thick wall, which should be no more than one metre (yard) high, running bond is usually used. Flemish or English bond, which have headers periodically binding the double thickness of brick, are used for higher walls. A more decorative bonding can be used on the facing side only of a 300mm (1 ft) wide wall. The crispness of the bond is either emphasized or subdued by the style of pointing and the colour of the mortar used.

Standard brickwork bonds

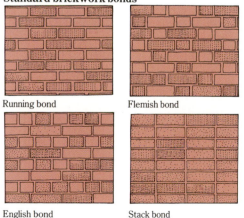

Running bond

Flemish bond

English bond

Stack bond

CONSTRUCTING A BRICK WALL

A wall must be built on stable and adequate foundations to eliminate any risk of subsequent movement. The depth of the foundations depends on the level at which frost or the movement of ground moisture occurs. In most cases, a depth of 450 to 600mm (18 to 24 in) is sufficient. For normal wall foundation work you need a concrete mix of 1:2:4–6, cement:sharp sand:aggregate.

The brick courses are built up from the foundations with great care taken to keep the wall square, both horizontally and vertically, and the amount of mortar used consistent. A suitable mortar mix for most exterior walls is 1:1:8–9, cement:lime:sand, although you might use a smaller proportion of sand for brickwork subject to water saturation or freezing temperatures.

The brick wall shown here, below, is being laid in English bond, with one course of headers and the next of stretchers.

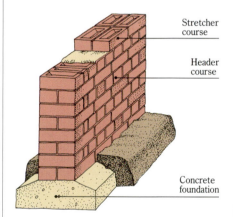

Stretcher course

Header course

Concrete foundation

Cappings, below

As most bricks are only weather proof on the finished face, it is usually necessary to put a protective capping, or coping, along the top of a wall. Brick-on-edge, below left, is the traditional method. Paving slabs are used, below right.

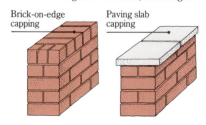

Brick-on-edge capping

Paving slab capping

Concrete block walling

Plain concrete blocks are hard to beat for their strength, economy, and speed of construction, and are now available in a variety of colours and finishes. Colours vary to match local brick or stone. They can be used in different ways to produce either a decorative finish or a perfectly simple one. Concrete blocks are available in a standard exterior heavyweight grade, or as lightweights composed of lightweight aggregate in a more porous texture. These last may have to be rendered for outside use but are ideal for roof garden construction where weight is a problem.

CONCRETE BLOCK WALLS

A concrete block wall is built more quickly and cheaply than a brick one. Piers are unnecessary for walls built of cavity walling blocks. Solid concrete walling blocks are half the thickness and will require the support of piers. A concrete foundation is also needed.

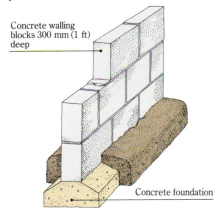

Concrete walling blocks 300 mm (1 ft) deep

Concrete foundation

Cappings

As with bricks, the block wall should have a protective capping, for example made of precast paving slabs, as shown below left.

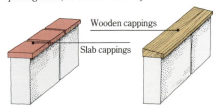

Wooden cappings

Slab cappings

Maintaining walls

Walls need looking after, particularly old walls with weak mortar, which the damp and aerial roots of climbing plants may cause to crumble. Damp walls need to be treated before they become unsound. Call on expert advice to locate the source of the damp.

Decorating walls

Outside walls can be painted, tiled, hung with ceramics and shelves, and so on, techniques that are particularly useful for brightening up a small outside space, while leaving maximum ground space for other uses.

In warm climates, walls are often colourfully painted to relieve the glare of the sun, while in duller climes, they can relieve the gloom. Pure white can turn to muddy grey when wet and may not be a good idea in drab conditions. Boundary walls painted in different colours or in several tones of the same colour will enliven a small enclosed space and counteract its oppressive feel. Abstract patterns of shape and colour or a realistic scene can be painted on walls for a dramatic effect.

Collections of pots, pebbles, and shells can be arranged on shelves attached to outside walls. Ensure first that the wall is strong enough to support the weight of the shelves and whatever is on them. This idea may be of particular use to roof-garden owners, where the weight on the floor of the garden can be reduced by putting container plants on shelves attached to the main structural walls of the building. Alternatively pots can be sited in metal hoops attached to the walls.

Dramatic combinations can be created by painting a wall in one colour and training a climber in a contrasting colour over it. Panels of trellis, covered with climbers or painted, can be used to disguise ugly walls or break up a large expanse of wall.

Over a long time self-clinging climbers like ivy will begin to erode the coursing of old walls built with lime mortar. Modern cement mortar, however, is more resilient, and climbers will have no appreciably adverse effects. All climbers, and particularly evergreens, should be clipped well back, in order to prevent dead foliage or birds' nests collecting, which may cause damp to penetrate the structure.

WALLING MATERIALS

There is a vast range of walling materials in brick, stone, and concrete, but their suitability will depend on your location. Local materials often make aesthetic as well as economic sense. The scale of each component is important and must be sympathetic to the scale of other materials already present in the surroundings.

Brick
Engineering brick is hardest and most resistant to damp. Flettons are infill brick, and the cheapest type. Facing bricks come in a variety of colours.

Reconstituted stone
Different areas produce different rock, which can be crushed and used as aggregate in the composition of reconstituted stone blocks. Reconstituted stone block is easier to transport and lay than natural stone.

Precast concrete walling units

Terracotta walling units

Open screen walling units
The scale, texture, and pattern of these units vary. An open screen is generally more successful when used sparingly. Perhaps, for example, to pierce a solid wall as a decorative element. Vast areas of it tend to become boring. The finer terracotta elements can be used on roof terraces as wind baffles.

Concrete block
The concrete block is a much maligned element for garden construction work. It is comparatively cheap, easy to erect, and an honest contemporary material. Hollow blocks or cavity blocks are approximately 300mm (1 ft) deep, while solid blocks are about half that. Finishes vary from coarse to smooth.

Stone
The scale and texture of various stones in the right surroundings cannot be bettered. The cost of labour, cartage, and handling difficulties, however, often prohibit its use.

Cavity block

Smooth solid

Rock-faced solid

Sandstone

Granite

Limestones

1   Engineering blocks
2–4   Flettons
5–10 Facing bricks
11–14 Split aggregate blocks
15–16 Precast blocks

Entrances and exits

There is a balance to be struck between welcome and privacy when styling entrances, and the most compelling entrances are a combination of structure and planting, tempting the visitor to see what comes next. Pedestrian entrances tend to be successful when treated as part of the incidental decoration of the garden and have most charm if their styling is understated and in complete harmony with the surrounding planting.

Designing a gate

Avoid the standard catalogue approach of cheap, overdecorative ironwork, and design your own gate to suit your house and garden.

Consider how the gate will be used. Should it prevent people from looking in or give a glimpse of the garden? Is it to keep children and pets in, or is it a security barrier? Should it be merely decorative, or a utilitarian entrance and exit for pedestrians and cars? With answers to these questions, decide on dimensions and whether the gate should be solid or openwork. Decide on style, considering the style of your house and type of boundary it will interrupt.

An entrance of character
Gates are most effective when they are in character with both the garden and the landscape beyond. The beauty of a classic iron gate like this one, above, is that it provides an effective barrier without impeding the view. The sun throws beautiful shadows through the gate onto the path.

WOODEN GATE CONSTRUCTION

Build your gate to take heavy wear from visitors. This timber picket gate, right, has both horizontal and cross braces to support the verticals. The horizontals are mortised into the hanging and closing stiles, and these are glued and secured with wooden dowels to avoid any rusting of screws.

Mortise and tenon, below
The mortise and tenon components of this useful joint must be cut with great accuracy.

Timber picket gate

Latch

Tenon
Mortise
Wooden dowel

Cross brace
Hanging stile
Rail
Pale
Closing stile

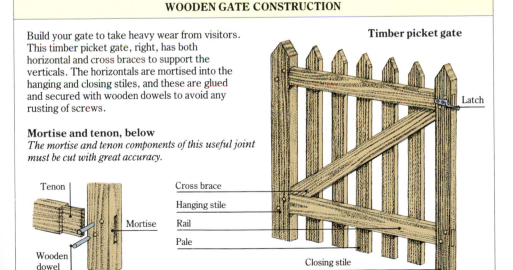

Surfaces

Now that the garden is shaped up with all its walls, changes of level, and steps positioned and built, you can get down to filling in the areas of ground pattern. The choices are many: the hard surfacing of brick, stone, concrete, granite setts, cobbles; the soft surfacing of washed pea shingle, gravel, bark chippings; timber surfacing or decking; or the soft surfaces of ground cover plants or clipped or rough grass.

Hard surfacing

Hard surfacing can have several functions in the garden, on the one hand providing a textural and visual link between buildings and the soft, planted areas of the garden, and on the other serving the purely practical purpose of getting from A to B. It also provides hard standing for furniture, pots, sculptures, sandpits, and other elements, and can act as a neutral backdrop or as a feature in its own right. Detailing can be fine, as in brick paving, or non-existent, as in smooth concrete.

TYPES OF HARD SURFACING

Precast paving slabs
Most pavings for family pedestrian use will need a hardcore base of about 100mm (4 in). Over this the slabs should be laid in 50mm (2 in) of builder's sand if the individual paving elements are heavy or sand and cement if the slabs are smaller and require firmer support. Assuming the slabs themselves to be 50mm (2 in) thick, you will need to excavate to a depth of at least 200mm (8 in) to achieve a finish flush with surrounding levels. Brush sand or dry sand and cement into joints.

Poured concrete
Concrete laid *in situ* is only suitable for perfectly stable soils that are not liable to frost upheaval or where the water table is high. First make a frame, out of wood if temporary or brick or paving stone if permanent. A temporary frame is constructed from 75×25mm (3×1 in) timber held rigid and level by stout pegs, allowing for the necessary fall, over a well-consolidated 75mm (3 in) base of either fine hardcore or binding gravel. Next pour in newly mixed concrete.

Temperature changes will make a poured concrete surface crack if its area is too large for its thickness. A good thickness is 100mm (4 in).

Stone
Quarried stone may be split and given a sawn or rubbed face for paving. Choice of stone will depend on durability, whether it becomes slippery underfoot when wet, and whether it fractures in frost. The thickness of stone flags will vary from 50 to 75mm (2 to 3 in).

On normal soils lay the stone flags on a 75mm (3 in) layer of clean hardcore, or other granular base material, blinded over with sand. Allow for a cross fall of 1:32 across the paved area. Brush in a dry mix of 1:1 sand: cement to seal the joints.

Random paving
Random paving describes paving where each unit is of nondescript shape. Foundations and jointing are as for precast paving slabs. Badly laid crazy paving soon becomes weed infested and uneven. Good laying involves tailoring sizeable individual elements to fit each other so that the joints are no wider than those of regular paving.

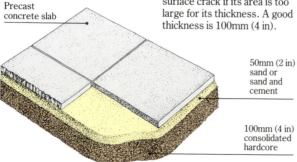

Precast concrete slab

50mm (2 in) sand or sand and cement

100mm (4 in) consolidated hardcore

Paving designs

First decide on a paving design. Work out the overall combination of shapes and the position of individual paving units within that design. Different paving designs can radically alter the look of a space, as shown in many of the gardens in Chapter one (pp. 12–63).

Paving patterns can be either static or dynamic. Static patterns hold the eye within the site – the effect might be of visually dividing the space into rooms. Densely patterned paving will hold the eye in one spot. A very bland or non-existent pattern will emphasize the overall shape of the paved area and act as a neutral backdrop to other aspects of the garden design. A static design suits an enclosed space with no one point of focus, such as a terrace used for meals outside.

Dynamic patterns on the other hand create a sense of movement and visual pull. In a larger garden space, pathways of hard surfacing threading through lawns and planting will lead the eye. In a smaller garden, the pattern of the paving stones within the paved area, perhaps the whole garden, can be used to create a dynamic effect. Linear paving patterns succeed where the visual pull has a satisfying conclusion, perhaps a pleasant view or a sculptural feature, or a practical function, perhaps leading to the front door.

A simple paving pattern with other garden features scaled-up will make a space appear larger, while an elaborate pattern will create a busy effect and make an area appear smaller, particularly if groupings of container-grown plants and other features are sited on it.

Planning practicalities

Paving near the house has the additional purpose of setting off the building, and the paving material needs to be sympathetic with the house building material. Paving laid adjoining a building should only butt the wall if it is 150mm (6 in) or more below the damp-proof course. Otherwise allow a gap of approximately 75mm (3 in) between the two and fill it with clean pea shingle.

All paving should be laid with a slight fall across its surface (away from the house in adjacent paving), of no less than 50mm (2 in) in 2m (6½ ft). Over a small area, allow a drain off into neighbouring planting or to a lawn if your soil drains well. For larger areas, lay a drain run at the edge of the paved area, linked to a soakaway (see *Drainage*, p. 90). If this is not possible, as for example in an enclosed yard, lay the paving to fall to a central gully, which might link to a soakaway or to surface water drainage from the house.

Whatever paving you choose, try to avoid having to cut too many elements. Keep the outlines of paved areas simple and consider the possibility of working out the framework grid for your garden design (see *Evolving a framework*, pp. 76–7) to fit multiples of the paving unit dimensions.

SMALL UNIT PAVING CONSTRUCTION

Small units, such as bricks or granite setts, allow you to pave awkward shapes in the garden more easily and provide a richer surface texture and an attractive feature in their own right. They do need to be laid well, however. Badly laid units can become weed infested, uneven, and dangerous to walk on.

Any small paving unit is prone to shift after laying because of its relative light weight and small surface area. To prevent this and for normal wear, each element needs to be buried in a 25mm (1 in) mortar base, over a 75mm (3 in) consolidated hardcore base. Brush a 4:1 sand:cement mix in the joints. This mixture will gradually take up moisture from the ground and slowly set. Before it dries completely, run the rounded end of a stick along the joints to produce a neat, concave finish between each unit. Before fixing a single element, make sure that your pattern will work by laying out the bricks or setts loose.

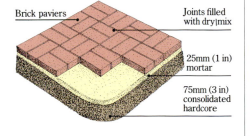

Brick paviers

Joints filled with dry|mix

25mm (1 in) mortar

75mm (3 in) consolidated hardcore

Combining paving and plants

Including plants among paving can create a very pretty effect, although it will restrict the usage of the paved area. The effect is strengthened if only one type of plant is used. Plan open joints for planting carefully so that the character of the paving is enhanced rather than obliterated.

Granite setts

Setts are a hard, quarried stone surfacing material, and are relatively expensive to use. They are grey and either roughly brick shaped or half-brick size and roughly cubic. They were originally designed as extremely durable road surfacing material, close-packed in sand. Granite is an alien material in many situations, so consider its use carefully.

Cobbles

Rounded stones or cobbles have been formed by glacial action or by the action of the sea. They are graded and sold in various sizes for use in the garden. Laid loose and contrasted with bold foliage plants, they create a Japanese effect. They are difficult to walk on and may be used as a deterrent, infilling corners which would otherwise be trodden on.

Brick paving

Brick paving which matches the brick of the house structure is a sure way to achieve integration of building and site, and will create a pleasant wraparound feel. Facing bricks for exterior walling (see p. 106) are not specifically recommended for exterior paving. Sooner or later they will flake and become uneven through frost damage. This may be the effect you want, particularly in a period setting. For a crisper, longer lasting brick surface, use brick paviers. These have been fired to become harder than walling bricks, and, although more expensive, are easier to lay because thinner, slightly wider, and longer. Engineering bricks are another alternative and again are more durable than facing bricks.

Take care not to lay too large an area of brick paving in fancy patterns. There is something special about good brick paving, but the mix can soon become too rich.

PATTERNS IN BRICK

Brick or brick pavier is an adaptable paving medium. It can be laid face down to present the bottom, or bedding, face of the brick, or laid on edge to present a side, or stretcher, face. Bricks can be interlocked in a variety of ways and they can be cut, making possible a wide choice of pattern. Over larger areas the richness of colour and quantity of elements dictates a simple pattern.

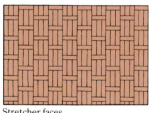
Stretcher faces

Stretcher faces

Brick paving designs
The five brick patterns shown here are all fairly elaborate and would suit smaller spaces. Simpler designs include all-aligning coursing and simple wall-bonding patterns, and suit larger areas.

Bedding faces

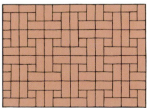
Bedding faces using halves

Bedding faces

PAVING AND EDGING CHOICES

Proprietary concrete paving blocks

Smooth, round concrete slab

The range of types of paving is bewildering. While natural, local paving materials are usually the best suited to the environment, most people settle for concrete in one form or another, persuaded by price and availability. Mixing materials can often be a good compromise.

Plain concrete edging

Two sizes of rough-edged granite sett

Hexagonal concrete paving slab

Fluted neo-classical edging

Engineering bricks – manufactured in many local clay colours, they create a clean, crisp effect

Wire-cut clay blocks

Glazed barley-sugar edging

Textured blue stock brick

Concrete coping

Soft surfacing

Soft surfacing provides an ideal textural transition between hard paving and areas of lawn or planting, as well as a cheaper alternative to stone or concrete. The effect is relaxed and maintenance is easy. The most common materials are washed pea shingle, gravel, and pulverized bark.

Gravel or shingle are ideal for surfacing tight spaces that are too awkward to pave, and for places where not much will grow, such as under trees. They can be used instead of small areas of lawn in urban spaces, creating a crisp, neat look in place of worn, shabby grass.

All soft surfacing materials need to be contained within a retaining edge, otherwise they tend to spill over onto adjoining lawn or paving. Within this retaining edge, gravel or shingle only require periodic maintenance.

Planting in soft surfaces
Shrubs, herbs, seasonal bulbs, and perennials will all grow happily through gravel, shingle, and smallish pebbles laid no more than 100mm (4 in) deep. The surface binding layer acts as a mulch and is an ideal medium in which seeds can germinate.

Planting in areas of gravel rather than bare earth confined to beds creates a random, relaxed look, linking planted areas more naturally with those of a paved area or neighbouring pathway. It also makes a small space appear larger – the fewer ground divisions there are, the less cramped it seems.

Textural combinations
Japanese gardeners have used gravel as a ground surfacing for centuries, raking it into abstract patterns that simulate marine eddies and currents swirling around islands of rock and moss. This technique requires regular, if not daily, care, because every shower of rain and every footprint erodes the pattern. On the positive side it gives you the freedom to change the pattern whenever you like. A combination of unraked gravel or pebbles with boulders and rocks can be just as effective and considerably less time consuming.

Gravel designs
Seventeenth-century French and Italian landscape gardeners also used gravel between areas of box hedging in their formally patterned *parterres*. Gravel can be used alongside well-defined areas of planting to create a textured, geometric pattern.

Different colours and sizes of gravel can be used to make patterns, varying from formal chequerboard to looser, more abstract shapes. Brick or thin strips of wood or aluminium are used to separate the different types of gravel. This technique of patterning gravel can be used on a roof that is viewed from above or to bring interest to a dark corner.

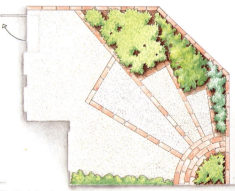

Abstract shapes
A swirling design for a walled area uses different coloured loose gravels divided by ribbons of aluminium, above.

Radial design
Two colours of gravel radiate outwards from an area of corner planting. The brick used to divide the gravel is an integral part of the design, above.

Shingle and gravel

Pea shingle consists of small chippings of stone that have been smoothed by the action of water. It is dredged from low-lying inland pits or taken from beach areas. Always stipulate washed single when ordering, so that it doesn't arrive with a covering of clay.

Gravel consists of sharp chippings of natural rock from a quarry. Both shingle and gravel have marked regional differences, depending on the type of rock they come from.

Laying gravel or shingle

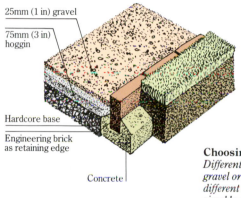

25mm (1 in) gravel

75mm (3 in) hoggin

Hardcore base

Engineering brick as retaining edge

Concrete

Soft surfacing choice

The cheapest type of soft surfacing available locally will probably be produced from rock native to your area. In mountainous areas this is likely to be quarried chippings; in coastal or river areas, it will be pea shingle.

Gravel colour choices range from white and creamy beige to grey, red, brown, and black. River-washed shingle or dredged pea shingle, both rounded by the action of water, is less extensive in range and can look just as good.

Both gravel and shingle suit just about all locations, but they tend to be swept up when snow is being cleared, and a pale gravel can produce a lot of glare in open areas exposed to harsh sunlight. Shingle and pea shingle are more suitable for children to play on than gravel, which has sharp edges. Pulverized bark or grass are even better choices and will produce fewer scraped knees.

Pulverized bark is a particularly good surfacing for woodland settings, underneath trees where not much will grow.

Choosing materials
Different colours and gauges of gravel or pebble will produce very different effects when laid over a sizeable area.

Bark can be laid through trees and shrubs to create a soft organic look

White limestone chippings (coarse grade)

Grey granite chippings

Fine-textured washed shingle

Washed pea shingle

White granite chippings

Fine horticultural grit

Honey-coloured rock chippings

Decking

Cost and climate are two factors that may determine whether or not you choose timber as a surface in your garden. In areas where timber is relatively cheap and plentiful, decking becomes an attractive method of surfacing and will provide a sympathetic link between garden, clapboard houses, and surrounding countryside. Ideal climatic conditions for timber decking are long, hot, dry summers, even if followed by extremely cold winters with heavy falls of snow. Long, moist winters, on the other hand, make timber slippery underfoot and unattractive.

Types of decking

The simplest type of decking is low level and provides an alternative to terracing. Supports are concrete piers or short timber or metal posts. Low level decking is often useful as a bridge between house and garden where there is a difficult level change between ground floor and outside space, as, for example, in turn-of-the-century town houses with basements. Decking is not always attached to a building, however – timber can be used as a surfacing material at ground level anywhere in the garden. Interesting patterns and satisfying textural contrasts can be created by combining small areas of deck with stone or concrete paving. Decking is also a sympathetic surface to have alongside water, around a swimming pool or pond.

Hillside decks create level space where none existed before. The deck extends out from the elevated first floor, and steps lead down to ground level. Correctly sited, a hillside deck can provide a platform for spectacular views. This type of deck is expensive to construct and may involve the services of an architect, particularly if the deck adjoins the house. An architect will also be aware of any local building regulations that affect the work.

A third type of decking is used to surface a roof garden where the original roofing material was unsuitable for walking on and for garden elements. Square timber panels the same size as paving slabs can be clamped together in a sympathetic flooring that is lighter than concrete or brick. The panels are laid on a timber base above the roof finish, so that water can drain to an outlet. Where any major construction is planned to convert a roof space for use as a garden, take the advice of an architect or structural engineer so that the load the roof can bear is established. Plant pots alone filled with wet earth are very heavy.

CONSTRUCTING A DECK

Low level decking is relatively easy to construct. It depends on firm, poured concrete footings, or foundations, below ground level. Dig out holes for the footings beneath the final positions of the piers of the proposed deck, and use temporary wooden formers to establish a substantial slab of concrete. Proprietary precast concrete piers are available which sit on the footings and provide the bases for the timber posts that will take the timber frame of the deck. The timber posts must be cut to allow for any changes in ground level so that the 100×100mm (4×4 in) beams which form the basis of the deck structure are indeed level. These beams support 100×50mm (4×2 in) joists which in turn support the decking planks. The structure is nailed together. The timber posts are nailed to nailing blocks let into the wet concrete of the footings.

Where decking is used at low level, weed growth beneath the deck must be suppressed. One method is to spread black plastic sheeting between the deck supporting posts.

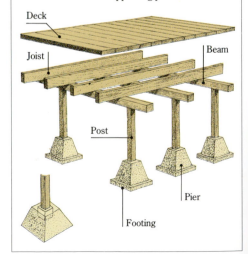

Deck

Joist

Beam

Post

Pier

Footing

Choice of timber

A successful deck depends on the quality of the wood used and proper maintenance. The wood should be resistant to decay, splintering, and warping. Redwood is ideal, but is only available in the United States. It doesn't require treatment with preservative. Red cedar is also durable and more widely available. Pine, larch, and spruce can all be used for decking, but require preservative treatment. It is essential that the wood can be sawn without splintering and will accept nails readily. Galvanized nails are used rather than screws.

A simpler pattern will use less wood than a more complex one and take less time to construct, and therefore be less expensive.

DECK DESIGN

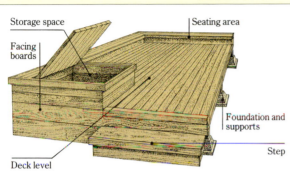

Storage space
Seating area
Facing boards
Foundation and supports
Step
Deck level

This design for a timber deck, left, gives useful terrace space which might adjoin any house. In place of a handrail or balustrading, the edges of the deck have been built up to surround the area and to provide casual bench seating. A further raised section, doubling as a table, lifts to provide useful storage space, possibly for cushions or garden equipment.

Raised garden space
The crisp lines of this timber deck, left, continue the feel of the house it adjoins and make an inviting extension to the inside living area as well as a stylish transition between ground floor level and garden level.
Decking patterns work best if they are related to patterns in neighbouring timber structures, such as fencing or clapboarding.

Structures

Whether you are planning a garden from scratch or making changes to your existing garden, building in structures sympathetically can be difficult. It may be a conservatory, a pergola, a greenhouse, or a shed, but it is the difference in scale between house and new structure that can be hard to reconcile. Particularly as the height of a pre-constructed building is often out of scale to its ground plan. Materials are another problem – whatever your new shed is constructed from may be completely out of keeping with the character of the house, and it will need to be sited well away and/or screened.

You may choose either to buy a pre-constructed structure or to build your own. The range of ready-made buildings is considerable. If you are considering more than one building, make sure they are made from the same materials or come from the same manufacturer, otherwise the overall effect will be haphazard.

Unity can be achieved by grouping structures – perhaps a shed, a greenhouse, a frame, a compost area, and possibly an oil tank – in a service area that is served by one path. Alternatively employ a windowless wall to support lean-to structures. The rule is to *build in* new structures rather than just add them.

Conservatories

Although usually attached to the house, the conservatory is part of the garden. It is a place for growing decorative plants under glass. Furnishing and flooring will therefore have to sustain frequent watering, including spraying, and general plant husbandry. It is distinguished from the garden room, which is an extension to the house and is furnished very much with people in mind rather than plants.

Building a new conservatory along traditional lines involves major expense, but you might be lucky enough to inherit one that will respond to a little judicious renovation. You may decide to heat it, bearing in mind that warming a single-glazed house to even a modest temperature is an expensive business. It is possible to bring on early spring and summer flowers with great success with no heat at all.

A wide range of ready-made conservatories is on the market, from traditional Gothic to modern style. Most conservatories are

CONSERVATORY OR GREENHOUSE STAGING

Staging provides surfaces at different heights both for working at and displaying container-grown plants. Staging systems are commercially available, but may not fit into awkward spaces. If you decide to build your own, it must be of stout construction to support the considerable weight of gravel and pots when filled and watered.

Use 50mm (2 in) angle-iron both for the legs, which should be set in concrete, and the tray, which must be welded to the legs and hold corrugated asbestos sheeting. Fit braces under the sheeting and at an angle between the legs and the horizontal tray. Paint the iron to protect against rust. Next cover the corrugated sheet with a layer of fine, washed gravel into which pots can be set. The gravel will soak up surplus drainage moisture and help maintain moisture in the pots, and the plants will soak up water by capillary action.

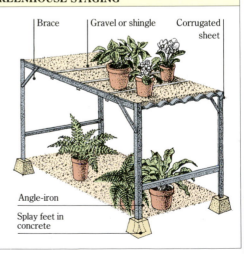

Brace | Gravel or shingle | Corrugated sheet

Angle-iron

Splay feet in concrete

constructed of softwood and painted white, and need regular maintenance and re-painting. Plants may be sited in beds or in pots, on the ground or raised on shelving. An automatic watering device will make plant care considerably easier in warm weather, when plants may need watering twice a day.

A conservatory will house a growing garden through the long dark days of winter, with hyacinths and narcissus, cascading mimosa (*Acacia* sp.) or a Banksian rose (*Rosa banksiae*), as early as January.

For best effect, keep your planting and furnishing to a particular style, and on no account let the conservatory degenerate into a collection of potted oddments. Make it tropical with large-leaved plants or light and pretty within a particular colour range. A large conservatory can even become an occasional dining room in the summer months, for exotic eating out.

The plant grower's conservatory
This conservatory, above, has been designed more for plants than for family use, but space has been found for some incidental seating within a bower of planting, in the nineteenth-century manner.

A GARDEN PAVILION

If you decide against an exotic plant collection, you might settle for a structure with large, glazed areas in the walls so that it can function as a greenhouse, but with a traditional roof of tiles, slates, or shingles. Such a structure might be called a pavilion and can be sited away from the house, perhaps adjoining a terraced area, to provide shelter or shade. Below is a construction idea for a pavilion linking two terraces bounded by an existing high brick wall. The pavilion is hexagonal with brick elevations to match the walling, pierced by large windows and a matching double door for access. The pitched roof is tiled. The stone flags used to surface the two terraces also make up the treads of two steps that follow the line of the building. It is important that surrounding planting is full and allowed to flop on to the paving, softening the overall look of the building and the hard surfacing, and integrating the new structure with the rest of the garden.

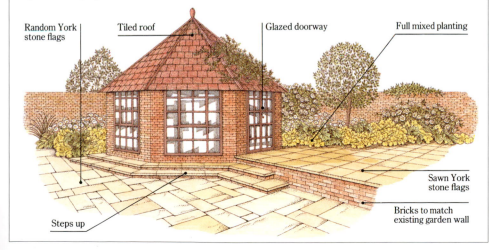

Random York stone flags

Tiled roof

Glazed doorway

Full mixed planting

Sawn York stone flags

Bricks to match existing garden wall

Steps up

Pergolas

The vine-entwined Mediterranean structure, providing shelter from the hot afternoon sun and connecting one building with another, is one image of the pergola. In other contexts the pergola can form a semi-covered room, a plant-smothered arbour, or be used to strengthen some aspect of a garden design.

Directional pergolas

A dynamic or directional pergola is one that leads from one space to another. In contrast, one that defines a space rather than leading through it can be described as static.

A freestanding directional pergola draws the eye down its length and shortens the foreground perspective. It might lead to and frame a view or entrance where it is constructed over a path. Attached to the side of a building, a pergola creates a colonnade effect and can be useful for covering an entrance, keeping the sun from rooms inside, and providing shelter for outdoor seating.

A pergola covering a terrace or even the entire garden provides a ceiling and can be styled to extend the mood of the interior, and create an additional room outside.

Static pergolas

A static pergola may be freestanding, but the horizontals are more likely to be connected to a wall at one end, and sail outwards to meet the verticals which rise from the far edge of the covered space. Uprights may not be required at all if the horizontals simply bridge the gap between two walls.

A pergola on the roof

Roof gardens tend to be rather exposed to the wind and the great expanse of the sky above, as well as to surrounding buildings. A pergola construction can lend a sheltered feel to a roof garden and some protection from sun and wind.

Always check the load-bearing strength of a roof before constructing a pergola and whether you need planning permission. Metal frames are more suitable for roofs. Metal wires or ropes can be used for horizontals.

CONSTRUCTING A PERGOLA

Stained softwood beams and scaffolding poles can be used to make a simple pergola, as shown below right. The beams sit in proprietary metal joist shoes where they meet the supporting wall. At the opposite end of each beam, scaffolding poles are let into the timber for half the thickness of the beam. These poles must be firmly bedded in concrete foundations beneath the surface they pierce. The run of beams is braced laterally with a metal tie. Plant support wires can be run along the underside of the beams. Terrace paving units beneath the pergola can be spaced so that the pergola verticals coincide with a joint, thereby unifying all sides of the structure.

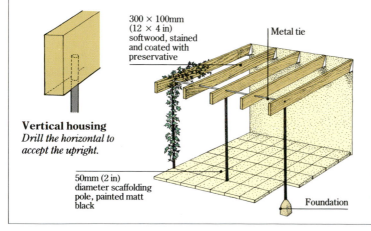

300 × 100mm (12 × 4 in) softwood, stained and coated with preservative

Metal tie

Vertical housing
Drill the horizontal to accept the upright.

50mm (2 in) diameter scaffolding pole, painted matt black

Foundation

Metal shoe fixing
A pergola adjoining masonry can either be let into the structure or sit into an L-shaped metal shoe. The metal joist shoe is let into the wall and fixed to the mortar.

Planting

One of the most attractive aspects of a plant-covered pergola is the dappled light that filters through. Climbers will soften the overall effect of the structure and help provide shade and privacy. Consider the weight of whatever you are planting in its mature state, particularly if you are training it along wires or rope. Consider also density of foliage and how long it is in leaf. A leafless climber will not provide much shade. Evergreen climbers may provide too much shade in the winter months, when you want maximum light.

Proportions

Garden spaces in urban areas are often not in scale with surrounding buildings. Pergola horizontals can be used here to lower the height of the space and create an aesthetically pleasing and well-proportioned area that is comfortable to be in.

The proportions of the different parts of the pergola should balance. The verticals should not be disproportionately large to the horizontals. The scale of the timber horizontal will depend on the length it has to span between supports, and this will depend on the type of timber being used. As a rule of thumb, the span should be no more than 3–3.5m (10-12 ft). If the timber is too large in section, it becomes oppressive, and if it is too narrow, it has a tendency to warp.

Materials for pergolas

As with all garden elements, the materials chosen for a pergola must be in sympathy with the mood and style of the buildings around it. Materials can be treated in different ways to create very individual looks. Wood can be painted, stained, or just treated with a preservative and left its natural colour. The ends of the horizontals can be shaped to echo architectural features.

In the British Isles, timber horizontals are traditionally massive oak spars. Further south in Mediterranean areas unsawn softwood is also used. Other choices include stained or painted softwood, or cedarwood, which turns an attractive grey with age. Hardwood is less liable to warping or cracking but is extremely expensive. Tensioned wire or brightly coloured chandler's rope provides cheaper, lighter, and simpler alternatives. Vines or hops trained along wires or ropes will give shade in summer and let light through in winter.

Pergola horizontals
Consider shape, colour, materials, and the shadows that the horizontals will cast.

Sawn softwood

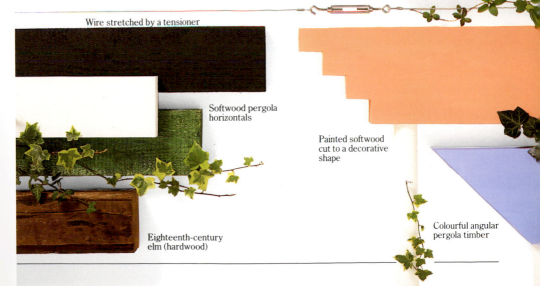

Wire stretched by a tensioner

Softwood pergola horizontals

Painted softwood cut to a decorative shape

Eighteenth-century elm (hardwood)

Colourful angular pergola timber

Storage structures

All kinds of things need dry storage in the garden – tools, outdoor furniture, bicycles, toys, and so on. Discarded toys and leisure equipment quickly accumulate, as do gardening items. Fertilizers and pesticides need waterproof storage out of reach of children, and preferably under lock and key. There may be a range of composts – mixes for seeds, mixes for cuttings, and mixes for house plants. Gardening coats, hats, boots, and gloves all need hooks and shelves.

An existing outbuilding is the perfect solution. Consider building a new one within your garden plan, perhaps adjacent to an existing wall or fence. Or you might decide to build a storage shed, making sure you first consult local bye-laws about where and what you can build. A simple structure built as part of a plan can be surprisingly inconspicuous.

Built-in storage

In a small garden it is even more important to integrate storage space in the overall design. Good use can be made of awkward corners where cupboards are tailored to fit neatly into the space and designed to meet your exact requirements. As part of the design of a door or gate, such practical solutions can be stylish features, as shown above right. Cupboards for storing rubbish must be accessible and easy to clean. Items for long-term storage can be

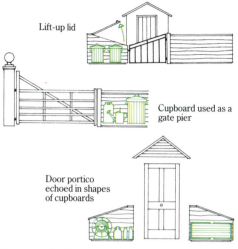

Lift-up lid

Cupboard used as a gate pier

Door portico echoed in shapes of cupboards

Design solutions
Three stylish designs for built-in storage.

successfully hidden in out-of-the-way places, for example in a hollow brick bench with a removable timber surface.

Screening

An openwork screen, such as trellis clothed with climbers, or a solid screen, such as closely lashed bamboo, can be used to divide off a small area for dustbins or for a compost heap. Hedging plants make equally effective screens. Choose evergreen screening plants, or you will find yourself with a seasonal rather than a permanent screen.

DIFFERENT TYPES OF GARDEN SHED

The structures illustrated below give an idea of the range available. Choose a unit in scale to the garden. As a general rule, however, it is always easier to integrate a larger unit into a layout than a smaller one. Consider siting your shed next to an existing freestanding structure, such as a garage or greenhouse, to avoid too many service paths and too much hard surfacing.

Wide-doored shed in metal and plastic

Simple timber shed

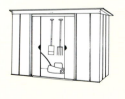

Metal section shed with sliding doors

Half-sized shed in metal

Greenhouses and frames

Appearance and function will influence your choice of greenhouse. Construction materials can be painted or stained softwood, cedar, or metal. Shapes include the ridge type, the lean-to, the hexagonal, and the dome.

Sophisticated modern greenhouses offer fully automatic watering, ventilation, and shading. Most people, however, settle for a greenhouse which they can use for over-wintering, seed sowing in spring, and propagation of cuttings for later summer use. Tomatoes and peppers can be grown throughout the summer, but watering will be daily and time consuming.

Frames

A frame with underground heating will provide most people with all the glass they really need. A limited range of frame types is available, but it is reasonably easy to build your own of brick or timber, with a simple lift-up framed glass top. Unheated or cold frames can still be used to harden seedlings.

Siting

Both frames and greenhouses will need to be sited in full sunshine, away from the overhang of trees. Any snow that builds up on a greenhouse roof must be cleared regularly. Overhanging trees would deposit collected snow with potentially disastrous results.

Service paths to frames and greenhouses should be hard and dry and wide enough for a wheelbarrow. Allow plenty of space around them for standing pots and boxes.

COLD FRAME CONSTRUCTION

Cold frames are used to harden off plants between greenhouse and open ground or to germinate annual or vegetable seeds. A simple cold frame made of a wooden, sloping-sided box, say, 1.2m (4 ft) square, with a glazed panel lid is easy to construct.

Treat the wood with a "safe" preservative – creosote fumes will kill seedlings – and give the frame plenty of time to dry. Alternatively, paint the frame, perhaps to match the greenhouse. If it is used for growing plants in containers rather than in the earth, it can be positioned on hard surfacing and will be less prone to rot.

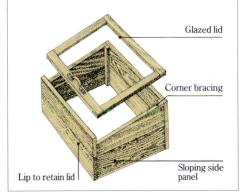

Glazed lid

Corner bracing

Lip to retain lid

Sloping side panel

GREENHOUSE TYPES

The basic types of greenhouse for average size gardens are shown below. They may be constructed in metal or cedar (both needing little protection) or softwood (needing regular painting) or a combination.

Site the greenhouse to ensure adequate sunlight. Ideally position the longest axis north/south so that the sun crosses it during the day, giving equal shares to both sides. Also take account of water and power provision when choosing a site.

Timber-walled

Metal frame, glass-to-floor

Lean-to on brick base

Metal-framed dome

Features

Having established the basic layout and working areas of your garden, you can now think about realizing any eye-catching features you may have incorporated in your plan – raised beds, rockeries, water features, even a swimming pool, cooking and eating areas, play areas for children, and flights of fancy.

Few modern gardens are large enough to accommodate many features. In a small area, the special feature should set the character for the whole garden. Avoid creating a series of unrelated exclamation marks, divided by grass or planting, which will look like a collection of oddments and never a harmonious whole. Always treat the garden as a single picture.

Misjudgement of scale is the most common error. The rockery, for example, must look natural, as though it were an escarpment of rock exposed through the action of wind and rain, rather than just sit on a lawn as if it came from nowhere. Water incorporated with rock outcrops can look charming, but can easily become pretentious unless the concept is kept bold and simple.

Rockeries and raised beds

A natural-looking rock grouping has the rock placed in strata and uses rock indigenous to the area. The build-up of land to the outcrop should also look natural. A rockery on flat land needs considerable space to allow for a gradual build-up as well as the rock grouping itself. In a smaller space you can grow alpines in contrived changes of level which create a series of raised beds. This sort of arrangement is far more at home in an urban setting than a rockery. A raised bed can provide the well-drained, open situation that alpines thrive in. In the wild many alpines root in scree or shale. Gravel or shingle provides a good substitute for the real thing in the garden. You might consider incorporating raised beds in a terrace to provide shelter from draughts and screening.

CREATING A ROCK OUTCROP

You don't need a mountain of earth to make a realistic rock outcrop. You can use any gentle gradient in the garden. In a flat area you can change levels either by creating a simple mound or by constructing a retaining wall (see p. 97). The mound should not be too high, however, nor too cramped. Try to use slabs of rock to let in to the bank, creating the impression of naturally occurring strata. Much of the rock will be covered by backfilling with earth and gravel or other scree substitute. The backfill must be well drained for alpines to thrive, but it need not be rich. Soil accompanying granite or ironstone tends to be acid, while soil accompanying limestone is alkaline. Reflect this and choose your plants accordingly.

If you don't have room for both sides of the mound, the diagram on the right shows how you might fake the mounded effect with a low retaining wall. This construction is useful for siting a rockery at the edge of your garden. In this case, however, ensure that the retaining wall is hidden or the effect will be spoiled.

Rockery with retaining wall

Rockery set into a mound

Earth and gravel

Existing bank

SCREE BED CONSTRUCTION

In a natural situation a bed of scree is composed of chippings of the parent rock. It is difficult to walk on and liable to slip. It is well drained and dries out quickly. It supports a limited range of plants. Plants growing in scree tend to be in semi-shade in the lee of larger rocks, a situation which you might seek to recreate in your garden, building up the bed as shown below left.

You can site a scree bed in a similar position to a rockery, combine the two, or raise the scree bed within retaining walls of brick, stone, or railway sleepers to show off small alpine plants to best effect.

Below is a series of brick retaining walls backfilled with scree beds to support a selection of alpine plants which will crawl through the gravel finish and cascade over the low walls. Brick steps are incorporated for negotiating the bank which sweeps in on the right.

Scree beds in retaining walls
This corner idea, below, combines steps and retaining walls to provide raised beds for alpines. The stepped route across the beds encourages the visitor to stop and study the plant groups.

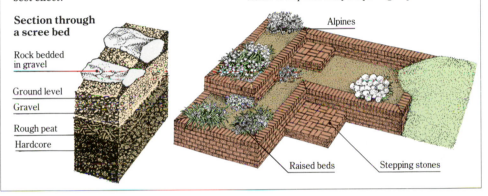

Section through a scree bed

Rock bedded in gravel

Ground level

Gravel

Rough peat

Hardcore

Alpines

Raised beds

Stepping stones

Natural rock grouping
Stone is well integrated in the garden surround here, above. The stone sits in a bank, looking as though *weather has exposed it. The stratification, or graining, of the rock runs in the same direction as it would if occurring naturally.*

Water

Water has a compelling quality and can bring the most uninspiring garden alive. It has almost the strength of a building in a garden layout, with the unique attribute of reflecting light. A well-integrated water feature can be the highlight of a garden, whereas water that is out of scale and style with the rest of the garden can easily become an irritation, rivalling other features of gentler attraction. Always use water with discretion and as part of the structure of the garden design.

Effects and impressions

An area of still water at ground level in a garden creates a mirrored setting for surrounding features. A dark internal lining at the bottom of a pool of water will intensify reflections further, whereas a light-coloured glazed tile finish will reduce them, tempting the viewer to look into the depths at plants or fish rather than at the surface. Sunlight playing on the surface of still water produces a Hockney-like, cellular pattern.

In another dimension, the sound of water running, splashing, or trickling can have a cooling effect on a hot day, a relaxing effect at any time, and can help to baffle background urban noise. Flat planes of water act as a foil to planting, either in the water or adjacent to it –

Formal pool, informal planting
Informal planting softens the rigid shapes of this L-shaped pool with wooden sleeper surround.

reeds and water lilies, for instance, or overhanging blossoms – linking the ground pattern of the garden to three-dimensional plant forms. Plants used with moving water create a more vibrant effect.

Planes of water can be contained at different heights to create a visual relationship between the ground plan and the boundary. The focus can be water flowing from one plane to another or, as in the "New York Plaza" effect, forming a sheet of water falling down a wall. Or it can be a steady trickle, snaking between carefully positioned plant groupings.

CONSTRUCTING A FORMAL POOL

Small pools are best constructed in waterproof concrete, incorporating an outlet to a soakaway (see *Drainage*, p. 90) for cleaning and as an overflow to prevent flooding in heavy rain. Where frost is likely, the concrete should be reinforced and the pool made with sloping sides to allow the ice to expand upwards as it freezes. Failing this, a softwood plank can be floated in the

pool as freezing temperatures set in, for the ice to expand into. Build in a shelf recess for marsh plants. You will need special containers or planting baskets, which are designed to hold a rooting medium and the root systems of water plants for planting in the water (see *Water plants*, pp. 160–163). You can use bricks to adjust container heights in the pond.

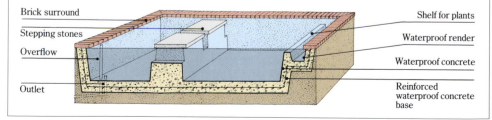

Brick surround
Stepping stones
Overflow
Outlet

Shelf for plants
Waterproof render
Waterproof concrete
Reinforced waterproof concrete base

Choosing a style

In small gardens it is probably better to use water in a formal way, in conjunction with the building or as a sculptural feature. Water used informally, in free-form shapes that imitate naturally occurring ponds, needs a lot of space.

Be absolutely clear about the kind of water feature you want in your garden: formal or informal, flowing or still, size and scale, whether it will be safe for any children using the garden. Small children and unsupervised water don't really mix in any event. In suburban or rural areas you may have to secure netting over your pool to prevent birds from stealing the fish and to prevent falling leaves from contaminating the water.

Decide on the depth of the pool according to its purpose. A shallow pool about 300mm (1 ft) deep will appear deeper if the sides are painted black with waterproof paint. You need a deeper pool to sustain pond life. Fish must be able to get under ice if the pond freezes in winter.

Keeping the water clean

Whatever style of water feature you choose, the water in it should be clear and sparkling. There are two ways of achieving this. You can install a pumped recycling system so that the water is always running. Or to save energy and promote ecology you can establish a balance of pond life including oxygenating plants (at least ten per square metre/yard of water surface), snails, and fish to create a food chain which excludes the green algae that stain surfaces and cloud water. Small water containers should be drained and refilled regularly.

Formal use of water

"Formal" in this context refers to geometrically shaped containers, pools, or channels used as garden features.

A formal pool can be still and reflective, its surface broken only by the occasional iris or rush clump or it may be agitated by a fountain. Keep any fountain display in scale. Wind can play havoc with fountains, quickly emptying the pool if the jet of water is too high. The height of the jet should be no greater than the distance from its source to the pool edge. Formally contained water can be most attractive when it is raised rather than sunken.

Informal use of water

Water used informally needs space to be successful. You are trying to simulate a natural pool with planting running into the water interspersed with beaches of shingle. Alternatively, choose a Japanese-style, informal boulder pool, backed with bamboos. A plain, planted circle of water in an informal setting can be attractive, where you are creating a contrast of form. The small scale dribbling stream and informal pool emanating from a rockery is never very convincing.

CONSTRUCTING AN INFORMAL POOL

The area of an informal pool must be larger than that of a formal one if the effect is not to be pretentious. A piece of butyl rubber sheeting makes an ideal lining for these amorphous shapes. The drawback is that you need to hide the edge of the sheeting carefully, as well as any folds. Two ways of edging are illustrated. The sheeting is laid on a 75mm (3 in) layer of sand.

On the left is the informal beach effect, where the gradient is shallow enough to hold the boulders laid over the sheet. An alternative is to lay the sheet over pre-formed steps, cut into the earth, to hold the beach. On the right a straight edging is achieved by wrapping the sheet over a block retaining wall and laying a brick or stone coping over the top of it.

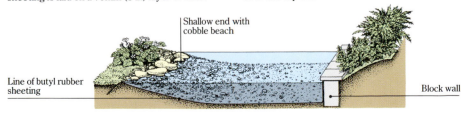

Shallow end with cobble beach

Line of butyl rubber sheeting

Block wall

Swimming pools

Nothing is so demanding in a garden as a swimming pool. It will always dominate its surroundings. Its shape should be carefully fitted into the overall garden plan. The simpler the shape of the pool and its terrace surround, the easier it is to integrate, and, from a practical point of view, the easier it is to heat, cover, and swim in.

The site for a pool must be open, sunny, and away from deciduous trees whose leaves would otherwise litter water and poolside. Check the level of the water table at any potential site. If the water table is too near the surface, the whole structure will be subject to movement. Easy access to the site will be needed for digging machinery and the excavated spoil will have to go somewhere. Storage space will be needed for maintenance gear, a site for the filtration plant, and ideally a place for changing.

Leave the structural work of building the pool to specialists. They will advise you which type of pool is most suitable for your needs. If you are contemplating a heated pool, consider using solar energy. Take advice on how to site the panels to catch the sun.

Alternative types of pool
Think realistically about how you will use your pool. Lap pools are perfect for exercising without taking up too much space. They need be no more than 3m (10 ft) wide and 7m (23 ft) long. Even a small garden might accommodate a pool of these dimensions, although there would not be much room for anything else.

Plunge pools are smaller – only large enough to immerse the body in – but for exercise purposes can be fitted with a wave machine which will create a force of water to swim against. They are ideal for cooling off in during warm weather.

Even smaller in scale is the jacuzzi and hot tub which can be sited in a sheltered spot. If they are close to the house, you can use them in winter. Immersing yourself in warm water with only your head in sub-zero temperatures is a stimulating, not to say bizarre, experience.

A feature of beauty
Few have such a dramatic location as this, below, for their swimming pool. This free-shaped pool above an Italian lake shows how successful the swimming pool can be as a garden feature.

DIFFERENT POOL-EDGING STYLES

The edging provides the trim to the pool. Above all it should not be slippery. Lighting and a scum trap can be well integrated into pre-formed proprietary mouldings. The first example shows a recessed scum trap below the level of the edging. The second example allows the raised pool surface to overflow into a surrounding scum trap. The third and fourth examples could equally well edge an ornamental pool. Concrete slab, quarry tile, or brick edgings better complement grey or black pool linings, rather than bright blue, and the overall impact is less jarring.

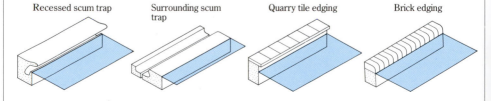

Recessed scum trap

Surrounding scum trap

Quarry tile edging

Brick edging

Outdoor kitchen

The barbecue area can become the centrepiece of a terrace garden in the summer months. Various forms of portable barbecue are available, but it is fairly easy to construct your own in brick. You can build in lighting, worktops, and cupboards, and design the whole thing into the terrace layout. Ensure that prevailing winds will not blow smoke into the house, towards the sitting area, or towards neighbouring houses.

Allow plenty of space surrounding the structure, both for the cook and for guests. On a chilly summer evening, hot charcoal becomes a big attraction and people will crowd round when the cooking is over. Flat, raised surfaces to the sides of the barbecue structure are useful for serving, depositing plates, for relishes, glasses, and bottles.

Dining alfresco
A well-designed area for preparing and serving food can be the perfect setting for outdoor entertaining. This integrated and inspiring food preparation area, above, with its wealth of storage space and worktops, is possible in a hot, dry, predictable climate.

CONSTRUCTING A BARBECUE

A barbecue for serving several people at once should have a cooking grill no less than 1m×500mm (3½×1½ ft). Anything smaller will guarantee some guests waiting for food while others eat. The grill can be held neatly in the coursing of a well-built brick structure, such as the one shown below. The charcoal tray slots below the grill. Both are removable. Allow at least a square metre (yard) of worktop to the right and left of the cooking area for preparation and serving of food. Make sure the worktop and cooking levels of the barbecue unit are at a convenient height, making a comparison with the height of the kitchen worktops. Build in cupboards with waterproof doors beneath the worktops for storing equipment throughout the summer. The barbecue structure will sit directly on a well-constructed terrace or on its own concrete foundation. A poured concrete infill beneath the grill is a useful protection.

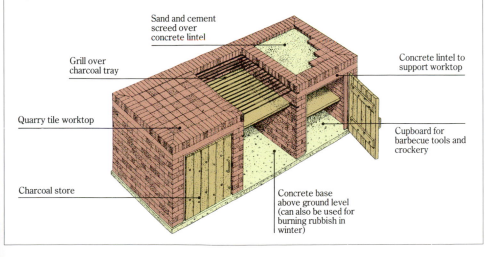

Sand and cement screed over concrete lintel

Grill over charcoal tray

Concrete lintel to support worktop

Quarry tile worktop

Cupboard for barbecue tools and crockery

Charcoal store

Concrete base above ground level (can also be used for burning rubbish in winter)

Children's play areas

Children can cause damage within a garden if it is not designed to accommodate their play. The garden may be the only safe outside area for their games, so make space for them. Draw ground rules early on: make clear where they can play and which areas are off-limits. The demands of children's play change as they grow older. Toddlers need a small grassed area in sight of the house, well away from water or steps. After a few years, they enjoy simple changes of level, such as grass steps or a gentle slope to roll, run, or ride down, sandpits, swings, climbing frames, and slides.

As children get older, they will want more space for their activities – a route for bicycles, somewhere to play ball games, space to tinker with machines, a corner for pets, and perhaps a patch of land for growing their own plants.

Children think of a garden as a place to have fun. They must be allowed to run about, kick a ball, cycle, and climb without being inhibited.

Entertaining gardens
For children a sandpit can have endless attraction. It doesn't need to be a piece of bright plastic jarring on the eye, it can actually be a bonus as in this garden, above.

FUN IN THE GARDEN

A sandpit should be large enough for more than one child to play in at once, well-drained, and filled with the correct type of sand. A depth of about 300mm (1 ft) is about right.

The structure can be of concrete, brick, or timber, laid on paving slabs, which in turn are laid over a layer of fine hardcore or ash. The slabs are not jointed to allow for drainage. Construct a simple lid – a timber surround infilled with netting – to protect the sand from cats.

Most shop-bought climbing frames quickly become defunct as children outgrow them. Try to build your own adaptable climbing frame from an old tree trunk. It will provide a point of minor sculptural interest and be far more aesthetically pleasing than a brightly painted metal frame. It can eventually be sawn for logs. Remove rough bark and splinters by wirebrushing. Add tyre swings, ladders, and planks to it for greater versatility.

Sandpit construction

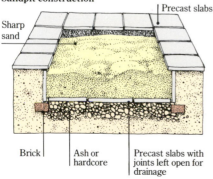

Sharp sand

Precast slabs

Brick

Ash or hardcore

Precast slabs with joints left open for drainage

An improvised climbing frame

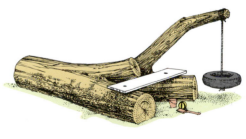

Special effects

There are a number of design tricks and devices, using paint, trellis, mirrors, and natural phenomena such as light and shadow, which can add an exciting and dramatic flavour to your garden. These techniques provide inventive ways of decorating spaces which are too inhospitable for plants to grow, and of creating illusions of space and grandeur.

Painted *trompe l'oeil*

The Renaissance Italians were the early masters of *trompe l'oeil*, painting lavish and apparently three-dimensional architectural scenes and rural idylls on walls both inside and out. Today vibrant and colourful murals are often used to enliven city landscapes. These ideas can be borrowed on a reduced scale and used in the garden. You could either commission a mural or paint one yourself. A garden door to suggest another garden beyond your own, a window with a real windowbox, or plants and trees where none will grow or to thicken up existing vegetation.

Exterior grade paint should be used on garden walls. Different effects can be achieved with matt or eggshell finishes and painting techniques such as stencilling or marbling.

Using shadow

Where natural light is strong, take advantage and position plants or architectural features where they will cast dramatic shadows on surrounding surfaces. Plants with architectural form, such as *Euphorbia characias wulfenii*, placed against a plain background, will throw their shadows to great effect.

Using mirrors

Reflections in glass and water (see p. 124) can be used to create an illusion of size. Strategically placed mirrors will reflect the area you already have and double the apparent size of your garden. Carefully positioned, they can create an impression of ever-receding space. Large areas of mirror are an effective way of brightening areas such as shaded basements or dark wells between city dwellings. Mirrors can also draw attention to a special feature, such as a statue or a collection of topiary.

Painted shadow
Where the sun is not strong enough to create real shadows, they can be imitated on walls or flooring with different shades of paint. Above, a shadow pattern of two tones of blue paint and the reflections of the pergola beams in a pool of water combine to create a cool-coloured composition.

Using reflections
Carefully positioned mirrors combined with framed trelliswork in a small courtyard, above, create an intriguing visual conundrum, promising the viewer cool, leafy spaces beyond the framed doorways. In reality the courtyard is small and damp.

Finishing touches

Planning the small, moveable features that will punctuate your garden design is the final stage before planting. Containers and pots, furniture, sculpture, and windowboxes can all provide detail and interest, harmonizing with and enhancing the ground structure and planting. A badly planned garden will seldom be rescued by adding attractive details but if a garden has been well conceived and executed, the right finishing touches can make it special – perhaps a single piece of sculpture or a simply styled, solid wood bench. You may not be able to afford everything at once, but you can decide on the overall style at the outset and gradually add to your collection of small garden features over time.

Pots and containers

Grouped pots, tubs, and other containers, either with or without plants, can provide incidental points of interest throughout the garden. Pot groupings may not be significant in a larger garden, but they can be very effective in a smaller, sectioned area of the garden or on roof terraces, decks and balconies.

The popular image of garden containers may be of Mediterranean-style terracotta pots flooding over with colourful annuals, but there are many variations on the relationship between pot and planting. The right pot with no planting at all can assume a sculptural quality. In the eighteenth century the boundaries between pot, plant, and sculpture were deliberately blurred in a fashion for lead plants in urns used as finials – adornment for gables and gate posts.

Simple stoneware pot, above
The bold shape of this pot contrasts well with the agave backed by Coronilla glauca. *As a general rule, simple modern pots need a bold planting style to match.*

Sculptural stone, right
There is a medieval simplicity about this arrangement of unplanted containers, the largest of which is an unused font.

Scale and style

Consider how the shape and style of a pot or grouping of containers will look against its backdrop. A jumble of pots can look charming in the right environment, but a jumble can easily become a mess. A classical-style urn may not fit in with a humble location. A pot that doesn't relate to the scale of the space or the overall style can ruin the total effect. With each individual pot, consider whether the pot or the plant provides the main interest, and treat the whole accordingly.

Materials

Almost any kind of container with adequate drainage holes can be used for planting. In the Mediterranean and in Mexico all sorts of cans, pots, and pans are colourfully planted and massed together, bringing colour and interest to doorways, alleyways, and courtyards. There is plenty of scope for inventive use of chimney pots, plastic food containers, and old sinks. Natural materials for purpose-made pots include stone, reconstituted stone, terracotta, wood, earthenware, and even slate. Other materials include concrete, metal, fibreglass, and plastic. Choose a frost-resistant material such as stone for containers that will stand outside all year round in cold climates.

Stoneware is very heavy and difficult to move once filled with earth and planted. Hand-made Italian terracotta pots are often attractive, but little of the pot itself may be visible once the plants have started to grow over the sides.

Pots above ground

Make sure that a roof terrace or balcony is not overloaded with pots. Check the load-bearing capacity of the site with a structural engineer if you are in any doubt. Containers filled with wet earth can be extremely heavy. Choose lightweight containers and position at the side rather than in the middle of a roof, resting their weight on side structural walls where possible. Pots above ground level need to be secured to prevent a sudden high wind from sweeping them groundwards.

Strong shape, above
A boldly shaped terracotta pot, simply planted with a pelargonium, tones perfectly with the baked earth colour of the wall behind.

Gothic vase, left
The delicate tracery of this container is complemented by the planting of a lacy species of pelargonium. Decorated pots need light planting.

Garden furniture

A garden seat may be the last thing you add to a garden, but the first thing that catches the eye and sets the mood and style. Garden furniture should be an integral part of your whole design.

The options are many. Tables and chairs for outside meals, chairs for relaxing and conversation, loungers for sunbathing. Materials include wood, cane or bamboo, stone, metal, either painted or plastic-coated, moulded fibreglass, and plastic. And for visual delight and pure enjoyment, a hammock slung between two apple trees is hard to beat. Some furniture becomes a permanent part of the garden, outdoors all year round – stone benches or heavy wooden chairs with removable cushions, for example. More lightweight chairs and tables need winter storage and can be moved around the garden as required.

Style considerations

Comfort and practicality on the one hand and stylish design on the other need not be mutually exclusive. It is worth hunting around

---

DIFFERENT TYPES OF FURNITURE

Metal
Well-designed metal furniture can be very comfortable. Its lines should be crisp and its appearance lightweight. Metal is durable and can be left standing outside all year round. Much metal furniture is plastic-coated and needs little maintenance. Painted metal needs repainting regularly to keep up its crisp appearance.

Plastic
Reinforced plastic furniture is light and weather resistant and available in any number of shapes. Bold, plain upholstery on a moulded plastic base is often ideal for a sunny terrace in summer.

Teak bench

Poolside
Choose loungers that can withstand moisture and hot bodies covered in suntan oil. Many loungers are covered with simple, fine-gauge nylon or even woven plastic coverings which allow water to drain through and air to circulate freely. Poolside furniture ranges from simple canvas and metal frame designs to ornate metal or plastic-framed versions with adjustable backrests. Most fold for winter storage.

Stone
Stone furniture will be a permanent feature and needs to be planned into the garden layout. It can be positioned to make the most of any sculptural quality it may have and sited against strong background planting to soften its lines and bulk.

Built-in furniture
Very successful seating can be built into the fabric of the garden as a permanent feature. Precast concrete units can be stacked or placed in a row to provide a bench, perhaps doubling up as steps or a retaining wall. A bench

Reinforced plastic chairs

section can be designed into timber decking. A raised pool edge can provide an inviting place to sit. Built-in furniture is low key and harmonious compared with the eye-catching quality of some moveable garden furniture.

Wood
A sturdy garden table sited close to the house will find itself used for many purposes other than as a dining table. Unpainted wood is an excellent choice for garden furniture, blending as it does so well with any background of planting, terrace, trees, or lawn. Painted wood has a very different character, and becomes part of the house rather than the garden.

for pieces that are functional as well as aesthetically pleasing. Consider how the colours of any furniture, and in particular upholstery, may be affected by the quality of natural light in your garden. A bright floral pattern may look fine in brilliant sunshine against an azure sea, but becomes depressingly gaudy in a grey-skied suburban garden. Furniture constructed from natural

materials, particularly weathered stone and wood, and upholstered in neutral colours tends to fit more happily with the natural forms of the garden, as do curving organic shapes. It may be, however, that the natural look doesn't match the architectural or interior style of your house. The hard lines of a sleek metal chair may suit the feel of your urban balcony and echo the chic style of the room opening onto it.

Sculpture

Sculpture may be the centrepoint of a garden or merely a side attraction, incidental to the whole. It may be deliberately overscaled for a dramatic effect or unobtrusive and in total harmony with the surroundings. It may be striking or incongruous, traditional in style or abstract. Groupings of pots or urns, boulders or stones, can all create a pleasing sculptural feature. Each location calls for a different style and treatment.

Successful settings

Sculpture can give pleasure not only in itself but also in its setting. This Italian figure of fibreglass impregnated with lead, right, would look good in either a modern or a traditional garden. Here it sits on nicely detailed, brick paving, backed by an architectural plant grouping.

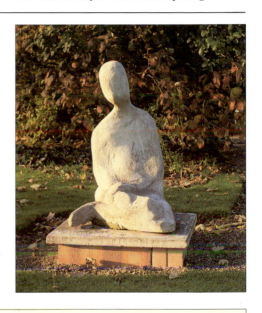

SITING SCULPTURE

Sculpture located centrally in a garden commands attention. Placed to one side, it becomes part of the incidental interest of the garden. If it is sited

as part of a group, the garden space will seem to flow around it. Wrongly sited sculpture can easily upset the balance of a garden design.

Sculpture as the focal point
A classical urn and plinth placed centrally and to the rear of an oblong plot dominate the garden and immediately draw the attention.

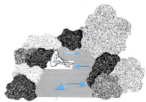

Sculpture to create a balancing feature
A seated figure strengthens one side of the garden, giving it importance equal to the planted masses on the other side.

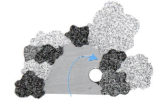

Sculpture to provide strong foreground interest
A sphere strengthens the foreground grouping considerably and encourages a feeling of movement around the group.

Windowboxes

For many urban dwellers, the windowbox is his or her only contribution to the landscape, but a row of houses ablaze with windowbox colour can be a wonderful sight in a town.

The most appropriate windowbox will depend on the type of window and how it opens. You may choose to have your box inside, perhaps herbs on the kitchen sill. Where a window opens outwards, the box needs to be suspended on strong metal brackets far enough below the window so that plant growth doesn't impede the opening. Inward-opening and sash windows make the whole business of a windowbox much simpler. Boxes can be secured with a brace on either side attached to the window surround.

The best boxes are made of timber, but with a lift-out metal lining for easier planting, which insulates the plant roots from what can be lethally intense sunshine. A thin layer of lining plastic is not enough to protect them.

Compost for a windowbox should be rich in organic material or peat to retain moisture, and plants will need regular feeding with a proprietary liquid fertilizer. Frequent watering will leach out minerals fairly quickly. Drainage

Conventional display
An attractive, traditional windowbox planting of evergreens and conifers, together with begonias and trailing lobelias, above.

needs to be good – a 50mm (2 in) lining of broken crock or terracotta pot in the base of the box, with drainage holes through the base. Standing water in an undrained container will cause roots to rot and eventually kill the plant. Place turf or other organic matter over the crock to prevent the compost from percolating into the drainage layer. Consolidate the compost to 50mm (2 in) below the rim of the box to allow for watering.

CONSTRUCTING A WINDOWBOX

Where possible use hardwood, which will last much longer. Alternatively use seasoned timber that has been treated with preservative under pressure and allowed to stand for several weeks. Use zinc-coated screws, counter sunk in the construction. Ensure adequate drainage, fitting plastic inserts through the drainage holes to prevent damp from seeping into the end grain of the timber. Make the structure stoutly – wet earth will exert considerable outward pressure on the box. Line the container with a removable metal tray for easy planting.

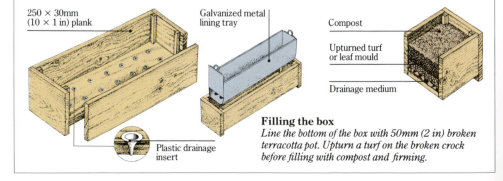

250 × 30mm (10 × 1 in) plank

Galvanized metal lining tray

Plastic drainage insert

Compost

Upturned turf or leaf mould

Drainage medium

Filling the box
Line the bottom of the box with 50mm (2 in) broken terracotta pot. Upturn a turf on the broken crock before filling with compost and firming.

Garden lighting

Outdoor lighting will maximize the pleasure you get from your garden, enabling you to eat, read, or simply potter about outside on warm spring and autumn evenings, and enjoy a night-time view of it all year round.

Outside lighting is essential in places where darkness falls early and the heat of the day makes escaping into the cool evening air a necessity. Even where summer evenings are long and light, subtle artificial lighting will enhance the atmosphere of a meal outside or a party on a terrace and enable you to use your outside space to the full.

Creative and functional lighting
Spots can be used to create a gentle glow in the tracery of a fine specimen tree, to illuminate a group of pots, or to spotlight a piece of statuary, even in winter and under snow. Lighting in a rural garden will offer a hint of the wildness beyond your own cultivated plot.

Other types of lighting are primarily functional – to illuminate the path between garage and front door or a flight of steps, and for security purposes.

Creating the right effect
Each type of lighting needs a different treatment. Functional lighting needs to be direct. Position the light fitting near the area to be lit, but low to avoid creating an eerie effect. Bulkhead fittings let into walls do the trick

perfectly. A simple outdoor table lamp will do for eating or reading. Install waterproofed sockets in different places so that the light can be moved around. For special occasions there is nothing more pleasing than the gentle flicker of candlelight. Various designs of garden candle are available, including candles on sticks, which are simply pushed into the soil.

Fittings and installation
Choose practical fittings in a sympathetic style. Wherever possible, stick to simple, strong, and unobtrusive designs. Use light fittings designed for outside use and make sure they are installed to a professional standard. All light fittings, cables, and power points must be waterproofed and armoured where they might be damaged by garden tools.

Night-time effects
Interior lighting combined with external fittings give this narrow decked area, above, a warm glow. Very atmospheric for evening entertaining.

THE DIFFERENT EFFECTS OF LIGHT

Light can be used to create atmosphere, to produce a theatrical effect, or for practical reasons in the garden, as shown below. Further effects can be created using combinations of the different lighting schemes, with additional lighting thrown from the house, or in the form of small lamps and candles. It is worth experimenting to get a good combination.

Giving a clear view

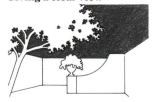

Dramatic light and shadow

Subtle overall illumination

CHAPTER FOUR

PLANTS AND PLANTING

The hard structure of your garden will now be in place, ready to be brought to life by plants. Choose plants in scale to the layout and features of the garden. Use distinctive shape, form, texture, or smell to give year-round strength to your planting. Consider the composition of each grouping of plants, and plant in masses rather than singles.

Groups of plants have particular characters shaped by their native location. The cultivated forms of a native range of plants may form the backbone of your garden selection. In a garden with acid soil, for example, you might plant heaths and heathers. In a hot climate, the herbs and shrubs with resinous stems typical of the Mediterranean regions, could form the basis of the planting. Plants from different natural locations can be mixed, but carefully. A yucca will probably grow quite well next to a fern, but they will not look natural together.

As you formulate your plan in your mind's eye, consider first leaf shape and overall plant shape, characteristics that remain constant throughout the year. Only then decide on flower colour, which often puts in a very brief appearance. Work towards a controlled but ever-changing plant arrangement to make up your garden mass.

Dramatic colour, strong shape
A limited palette of yellows and greens produces an eye-catching combination, strengthened by the striking but relaxed form of Euphorbia characias wulfenii.

Principles of planting

Until a garden is planted it remains incomplete. The plants you choose and how you group them will depend on many factors. Planting can be used to fulfill a specific purpose: to screen an unsightly view or fill a damp and shady corner, to provide food or shade, or to produce wonderful scents. More often, however, plants will be used to make up the green bulky infill of the framework, extending the design concept while giving pleasure with seasonal changes of colour and texture in foliage, stems, fruits, and flowers.

Although the garden is a contrived place and does not pretend to duplicate natural vegetation (as does the ecologist's wild garden, for example), it often contains features that imitate Nature.

Different areas, whether a pine woodland or heather moor, often get their feel from one or two dominant species, with only the occasional intrusion of others. Similarly, simple and discreet planting schemes in the garden make it a relaxing place, where things look and feel right. You don't need to fill every corner with a

DRIFT AND FLOW EFFECT

Drift and flow describes the evolution of a bed over a season and from one season to another. Shrubby material makes up the skeleton

framework, gradually assuming its planned role in the overall grouping. Perennials and annuals are less predictable components.

First year, right
The scheme starts out looking sparse. Perennials and annuals (among them Alchemilla, Stachys, Ajuga) *flow around the evergreen bones (a yew, a cotoneaster, and a shrub rose).*

The newly planted bed

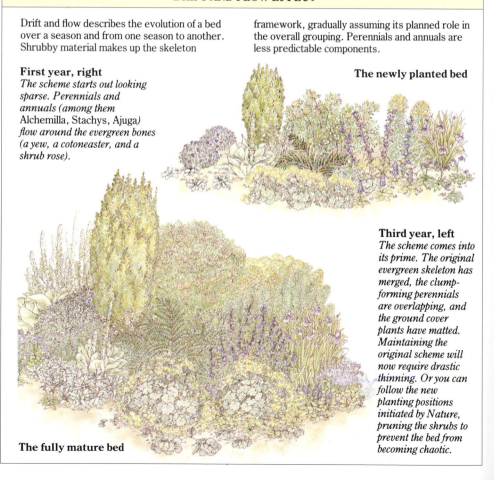

The fully mature bed

Third year, left
The scheme comes into its prime. The original evergreen skeleton has merged, the clump-forming perennials are overlapping, and the ground cover plants have matted. Maintaining the original scheme will now require drastic thinning. Or you can follow the new planting positions initiated by Nature, pruning the shrubs to prevent the bed from becoming chaotic.

PLANT CLASSIFICATION

Scientific Latin names are used to identify plants because common names can vary widely from region to region and country to country. They seem daunting at first, but the more you learn and read about plants, and particularly the more you grow them yourself, the more familiar and less mystifying they become.

The first word in a plant classification is the genus name, for example *Acer, Berberis*, or *Cotoneaster*. There are, however, approximately seventy types of cotoneaster, of which half are generally available. Some are barely 25mm (1 in) high, while others become trees. The second Latin name identifies the species of a genus, for example, *Cotoneaster horizontalis*. This name often describes the character of the plant. You will often see "sp." after the genus name, as in *Cotoneaster* sp. This is the accepted abbreviation of *Cotoneaster* species and refers either to all species of the genus *Cotoneaster* or to one of the species of the genus *Cotoneaster* without specifying which. If there is more than one natural variety of the same species, there will be a third Latin name to identify each, as in *Cotoneaster bullatus macrophyllus*.

If a variety has been produced by human intervention it is known as a cultivated variety or cultivar. Cultivar is usually abbreviated to "cv". In this case the third name will be in a modern language, and may be something like 'Crimson Rose'. Sometimes two genera or two species are crossed or hybridized. A hybrid is usually denoted by an x for "cross" before the species name, as in *Cotoneaster* x *watereri* 'John Waterer'.

different species of plant. The horticulturalist will have different interests, but even here, certain parts of the garden can be set aside for growing show specimens and for nursery beds, while other areas maintain the gentle spontaneity of natural plant grouping.

For people who have neither time nor inclination to garden intensively, the obvious answer is to settle for relaxed planting that allows Nature to influence the result, perhaps leaving wild plants alongside their hybridized relatives, and complementing the scheme with gravel surfacing or a combination of cut lawn and rough grass.

Rural harmony
The foreground planting in this damp spot, below, is domestic, but it reflects its location. Over the mown path, wild planting folds naturally into the background of trees, with incidental sculptural elements on the left, such as the fern.

Form, colour, and texture

Once you have decided on the scale of the plants you need to achieve the overall shape of your planting, next consider other plant characteristics. For example, whether a plant is deciduous, evergreen, or semi-evergreen.

Consider the form of each plant, particularly in relation to the grouping as a whole. Some plants are dense and compact, others are leggy and need staking. They may be low-growing and form clumps or be broad and bushy. Look at how the leaves orientate themselves – whether they weep, like grasses or bamboo, creating a fountain effect, or grow outwards, holding their shape, like hosta leaves.

Think about flower colour and flowering period in relation to that of other plants in the grouping. Leaf colour may change through the seasons, beginning the year as pale green or gold and becoming green in the summer, or starting green and later taking on glowing autumn colours. Stem colour can be very attractive in winter when, for example, thickets of pollarded *Cornus* and *Salix* sp. may range in colour from chrome yellow, through orange and red to dull burgundy. After the colour of flowers, consider fruit and berry colour for autumn and early winter interest.

Think also about texture, both of leaf and stem. The different textural qualities of leaves are the result of adapting to their original habitats. Many of the hairy, grey leaves, which are invaluable for mixed borders, are from the southern hemisphere and have strong visual and tactile qualities. One of the most appealing is the silky grey leaf of *Convolvulus cneorum*. Smooth and glossy textured leaves, like those of the holly (*Ilex* sp.), contrast with the crisp leaves of Mediterranean culinary herbs.

Planting for form
The dominating feature in this bed, below, is form. The leaves of Hosta glauca *and* Crocosmia sp. *are enclosed by tall* Lysimachia thyrsiflora.

Designing the planting

It is one thing to compose a small plant grouping on site, but it is quite another to visualize a whole border and take into account the various characteristics of all the plants you want to include. It is far better to get an outline down on paper first.

Using your final garden layout (see pp.78–9) as an underlay, trace off the areas to be planted and work on the plan to scale. First decide what your key plants are going to be – your special feature trees or shrubs. These can provide a visual link between planting and the surrounding architecture, for example a weeping cherry curving over a pool wall. On a smaller scale, the "special" might be a yucca acting as an evergreen pivot in a group of perennials. You might have a major and a minor "special", counterbalancing one another within the overall design. Next choose skeleton planting – the evergreen backdrop to the rest

of the planting, providing screening and shelter wherever necessary. Plant in groups or masses, rather than just one of each type of plant. Note how many of each you are planting. Perhaps three of some plants and five of others. You can plant through these with a couple of standard trees for height and density, bearing in mind that they will put the plants beneath them into shade. Use plenty of evergreen so that the plan will continue to work throughout the year.

Your plant catalogue will provide you with ultimate heights and spreads (also see *Plant selection guide*, pp. 194–216), which in turn will indicate planting distances (see p. 176).

Once you have decided on screening shrubs, start composing groups of decorative species in front of them. Think first about strong architectural forms (*Phormium* and *Yucca* sp., for example) for sunny areas and bold-leaved

A PLANTING PLAN FOR THE WHOLE GARDEN

Your planting scheme should be conceived in relation to your overall design and used to soften and overlay its hard structures. Before producing plans for individual beds, make a plan for the whole garden, taking into account the seasonal

ebb and flow of colour and life from one area to another. One way of planning your planting is by indicating the position and spread of plants in maturity on a scaled plan, using the system of symbols shown below left.

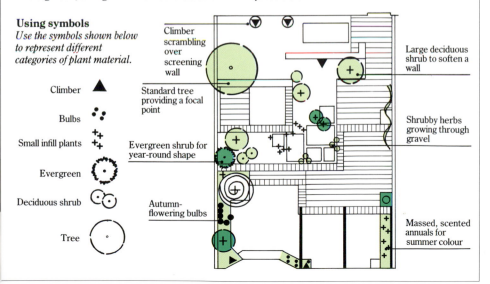

Using symbols
Use the symbols shown below to represent different categories of plant material.

Climber

Bulbs

Small infill plants

Evergreen

Deciduous shrub

Tree

Climber scrambling over screening wall

Standard tree providing a focal point

Evergreen shrub for year-round shape

Autumn-flowering bulbs

Large deciduous shrub to soften a wall

Shrubby herbs growing through gravel

Massed, scented annuals for summer colour

hostas and bergenias for the shadier parts. Contrast these strong shapes with softer, fluffier plants flowing around them. At this stage consider colour as well as form. Compose in ranges of colour. Plant and flower colours help to set the mood of the garden, which in turn will be suggested by the house and its location. Consider herbaceous planting, not necessarily restricting herbaceous plants to one border. Decide on bulbs. Spring bulbs, summer lilies, autumn crocus. Site a rose or two against an old tree or a Virginia creeper against a blank or ugly garage wall.

Put all this down on paper, making sure you include all your favourite species. At this point be ruthless and eliminate about half the number you have selected. A common mistake among inexperienced gardeners is to plant too much.

WORKING TO A COLOUR SCHEME

Limited-palette colour schemes provide a good framework for planning a bed. Schemes might be based on purple foliage, gold and yellow foliage and flowers, white flowers, or silver and grey foliage as here, right and below.

There are many plants with grey and silver foliage, and planted together they create a light and airy atmosphere. Flower colour provides transitory interest and contrast, with the yellow daisy-like flowers of *Senecio laxifolius* and the gentle pink blooms of *Ozothamnus* sp.

This bed was planted according to the plan shown below right, with plenty of space left between plants for them to spread, right. The mature bed, two years later, is shown below.

Planting a small bed
The feature shrub in this scheme is the yucca. Its sharp, sculptural shape is balanced in the opposite corner by the rounded form of a grey Ozothamnus sp. *Foliage in the planting ranges from light silver to grey-green, and gives the bed its year-round impact. Flower colour ranges through yellow, white, purple, and pink, and is always subtle.*

Planting plan

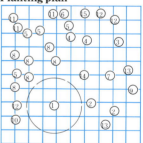

Key to planting plan:
1 Yucca *sp.* 2 Senecio laxifolius. 3 Ozothamnus *sp.* 4 Artemisia '*Powis Castle*'. 5 Ruta graveolens '*Jackman's Blue*'. 6 Achillea filipendulina '*Gold Plate*'. 7 Verbascum bombyciferum. 8 Erysimum variegatum. 9 Hosta tokudama. 10 Hedera helix. 11 Lamium maculatum. 12 Anthemis cupaniana. 13 Digitalis grandiflora. 14 Senecio *sp.* 15 Artemisia *sp.*

Planting a border

STAGE 1 – Feature trees and shrubs, below

Select a feature tree that will either become the focal point of the planting area, or at least counteract another strong feature, such as the house itself or a view. In this example, two *Phormium tenax* counter-balance the feature tree, *Acer negundo variegatum*.

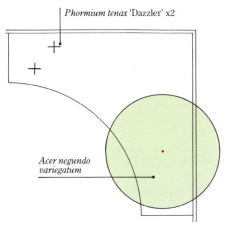

Phormium tenax 'Dazzler' x2

Acer negundo
variegatum

STAGE 2 – Skeleton planting, below

Add evergreen peripheral planting of shrubs and climbers that will contain the site, giving privacy and shelter and making the green walls against which decorative planting is seen. This skeleton principle should also apply to smaller plants, including ground cover material. Here, hellebores, bergenias, and an iris have been included as a framework.

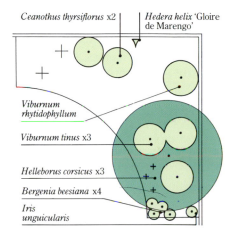

Ceanothus thyrsiflorus x2

Hedera helix 'Gloire de Marengo'

Viburnum
rhytidophyllum

Viburnum tinus x3

Helleborus corsicus x3

Bergenia beesiana x4

Iris
unguicularis

STAGE 3 – Decorative shrubs, below

Fill in with decorative shrubs of a smaller scale, considering colour harmony and contrast, height, shape contrasts (winter and summer), leaf shapes, textures, and stem qualities. Work down in scale, adding decorative herbaceous material in amongst the shrubs (not included here) and finally ground cover for edging and filling gaps.

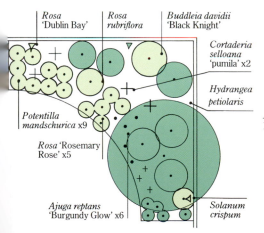

Rosa
'Dublin Bay'

Rosa
rubriflora

Buddleia davidii
'Black Knight'

Cortaderia
selloana
'pumila' x2

Hydrangea
petiolaris

Potentilla
mandschurica x9

Rosa 'Rosemary
Rose' x5

Ajuga reptans
'Burgundy Glow' x6

Solanum
crispum

STAGE 4 – Splashes of colour, below

Include annuals, biennials, and bulbs for bright splashes of colour if necessary. Here bulbs have been used exclusively. Use this additional colour with discretion, especially if your composition already includes species chosen for colour. You can always add more colour the following summer if you are not happy with the first year's showing.

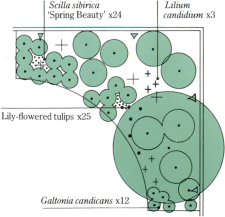

Scilla sibirica
'Spring Beauty' x24

Lilium
candidum x3

Lily-flowered tulips x25

Galtonia candicans x12

Plants for colour

Colour rejuvenates and revives the spirits. For those of us in northern climes, spring colour brings light at the end of the long winter months. We pore over plant catalogues in anticipation, all too often selecting a host of ill-assorted shrubs, perennials, and annuals to brighten a far-off summer scene. The location of your garden will influence your choice of plant colour. Many urban dwellers quite rightly use bright flowers to relieve the monotonous greys and browns that surround them. In a country garden, however, the fairground palette is less appropriate and it makes more sense to use colours that harmonize rather than compete with Nature's own.

When you are planning colour, consider not only the temporary flamboyance of annual flower colour, but the more permanent displays of foliage, stem, branch, and bark. Foliage colours range from all the many shades of green, through to gold, bronze, purple, and silver, while stem and branch colours include yellows, greens, browns, and reds. These should be combined to create year-round displays that will provide a foil to seasonal flower colour (see also *Using colour*, pp. 72-3).

The small urban garden

Whether your garden is limited to a few pots on a balcony or a few planters in a basement entrance, choose plant colour to blend well with the surroundings. Every element in a small garden, from walls and paving to chair-cover fabric, will contribute to the whole. Peppering a small space with many contrasting colours with nothing to link them to each other or to their surroundings, will create a random, disparate appearance. A harmonious composition, on the other hand, where colours have been carefully blended, will unify the garden and make it appear larger.

Colour and natural gardening

While your eye might forgive one or two exotic plant species in a natural garden, especially if they are harmonious in colour as well as form and texture, it will be offended by the violent oranges and purples of many species. Allow the colour of the plants within the garden to harmonize with the colours beyond it. In many country locations, everything is seen against the many shades of green, and virulent flower colour will tend to create discord.

Gold and yellow scheme, left
Two variegated flag irises (Iris pseudoacorus) *are the dramatic focal point of this scheme. Their strong vertical form contrasts with the small-leaved shrubs* Lonicera nitida *'Baggesen's Gold' and* Symphoricarpos orbiculatus *'Foliis Variegatis', which form a gentle golden backdrop and bulk out the composition. Golden elder* (Sambucus nigra *'Aurea') and gold* Physocarpus *sp. give height, and their well-defined leaf shapes provide a backdrop to the soft mass of golden sage* (Salvia officinalis *'Icterina'). Summer colour includes foxgloves* (Digitalis grandiflora) *and feverfew* (Chrysanthemum parthenium).

NATURAL COLOUR SCHEME

The strong purples and mauve-pinks of heather deserve space. This simple scheme brings the colours of the distant moor right into the garden. The shapes of the planting areas within the garden complement Nature's "moorland marquetry", formed by the combinations of patches of heather contrasted with patches of grassland and woodland.

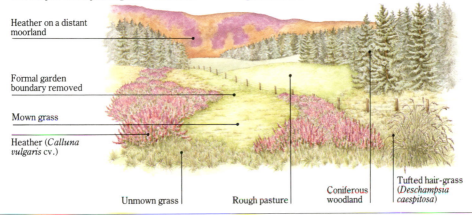

Heather on a distant moorland

Formal garden boundary removed

Mown grass

Heather (*Calluna vulgaris* cv.)

Unmown grass

Rough pasture

Coniferous woodland

Tufted hair-grass (*Deschampsia caespitosa*)

Colour can be used to unify a plant grouping very successfully, particularly when foliage provides the key colours of the scheme. Different colours create different moods. Golds and greens will brighten and warm any corner. Purple creates the quite opposite effect of moodiness.

Purple scheme, below
Purple is a demanding colour, difficult to incorporate in a mixed group. Here Berberis gagnepainii *'Wallichiana Purpurea' and purple elder (*Sambucus nigra *'Purpurea') provide backing to the huge leaves of* Ligularia dentata *'Desdemona'.* Foeniculum vulgare *makes a soft, feathery contrast with* Ajuga reptans *'Atropurpurea' and* Sedum maximum *'Atropurpureum'.*

CHOOSING PLANTS FOR COLOUR

For a more comprehensive selection, see p. 198.

Brassica oleracea
DECORATIVE CABBAGE
For a dramatic display grow the purple-bronze *Coleus blumei* 'Autumn Splendour' around an exuberantly patterned cream and green decorative cabbage. *B. oleracea* is a biennial grown as an annual. Grow in a fertile, well-drained soil, lime-rich if possible, and full sun. Height and spread to 45cm (18 in).

Paeonia officinalis 'Rubra Plena'
PEONY
Peony blooms have long been valued for their striking colour, bringing subtle shades of pinks and reds to the border. 'Rubra

Plena' is a long-lived perennial, with double, vivid pinkish-crimson flowers. Prefers sun and rich, well-drained soil. Height and spread to 75cm (30 in).

Cornus alba 'Sibirica'
RED-BARKED DOGWOOD
The coral-red stems of this deciduous shrub are dramatic in bright winter light. The most intensive colour is in the young wood, so cut back the stems in spring before the leaves appear. White flowers follow in early summer. Fertile, well-drained soil. Full sun or semi-shade. Height and spread 3m (10 ft).

Euonymus alatus
WINGED SPINDLE TREE
The dark green leaves of this deciduous shrub turn to a brilliant red in the autumn, when they are accompanied by small purple and red fruits. It grows to a maximum height of 2.5m (8 ft) with a spread of 3m (10 ft), so is a perfect small garden species. Well-drained soil. Full sun or semi-shade.

Petunia, Recoverer series
PETUNIA
White petunias have a striking purity about them and make some of the finest annual bedding material. They need plenty of sun to do well, however. Height and spread to 30cm (1 ft). Grow in fertile, well-drained soil, in a sunny position, sheltered from wind. Dead-head regularly.

Vertical planting

Plants climb in one of three ways. Some have aerial roots that cling to a structure, like rampant ivies (*Hedera* sp.) or the climbing hydrangea (*Hydrangea petiolaris*). Some are twiners, like clematis, and twist their leaf stems around a support to hold themselves up. The third category, which includes all the honeysuckles (*Lonicera* sp.) and rambler roses, are scramblers. They have no means of supporting themselves except by pushing their long branches in amongst a host plant.

The range of plants that like the protection and shelter of a wall and can be trained to grow against it, such as *Pyracantha* sp., *Ceanothus* sp., and forms of trained fruit tree, also come into the category of vertical plants.

A few climbers are evergreen and are ideal for screening. Large or small-leaved ivies, green, silver, or gold variegated, are all easy to establish and will grow facing any direction. There is an evergreen clematis (*Clematis armandii*) that flowers early in the year in a sheltered corner, and some evergreen honeysuckles, such as *Lonicera japonica* 'Aureoreticulata', with conspicuously veined leaves, and *Lonicera japonica* 'Halliana', both with fragrant yellow-white flowers. Other evergreens in this category are mostly wall shrubs, which can be trained to a considerable height. Suitable plants include *Coronilla*, some *Cotoneaster*, *Escallonia*, *Euonymus*, *Garrya*, and some *Viburnum* sp.

Fast growers tend to be deciduous. Remember that they will not stop growing when they have covered your fence. The most invasive is Russian vine (*Polygonum baldschuanicum*), which grows as much as 6m (20 ft) every season, quickly smothering an outhouse or clothing a tree with a froth of creamy flowers. Another vigorous twining climber is *Aristolochia macrophylla*. Then there is the ornamental grape vine, *Vitis coignetiae*, which has huge leaves that change colour in autumn to brilliant orange and crimson shades.

SUPPORTING CLIMBERS

Different types of climber need different degrees of support. Clingers adhere to vertical structures with aerial roots and need no extra support system. Twiners have tendrils that need a support system of wires or trellis to entwine.

Some climbers, like climbing roses and shrubs that grow vertically against a wall, not only need a support system, but also need tying in to support their bushy form of growth. Make sure any support system is sturdy enough for its plant.

Self-supporting clinger
The aerial roots of a climbing hydrangea cling to the wall without any artificial support.

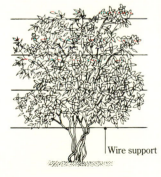

Wire support

Supporting a twining climber
Clematis tendrils twine around wires to hold the plant up.

Trellis

Supporting a scrambler
A honeysuckle cannot support itself and needs a trellis to scramble through.

CLIMBERS ON HOUSE FRONTAGES

Buildings of any period can often be considerably enhanced by climbing plants scrambling up the walls and around windows and door frames. *Wisteria* sp., Virginia creeper (*Parthenocissus quinquefolia*), clematis, and ivy (*Hedera* sp.) are all good choices. The supports that you choose for a house front should not dominate or be at odds with the symmetry of the house frontage.

Match the scale of the support to the scale of the climber – a bold support needs bold foliage, while a fine tracery of leaves needs a fine support. Against masonry walls, consider running wires, supported on "vine eyes", parallel with the mortar courses. Choose timber latticing to coincide with the proportions of windows and door frames, and of the frontage as a whole.

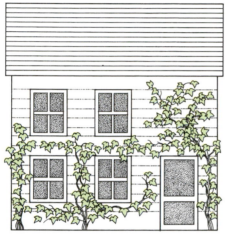

Wire support, above
Here horizontal wires, supported on "vine eyes", run parallel with the mortar courses.

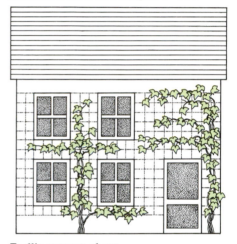

Trellis support, above
Squared trellis is spaced to match windows and door. It could be limited to half the frontage.

Climbing rose, above
Much of the charm of this old brick wall is created by the climbing rose, which is attached to imperceptible wires that run parallel with the courses of the wall.

Climbing roses need a certain amount of maintenance. Pruning involves detaching the rose from its support, taking out dead wood and shortening new growth to leave a clear framework, and then re-attaching the plant.

Scrambling honeysuckle, above
*A honeysuckle (*Lonicera sp.*) clothes a high wall that would otherwise be a very dominating feature. Like the rose, the honeysuckle runs along invisible wires. As it grows, its new shoots need tucking under the wires. Pruning is only needed to remove dead shoots and restrain growth.*

An evergreen honeysuckle is an excellent choice here, providing year-round cover. Other evergreen climbers include ivy and Passiflora caerulea.

CHOOSING CLIMBING PLANTS

For a more comprehensive selection, see p. 199.

Actinidia kolomikta
KOLOMIKTA VINE
The tips of *A. kolomikta*'s green leaves look as if they have been dipped in pink and white paint. Trained on wires, it will cover walls with an elegant mass of foliage until autumn. The leaves are most colourful when the plant is grown in calcareous soil. Full sun or partial shade. Height to 4 m (12ft).

Hedera helix 'Goldheart'
ENGLISH IVY
English ivy is one of the most useful evergreens for covering vertical surfaces. The growth of the large-leaved Persian ivy becomes too rampant. 'Goldheart' grows well in shade and will brighten up walls in dingy corners. Prefers well-drained, alkaline soil. Height to 6m (20 ft).

Humulus lupulus 'Aureus'
COMMON HOP
This golden-yellow hop has a phenomenal annual growth of up to 10m (33 ft), and will give a lush green appearance to an area in a short time, while taking up very little ground space. Useful for covering unsightly sheds or tree-stumps. Grows happily on walls of all aspects in well-drained soil.

Lonicera brownii
SCARLET TRUMPET HONEYSUCKLE
With support, most varieties of honeysuckle will grow up structures. *L.b.* 'Dropmore Scarlet' bears a profusion of brilliantly coloured flowers between spring and late summer. It grows best in light shade, in fertile, well-drained soil. Height to 4m (12 ft).

Parthenocissus tricuspidata
BOSTON IVY
The brilliant foliage of Boston ivy provides excellent autumn colour. It will grow vigorously up walls of any aspect, to a height of up to 15m (50 ft), and is tolerant of atmospheric pollution and suitable for urban gardens. *P. quinquefolia* cultivars also have bright foliage. Well-drained soil.

Rosa 'Mme. Alfred Carrière'
CLIMBING ROSE
The fragrant blooms of climbing roses will give just as much pleasure as those of shrub roses, without using up as much ground space. *R.* 'Mme. Alfred Carrière' is resistant to atmospheric pollution. Prefers an open, sunny site and moist, well-drained soil. Height to 5.5m (18 ft), spread 3m (10 ft).

Ground cover and grass

Ground covering plants are both a practical alternative to grass in a small area, particularly leftover or awkward shapes, and excellent for suppressing weeds. They can be used to link taller growing plants within a small, mixed planting scheme, or on their own to contrast with hard surfaces or areas of gravel. Avoid plants described as rampant or invasive, such as *Vinca major* and *minor*, for confined areas – you will have difficulty keeping them under control. Low-growing ground cover plants include species of *Ajuga*, which form a

MAINTAINING A LAWNED GARDEN

Proper maintenance of the lawn will keep the garden looking trim and attractive as well as increasing the health and vigour of the grass itself. Weekly mowing throughout the growing season is essential. The mower blades must be sharp, properly set, and at the correct height. Watering is necessary every seven days during drought and every ten days in spring. Always give the lawn a good soaking. Feed with a nitrogen-rich feed in spring to replace soil nutrients drained by constant cropping. Rake with a spring-tined rake to remove surplus and

dead surface foliage and to open up the thatch of matted stems, which otherwise encourage moss and weed invasion. Brushing with a stiff broom also helps. Scatter worm casts with a besom-type brush before mowing.

Aerate the lawn with a fork at least once a year to break up the surface layer and improve drainage. Top-dress the lawn in autumn with a mixture of peat, loam, and sand to improve the ground on which it feeds, particularly if the topsoil is poor, and use a balanced feed to build up roots and increase resistance to disease.

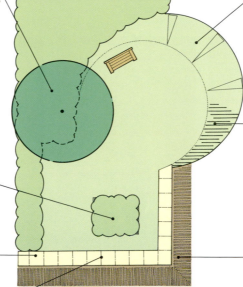

Areas beneath trees
Deprived of food, water, and light, these areas will suffer. Removing lower branches of the tree may help. Yearly reseeding of grass may also be necessary. Alternatively turn into a bed and plant with shade-loving shrubs, or pave under the tree with decorative brickwork.

Isolated beds
These must be in proportion to the lawn, and their shape related to the overall pattern.

Access areas
Ensure that the hard-surfaced entry to the lawn is of generous proportions, otherwise the grass around it will quickly become worn and unsightly.

Paths
Paths should run around a lawn rather than into it, or the junction of path and
grass will rapidly become worn. Paths should be slightly below the lawn level for ease of mowing.

Banks
Modern machines make banked lawns easy to mow, provided the slope is not more than about 30°. Sharper gradients should be dug and planted with ground cover for easy care.

Bulbs
Daffodils always look good in a lawn, but the leaves must be allowed to die down for vigorous growth the next year. In a smaller garden, site them within an overall pattern of rough grass.

Edging
Paving between the edge of the grass area and surrounding walls or flower beds creates a mowing edge, making the task much easier.

dense mat of small leaves, *Bergenia*, which have large, eye-catching foliage, and the furry-leaved *Stachys lanata*. For year-round cover choose an evergreen shrub such as the low-growing *Cotoneaster dammeri* or even a tall-growing evergreen with dense ground-level growth, such as Mexican orange blossom (*Choisya ternata*).

Lawns can be closely mown and time consuming or rough cut and easy to maintain. By allowing the grass to grow longer and mowing only paths through it, you will encourage flowers to grow within the rough area. Grass left uncut can successfully hide the raggy look of bulbs as their leaves are dying down after spring flowering.

Wild flowers in grass
Establishing wild flowers in a lawn is not simply a matter of scattering seeds. The grass will swamp the tiny seedlings. Plant young plants by hand through the grass in drifts to establish a good coverage of wild flowers. To create a real flowery or alpine meadow, first cultivate the ground and then sow a flower seed/grass mix suitable for the soil type. The grass needs to be slow growing so that the flower seedlings can compete. Coarse grasses will quickly swamp flowering plants and ruin the effect (see also *Wild flowers*, p.171).

Aromatic ground cover
Between informal ground cover planting and lawns are intermediate types of ground cover that can be walked on. These include aromatic herbs that will release perfumes. Chamomile has been used as ground cover since the Middle Ages. Choose a non-flowering variety , such as *Chamaemelum nobile* 'Treneague'. It tends to look bedraggled in winter, however, and doesn't like snow. Mixed low-growing thymes are hardier and can create a furry-textured, grey ground cover, streaked with waves of flower colour. *Thymus serpyllum coccineus*, for example, has tiny crimson flowers that bloom in mid-summer.

GROUND COVER PLANTING DESIGN

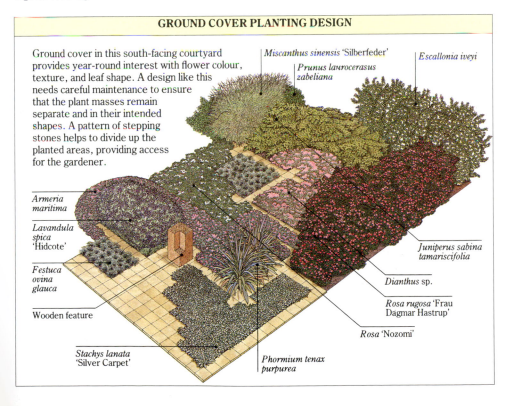

Ground cover in this south-facing courtyard provides year-round interest with flower colour, texture, and leaf shape. A design like this needs careful maintenance to ensure that the plant masses remain separate and in their intended shapes. A pattern of stepping stones helps to divide up the planted areas, providing access for the gardener.

Miscanthus sinensis 'Silberfeder'

Prunus laurocerasus zabeliana

Escallonia iveyi

Armeria maritima

Lavandula spica 'Hidcote'

Festuca ovina glauca

Wooden feature

Juniperus sabina tamariscifolia

Dianthus sp.

Rosa rugosa 'Frau Dagmar Hastrup'

Rosa 'Nozomi'

Stachys lanata 'Silver Carpet'

Phormium tenax purpurea

CHOOSING GROUND COVER PLANTS

For a more comprehensive selection, see p. 200.

Euonymus fortunei
EUONYMUS
The bright evergreen foliage of the shrub *E. f.* 'Emerald 'n' Gold' gives a cheerful appearance all year round. Like the cultivar 'Silver Queen', it has a low, hummocky form of growth and makes good ground cover. Well-drained soil, sun or semi-shade, height 5m (15 ft), spread indefinite.

Chamaemelum nobile
CHAMOMILE
Chamomile is an aromatic herb and useful as a grass substitute for lawns. Plant individual plants 10–15cm (4–6 in) apart. A non-flowering form, *Chamaemelum nobile* 'Treneague', is best for lawns, as the species chamomile needs to be de-flowered. It prefers full sun, and light, well-drained soil.

Ajuga reptans 'Atropurpurea'
BUGLE
The growth of this low-growing, shade-loving perennial can easily be kept under control. In spring it is studded with blue flowers against lustrous, purple-bronze leaves. It combines effectively with shade-loving primulas. Tolerates any soil. Height 38cm (15 in), spread 60cm (2 ft).

Lamium maculatum
SPOTTED DEAD NETTLE
L.m. 'Beacon Silver' is a perennial with heart-shaped, silvery leaves that brighten shady corners and will grow in sun too. Bright pink flowers appear in late spring. It grows fast, but is not as invasive as *L. galeobdolon*. Moist, well-drained soil, height 20cm (8 in), spread 1m (3 ft).

Stachys lanata
LAMB'S EARS
The charming, woolly grey foliage of the mat-forming perennial, *Stachys lanata*, provides excellent ground cover or border edging. Mauve-pink flowers are borne in summer. It prefers an open, sunny site and tolerates poor soil. Height 15cm (6 in), spread 60 cm (2 ft).

Plants for shade

Both urban and rural gardeners have shady corners to deal with. The shade may be cast by the solid structures of walls and buildings or it may be dappled light piercing through a tree canopy. Many of the plants that enjoy shade have gradually adapted themselves to life in reduced light by developing large leaves, often at the expense of brilliant flower colour. This characteristic makes them very attractive material to plant, the many forms of hosta being a fine example.

There are two types of shady garden area – damp and dry. A damp area might get no sun at all and be subject to drip from overhead trees. A dry area is sheltered from rain by dense overhanging plants that allow no drips through.

Plants for damp shade
Most of the maples (*Acer* sp.) do well in moist, shady conditions. As well as the more common Japanese type, the snake bark forms provide good winter interest. Other successful plants are alder (*Alnus* sp.), thorns (*Crataegus* sp.), poplars (*Populus* sp.), willows (*Salix* sp.), and the bird cherry (*Prunus padus*).

On a smaller scale, Goat's beard (*Aruncus sylvester*) will put on a huge show of creamy yellow flowers each summer. In a sheltered location and in neutral to acid soil, camellias do well in moist shade.

The whole range of *Cornus* sp. are good in leaf and retain attractive coloured stems throughout winter, providing a hardy stand-by for damp shade. The large-leaved *Fatsia japonica* thrives here too, putting on a mass of green flowers in late summer. For late winter flowers that stud their bare stems, consider witch hazel (*Hamamelis* sp.), whose scented, twisted flower heads are long-lasting and immune to frost.

Among the perennials there are *Helleborus* sp. for early spring flowering, *Hosta* sp., and the dramatic leaves of *Rheum palmatum* 'Rubrum', a decorative rhubarb. The hardy ferns are easy to grow, not fussy about soil, and prefer the cool, light-shaded, moist conditions on the north side of many gardens. And there are bamboos and ivies.

Plants for dry shade
The range of plants suitable for dry shade is smaller, but interesting. Trees include the genera *Caragana*, *Gleditsia*, and *Robinia*, apart from the golden forms. Among shrubs are *Amelanchier lamarckii* for spring and summer interest and many forms of *Berberis*.

Ground cover plants for dry shade include many of the large-leaved *Bergenia* sp. and perennial blue *Brunnera macrophylla* that flower at about the same time.

Many grasses grow well in dry shade. Most are easy to cultivate and many are evergreen. Pampas grass (*Cortaderia selloana*) is a standard favourite and thrives in dry shade, as do forms of *Festuca* and *Luzula* sp.

Semi-shaded glory
Alchemilla mollis, Polygonum, *and* Angelica *sp. make up the perennial ground cover of this richly coloured and inviting semi-shaded corner, below.*

CHOOSING PLANTS FOR SHADE

For a more comprehensive selection, see p. 201.

Anemone x *hybrida*
WINDFLOWER
A. x *hybrida* 'Honorine Jobert'
has a simple flower shape, tall,
elegant stems, handsome
foliage, and will grow in light
shade. It is a long-lived
perennial, but resents
disturbance once established.
Thrives in well-drained, humus-
rich soil. Height 1.5m (5 ft),
spread 60cm (2 ft).

Aucuba japonica
JAPANESE LAUREL
The gleaming green leaves and
bright red berries of this
evergreen shrub, *A.j.*
'Salicifolia', will bring a breath of
life to the driest and shadiest of
corners (variegated forms such
as *A.j.* 'Variegata' thrive better
in light shade). Tolerant of
pollution, grows in any soil,
height and spread 2.5m (8 ft).

Helleborus lividus corsicus
CORSICAN HELLEBORE
The grey-green foliage and pale
green flowers of this evergreen
perennial bring immense cheer
to shady corners during the dull
days of late winter and early
spring. It looks effective against
a dark-leaved evergreen such
as *Aucuba japonica*. Prefers
moist, well-drained soil, height
and spread 45cm (18 in).

Hydrangea macrophylla serrata
LACECAP HYDRANGEA
Hydrangeas are excellent urban
shrubs. They can be grown in
containers, they are unaffected
by atmospheric pollution, and
thrive in sheltered, lightly
shaded sites. However, they do
need moisture. The blooms
grow blue in acid soil and pink in
alkaline soil. Height 1m (3 ft),
spread 1.2m (4 ft).

Liriope muscari
LILY TURF
This evergreen perennial can
be grown in containers and
enjoyed in the smallest of shady
sites. It also makes excellent
ground cover. By early autumn
the tall stems that rise from the
elegant leaves are covered with
tiny droplet-shaped flowers.
Prefers well-drained soil, height
30cm (1 ft), spread 45cm (18 in).

Polystichum setiferum
SOFT SHIELD FERN
Ferns are indispensable shade
lovers – their fronded foliage
and arching form bring
atmospheric interest to all
manner of awkwardly shaped
nooks and corners. Most useful
are those that are evergreen,
like *P. setiferum*. Does best in
moist, well-drained soil, height
60cm (2 ft), spread 45cm (18 in).

Plants for exposed sites

Plants on roofs, balconies, and high windowsills are exposed to far greater extremes of heat, cold, and wind than those at ground level. The wind buffets plants and, together with the sun, dehydrates their soil. A considerable range of plants is able to withstand such inhospitable conditions, and there are many others that can survive a season or longer if shelter is provided by a fence, canvas windbreak, or tough shrub.

Tough permanent planting

Shrubby material can be used for background year-round interest and to shelter you and your less hardy plants from the wind. Viburnums are tough shrubs, and in particular *V. betulifolium*, with its white flowers in early summer. Look at what has adapted to survive conditions on exposed coastal, heath, or mountain sites. The broom family are tough (*Cytisus* sp., *Genista* sp., and *Spartium* sp.), as are the gorse family (*Ulex* sp.), various heaths and heathers, evergreen and evergrey herbs, most conifers, and many grasses.

Climbers in exposed locations are likely to take a considerable buffeting. Choose deciduous climbers that are naturally tougher than evergreen ones, such as Virginia creeper (*Parthenocissus* sp.), and honeysuckle (*Lonicera* sp.). Alternatively use resilient evergreen climbers like ivy (*Hedera* sp.).

Plants for seasonal interest

Many plants will survive a season on a balcony, windowsill, or roof. Mass spring and summer bulbs and annuals in containers to add a flamboyant dash of seasonal colour. Plants with a daisy flower are usually tough.

CHOOSING PLANTS FOR EXPOSED SITES

For a more comprehensive selection, see p. 204.

Cytisus nigricans
BROOM
A species of *Cytisus*, with its long, spiky, yellow flowers appearing unusually throughout late summer. Other genus members flower in late spring. All brooms are hardy shrubs, able to thrive in poor soil, and to survive strong winds. Prefers full sun, height 1.5m (5 ft), spread 75cm (2½ ft).

Santolina pinnata
COTTON LAVENDER
A hardy evergreen shrub that thrives in full sun, dry soil, and withstands strong winds – the perfect roof and balcony plant. It has fully divided green leaves and tiny cream flowers. It can be grown in troughs as a low hedge. Cut back hard in spring. Height 75cm (2½ ft), spread 1m (3 ft).

Sempervivum hirtum
HOUSELEEK
This rock plant grows best in poor, fast-draining soil, so add grit to the compost mix. It looks effective grown *en masse* in a shallow container. There are many species of *Sempervivum*, varying in size from the tiniest rosette to the size of a saucer. Does best in full sun, height to 15cm (6 in), spread 10cm (4 in).

Architectural plants

Architectural plants have a strong overall form created by dramatic leaf, stem, or branch shape and can be used in isolation to make a single bold statement or to give structural backbone to a mixed scheme of loosely formed planting.

The Italian cypress (*Cupressus sempervirens* 'Stricta') has a slim, elegant form that makes an eye-catching outline against urban landscapes and open skylines. Irish yew (*Taxus baccata* 'Fastigiata') does the same in a more robust way. Architectural shrubs include *Fatsia japonica* and x *Fatshedera lizei*. Both can be grown in containers and have flamboyant foliage that particularly suits urban locations. *Choisya ternata* gives a pleasing, rounded outline, and the bold leaves of yuccas and phormiums create spiky silhouettes.

Perennials with architectural merit include hostas and *Bergenia cordifolia* cultivars. Planted in bold masses they will punctuate and steady the blurred accumulation of other perennials, whose fleeting merit is in their flower. Although invasive, Giant hogweed (*Heracleum mantegazzianum*) is worth growing for its dramatic flower heads and foliage. Climbers with strong leaf shape, such as the rather vigorous, ornamental grape vine (*Vitis coignetiae*), bring excellent shape and pattern to all manner of vertical surfaces.

Architectural contrast
Among softer plants, the robust form of the agave provides a horticultural exclamation mark. The strong sculptural forms of the agaves en masse *complement the craggy outlines of stone buildings, below.*

CHOOSING ARCHITECTURAL PLANTS

For a more comprehensive selection, see p. 206.

Allium rosenbachianum
ALLIUM
Spherical heads of tightly compacted, mauve-pink flowers appear in mid-summer, making this bulb a plant for seasonal architectural interest. It looks particularly effective rising out of a plant with a low-spreading habit. Full sun and well-drained soil. Height to 1m (3ft), spread to 20cm (8 in).

Choisya ternata
MEXICAN ORANGE BLOSSOM
This evergreen shrub has a gentle, rounded form. In late spring its glossy foliage is offset by large clusters of fragrant white flowers. Flowers again in autumn. Prefers sun or light shade, well-drained soil, shelter from sharp winds. Height and spread 2.5m (8 ft).

Hosta sieboldiana
PLANTAIN LILY
Hostas all have a strong overall pattern of ribbed, textured leaves that will bring sculptural strength to shady spaces. *H. s.* 'Frances Williams' shown here has yellow-edged leaves and is slow-growing. Prefers shade and moist, well-drained, neutral soil. Height 1m (3 ft) or more, spread 1.5m (5 ft). Perennial.

Iris laevigata
JAPANESE WATER IRIS
The architectural strength of the perennial *I. laevigata* lies in the shape of its vertical leaves which form a spiky mass and make a striking backdrop to the rich purple flowers that appear in early summer. It grows best in shallow water or very moist soil. Height to 1m (3 ft) or more, spread indefinite.

Rheum palmatum
ORNAMENTAL RHUBARB
Huge, eye-catching leaves up to 1.2m (4 ft) across and mid-summer, foaming spires of rust-coloured flowers up to 1.8m (6 ft) high give this perennial an energetic outline. For maximum effect grow it in isolation from other plants. Its leaves tend to wilt in the sun, so plant in a moist, shady place.

Rodgersia podophylla
RODGERSIA
This perennial has enormous leaves, up to 30cm (1 ft) across, and spires of creamy flowers. It grows well in moist conditions, sheltered from the wind, and complements water plants with a vertical form, such as *Iris laevigata*. Tolerates sun or semi-shade. Height to 1.2m (4 ft), spread 1m (3 ft).

Scented plants

Scented garden flowers are wonderfully alluring and luxurious, particularly on a warm evening as the sun is going down. Their fragrance can be enjoyed outside or from inside through an open door or window. Roses around a bedroom window, aromatic herbs on a sill, or fragrant lilies in a container on the doorstep will all waft their scents into the house. Every season has its scents. Spring has the fresh fragrance of hyacinths (*Hyacinthus orientalis)* and daffodils (*Narcissus* cvs.), both ideal for containers, and the sweet scents of *Wisteria* sp., *Clematis montana*, and lilac (*Syringa* sp.), mingling with the light summer scents of roses and pinks (*Dianthus* sp.). These make way for the heady perfume of lilies (*Lilium auratum* and *L. regale* can be grown in containers), and *Buddleia* sp. The exotic scents of jasmine (*Jasminum officinale*), gladioli (*Gladiolus* sp.), and tobacco plants (*Nicotiana* sp.) overlap with the lilies and last into autumn. During winter we rely on the blossom of shrubs such as sweet box (*Sarcococca humilis*) and *Daphne odora*, and the aromatic leaves of evergreen herbs such as *Rosmarinus officinalis* and sweet bay (*Laurus nobilis*).

SHRUB PLANTING FOR SCENT

Although many scented shrubs bloom early in the year, neither their flowers nor their shape are spectacular. *Sarcococca* sp., *Mahonia japonica* (which does have a good shape), *Choisya ternata*, and forms of *Daphne* are not particular about their site, and can be put in a corner near a door or a window where their perfume can be best appreciated. For a visually satisfying border with strongly scented shrubs, you need to include plants with stronger shapes, forms, or colours. In this example a corner bed is pinioned by two clipped pyramidal hornbeams (*Carpinus betulus*), counterbalanced by the *Pittosporum tenuifolium*. Around this point of emphasis are grouped shrubs that combine in form and colour as well as providing a variety of scents through the season.

A scented garden bed

Philadelphus 'Sybille'

Myrtus communis

Syringa chinensis

Carpinus betulus pyramidalis

Chimonanthus fragrans

Mahonia japonica

Pittosporum tenuifolium

Osmanthus delavayi

Sarcococca humilis

Elaeagnus commutata

Rosa rubrifolia

Azalea sp. (white)

Choisya ternata

Perovskia atriplicifolia 'Blue Spire'

Daphne odora aureo-marginata

Berberis stenophylla

CHOOSING PLANTS FOR SCENT

For a more comprehensive selection, see p. 207.

Cytisus battandieri
MOROCCAN BROOM
In high summer the flowers of
Moroccan broom exude a
sweet, pineapple-like scent.
A semi-evergreen shrub,
C. battandieri has a spreading
habit, and can be trained against
a wall. It prefers full sun and
fertile, but not over-rich, well-
drained soil. Height 4.5m
(15 ft), spread 4m (12 ft).

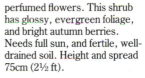

Daphne retusa
DAPHNE
In late spring *Daphne retusa*,
like many other members of the
daphne family, bears an
abundance of wonderfully

perfumed flowers. This shrub
has glossy, evergreen foliage,
and bright autumn berries.
Needs full sun, and fertile, well-
drained soil. Height and spread
75cm (2½ ft).

Matthiola incana Brompton
Series
BROMPTON STOCK
Brompton stock has a heavy,
luscious scent. Plant near a
window to enjoy the fragrance
on a warm mid-summer evening
or use as a colourful, scented
annual filler in a small bedding
scheme. Sun or semi-shade.
Prefers lime-rich soil. Height
45cm (18 in), spread 30cm (1 ft).

Rosmarinus officinalis
ROSEMARY
Rosemary, of which there are
many forms, has heavily
aromatic, evergreen foliage.
For the full benefit of its year-
round scent, grow near a bench
or under a window. *R. officinalis*
is also a good hedging shrub.
Needs sun and well-drained soil.
Cut back in spring. Height and
spread 2m (6½ ft).

Viburnum x *carlcephalum*
VIBURNUM
The spring flowers of *Viburnum*
x *carlcephalum* are sweetly
scented, and are followed by
brilliantly coloured foliage and
berries in the autumn. This
viburnum is a deciduous shrub.
It can be grown in full sun or
semi-shade, in fertile soil, but
not too dry. Height and spread
3.5m (11 ft).

Water plants

Water plants have different characters and different needs. Some like only damp roots and are known as marginal plants, while others such as reeds and rushes grow in up to 450mm (18 in) water. Aquatic plants like water lilies are mostly submerged, with only their leaves floating on the surface of the water. Others are fully submerged and act as oxygenators in the water.

Plant shapes

Many aquatics have large leaves and are excellent subjects for planting compositions. *Rheum* sp. and the larger *Gunnera* sp., for example, have enormous rhubarb-type leaves.

Horizontal-growing plants such as water lilies contrast beautifully with the vertical and spiky leaves of other aquatics such as Sweet Flag (*Acorus calamus* 'Variegatus').

The most striking groupings tend to be sparse and composed of two or three types of plant only, echoing naturally occurring water planting. Bold drifts of one subject against a mass of another will be effectively offset by areas of clear water between.

Planting techniques

First decide whether you want a natural look. Study local conditions to identify which weeds and floating plants are likely to become

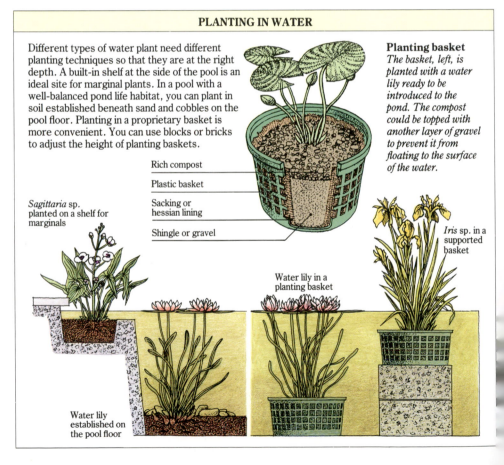

PLANTING IN WATER

Different types of water plant need different planting techniques so that they are at the right depth. A built-in shelf at the side of the pool is an ideal site for marginal plants. In a pool with a well-balanced pond life habitat, you can plant in soil established beneath sand and cobbles on the pool floor. Planting in a proprietary basket is more convenient. You can use blocks or bricks to adjust the height of planting baskets.

Planting basket
The basket, left, is planted with a water lily ready to be introduced to the pond. The compost could be topped with another layer of gravel to prevent it from floating to the surface of the water.

Rich compost

Plastic basket

Sacking or hessian lining

Shingle or gravel

Sagittaria sp. planted on a shelf for marginals

Iris sp. in a supported basket

Water lily in a planting basket

Water lily established on the pool floor

invasive. The best time of year for planting most aquatic plants is April to June, when plant life is starting to grow vigorously. By the following winter water plants will have established good enough root anchorage to survive really cold weather.

Water lilies are planted in containers and need rich compost to make good growth in one season. Without it the leaves will be stunted and plants will not flower. Ideally the compost should be made up of six parts turfy loam well mixed with one part of cow manure or coarse bonemeal. Cover the compost with a layer of

Plants and water, right
The horizontal planes of water and decking surround contrast with the vertical spikes of the rushes. Lush greenery and cool colours create a languid mood.

AN INFORMAL POOL PLANTING

This pool was built against a bank planted with hazels (*Corylus avellana*) and a holly (*Ilex* sp.). Its shape is an interpretation of naturally formed pools, which also allows easy access along one side and affords many different views of water and plants. The pool is 27.5m (90 ft) long.

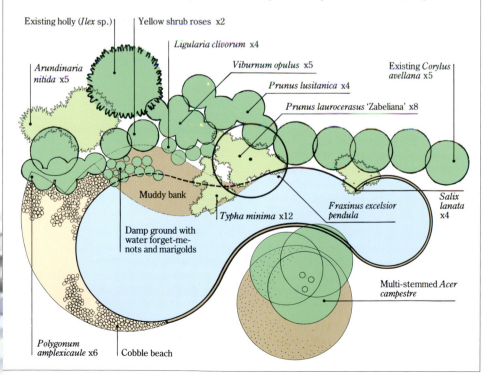

Existing holly (*Ilex* sp.)

Yellow shrub roses x2

Ligularia clivorum x4

Arundinaria nitida x5

Viburnum opulus x5

Prunus lusitanica x4

Existing *Corylus avellana* x5

Prunus laurocerasus 'Zabeliana' x8

Muddy bank

Fraxinus excelsior pendula

Salix lanata x4

Typha minima x12

Damp ground with water forget-me-nots and marigolds

Multi-stemmed *Acer campestre*

Polygonum amplexicaule x6

Cobble beach

Marginal planting
The bold leaves of Rodgersia *sp. form the background to this boggy planting, right, that includes* Primula japonica *in the foreground,* Astilbe *sp. on the right, and* Polygonum *sp.*

pure loam. Top with a layer of gravel to anchor the fine content when it is sunk in water, ensuring that the cow manure doesn't rise to the surface to decompose, foul the water, and poison the fish. Submerged oxygenators can be planted in pure loam, free of manure.

Filling the pool
Patience is needed here. When planting is complete, fill the pool gradually over a period of a few days. The shock of cold water to plants that have already been moved during their growing period can be fatal. Fill the pool slowly, at first to a depth where only the plant crowns are covered. Then leave it for a few days. To avoid disturbing mud when you complete the filling, direct the flow of the hose into an empty plant pot set on the bottom. Don't run the water too quickly. If you are introducing new plants into an established pool, lower them to their final position over a few days by altering brick heights beneath them.

Maintaining an established pool
It is neither necessary nor a good idea to empty and clean a pool frequently. Every time you do, it will need to re-establish a natural balance between water and pond life, including plants. Leaves need to be removed from the surface of the water or they will choke the plants. This can be done simply by threading some wire netting into the tines of a digging fork and using the fork as a scoop. In full sun,

algae growing in the water become a nuisance and must be cleared with a fine net, although proprietary chemicals are available for this task. Natural shade will solve the problem of algae eventually.

Dividing the plants
When you do eventually need to empty and clean your pool, take the opportunity to divide your plants before replanting them, in late spring if possible. Wash the plants thoroughly and cut out any weak or spindly growth. Strong stock should be divided and the tubers of water lilies cut into pieces, leaving one good crown to each plant. Leave only a short piece of tuber and cut away some of the old, fleshy roots.

The pond in winter
Plants and fish will be quite safe below ice during winter, provided the pool is deep enough – at least 60cm (2ft). You need to maintain a hole in the ice, however, about 60cm (2 ft) across, so that air can get to the water and the fish can be fed. Cut the hole as gently as possible – heavy blows on ice can injure or even kill fish.

Very small ponds can easily freeze solid in severe weather. Protect both plant and fish life within the pool by covering it with wooden boards and a layer of old matting or straw. Remove whatever covering you use as soon as the weather improves or the plants will be forced into premature growth.

CHOOSING WATER PLANTS

For a more comprehensive selection, see p. 208.

Acorus calamus 'Variegatus'
SWEET FLAG
The spiky, vertical form of this rush makes a clean contrast with the smooth, horizontal surface of still water. It is a perennial, marginal plant and grows in shallow water to a depth of 25cm (10 in). It prefers an open, sunny position. Height 75cm (2½ ft), spread 60cm (2 ft).

Alisma plantago-aquatica
WATER PLANTAIN
The long stalks of this perennial, shallow water plant hold its clumps of pointed green leaves well above the water line. Delicate flower stalks rise to a height of 60cm (2 ft) and a mass of tiny white flowers create a hazy background to the stronger shapes of the leaves. Prefers full sun.

Hosta lancifolia
PLANTAIN LILY
Plant hostas in damp soil to create a luxuriant surround to a lightly shaded water feature. *H. lancifolia* has small, elegant leaves. Its deep lilac blooms appear towards the end of summer and last into autumn. Hostas are perennials. Height 45cm (18 in), spread 60cm (2 ft).

Hydrocleys nymphoides
WATER POPPY
For a refreshing composition plant the yellow-flowered water poppy in a wooden tub, filled three-quarters with soil and one quarter with water. This perennial is a frost tender, deep water plant, grown for its floating foliage and attractive flowers. Likes plenty of light. Spread to 60cm (2 ft).

Lysichiton americanum
BOG ARUM
A handsome waterside plant with rich yellow flowers that appear in early spring. Its large, smooth leaves follow, growing to a height of 1.2m (4 ft). Its size and dramatic appearance make it a plant to be used on its own. Perennial, full sun or semi-shade. Spread 75cm (2½ ft).

Nymphaea 'Escarboucle'
WATER LILY
The strident colouring of this water lily – deep red petals with deep yellow anthers and dark green leaves – make it one that is best grown on its own. A single plant may spread to 1.8m (6 ft). It will grow in still water up to 45cm (18 in) deep and prefers an open, sunny site. It is a deciduous perennial.

Plants for rapid growth

Plants for rapid growth are ones that have an immediate visual impact and quickly come into flower. All annuals come into this category, as well as some biennials and fast-growing shrubs and climbers.

There will be gaps in the most carefully planned planting, particularly before the feature shrubs and plants have reached their maturity. Here annuals are indispensable. Some small space gardens, such as roof terraces and windowsills, rely entirely on annuals to provide colour, particularly where conditions are too harsh for overwintering. For quick infills use pot marigolds (*Calendula* sp.) and forget-me-nots (*Myosotis* sp.).

Evergreens take a particularly long time to establish – here fast-growing deciduous shrubs with a relatively short life span such as broom (*Cytisus* sp.) can be used as long-term infillers and moved when appropriate. Sunflowers (*Helianthus* sp.) and annual climbers such as runner beans (*Phaseolus coccineus*), hop (*Humulus lupulus*), and the cup-and-saucer plant (*Cobaea scandens*) are ideal for giving height to a maturing planting scheme.

Using biennials as instant plants requires a little more forward planning. They need to be planted one year to flower the next. Among those which reach a considerable height are foxgloves (*Digitalis* sp.), honesty (*Lunaria* sp.), and mullein (*Verbascum* sp.).

A bold arrangement
If you want to combine brightly coloured annuals in a parade of instant colour, be bold and flamboyant, arranging them in strong masses against a simple background as here, below.

CHOOSING RAPID GROWTH PLANTS

For a more comprehensive selection, see p. 206.

Buddleia davidii 'Peace'
BUTTERFLY BUSH
Buddleia grows up to 3m (10 ft)
in a season and is excellent for
filling in among newly planted,
slow-growing evergreens. Pull
it out after five years or so. For
maximum growth, cut back
hard after flowering. Buddleia is
a deciduous shrub and prefers
full sun and well-drained soil.
Height and spread 5m (15 ft).

Calendula officinalis
POT MARIGOLD
Pot marigolds are among the
easiest annuals to grow, and
their firm, bright blooms lend
themselves to a variety of
golden moods. *C. o.* 'Gitana'
has cream to orange daisy-like,
double flower heads from spring
to autumn. Needs sun and well-
drained soil. Height and spread
30cm (1 ft).

Helianthus annuus
SUNFLOWER
Sunflowers are giant, daisy-like
annuals that thrive in full sun.
They can grow more than 3m
(10 ft) tall and their flowers are
often as much as 30cm (1 ft)
across, and need staking. They
make dramatic infillers or
temporary screens. Gold is the
most common flower colour.
They prefer well-drained soil.

Nemesia strumosa
NEMESIA
The mixed colours of the
cultivar 'Triumph Mixed' create
a cheerful, cottage garden
mood. All cultivars of this
annual flower best in soil that is
fertile and moist. If it is grown
in a container, it needs
moisture-retentive compost.
Prefers full sun. Height to 45cm
(18 in), spread 15cm (6 in).

Passiflora caerulea
PASSION FLOWER
The passion flower is a rapid-
growing climber and its
evergreen leaves make a
handsome year-round screen,
enhanced by its summer display
of exotic flowers. Its tendrils
will cling to a lattice or wire
support. It will grow in any
fertile soil in sun or light shade.
Height to 10m (30 ft).

Polygonum baldschuanicum
RUSSIAN VINE
For an instant screen use
Russian vine. It is an extremely
vigorous, deciduous climber,
growing up to 3m (10 ft) in a
season. Bear in mind, however,
that it will grow the same
amount again in successive
seasons. Sun or shade and well-
drained soil. Height to
12m (40 ft).

Plants for containers

Just about any type of plant, be it a vegetable, a herb, or a small tree, can be grown in a container, provided it is given adequate root space and is well watered and fed. Pot-grown plants give you great flexibility in siting plant groupings around the garden. They can be used singly as dramatic punctuation marks or added to permanent plantings for a splash of seasonal colour.

Drainage holes in containers are essential. Sour water will collect in a sealed container and rot the roots. In winter any collected water might freeze and damage the roots and, quite possibly, the container. Always put a layer of broken crockery over the drainage holes.

The more compost you give a plant the more moisture and nutrients will be retained. Always use a good quality compost to avoid poor results. Revitalize established container plants by replacing the top layer of the mix with new compost each spring.

Plants grown in exposed sites or in hanging baskets should be fed and watered more regularly than those at ground level.

PLANTING IN CONTAINERS

Make sure the container has drainage holes. Cover these with a layer of crocks or pebbles and a layer of compost. Arrange your plants on these layers so that the crowns of their root balls are just below the rim. Backfill with compost, firm down gently with your hands, and water well.

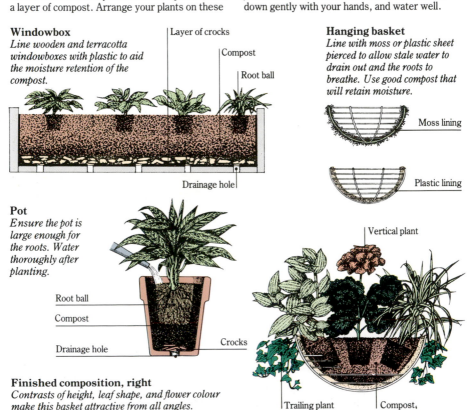

Windowbox
Line wooden and terracotta windowboxes with plastic to aid the moisture retention of the compost.

Layer of crocks

Compost

Root ball

Drainage hole

Hanging basket
Line with moss or plastic sheet pierced to allow stale water to drain out and the roots to breathe. Use good compost that will retain moisture.

Moss lining

Plastic lining

Pot
Ensure the pot is large enough for the roots. Water thoroughly after planting.

Root ball

Compost

Drainage hole

Crocks

Vertical plant

Finished composition, right
Contrasts of height, leaf shape, and flower colour make this basket attractive from all angles.

Trailing plant

Compost

IRRIGATION OF CONTAINERS

Plants grown in pots need more watering than plants in beds. An automatic irrigation system is a great time-saver if you have a lot of pots, and will ensure the survival of your plants when you are away from home.

The system
Automatic irrigation systems have a time-switched valve that regulates the flow of water from a tap which is left open, above right, and a hose with small outlets that lies over the pots, right.

Tap turned on

Time-switched valve

End of hosepipe sealed

Informal grouping of planted containers
The success of this grouping, above, stems from the combination of strong, sculptural plant forms and relaxed ones, arranged as carefully as plants in a bed.

CHOOSING PLANTS FOR CONTAINERS

For an additional selection, see p. 209.

Geranium sanguineum
BLOODY CRANESBILL
G. sanguineum, a spreading perennial, does very well in a container, forming a central mound and cascading over the sides of the pot. It bears deep magenta-pink flowers in summer, and is also useful for ground cover. It prefers sun. Any soil. Height to 25cm (10 in), spread 30cm (1 ft).

Nicotiana alata
TOBACCO PLANT
The creamy-white flowers of this elegant tobacco plant have a heady evening fragrance. It has oval, mid-green leaves. Plant in containers near a door or window to allow the scent to waft in. *N. alata* is a perennial grown as an annual. It needs sun and fertile soil. Height 60cm (2ft), spread 30cm (1ft).

Sempervivum tectorum
HOUSELEEK
The houseleek is an evergreen perennial often grown in rockeries and looks very effective planted in simple containers, which will show off the satisfying texture and pattern of its fleshy rosettes to best advantage. Happiest in full sun, thrives in poor soil. Height 15cm (6 in), spread 20cm (8 in).

Country garden plants

The popular image of the country garden is one of full, billowing outlines, gentle colours, soft fragrances, and an air of calm. Many try to capture these characteristics, whether in the country or in the city, among apartment blocks and busy roads.

Particular plants evoke the rural feel, many of them included in the plant choice on p. 170 and the plant selection guide on p. 210. No country garden is complete without, for example, mounds of *Alchemilla mollis*,

spreading its heads of bright green flowers onto paths. These plants can be combined to create a tapestry of country planting in a bedding scheme or even in containers.

Creating a country feel

At first glance the true country garden appears to have evolved naturally, produced by relaxed, almost random planting. It may certainly contain many self-seeded plants that have not been deliberately planted.

SEMI-WILD PLANTING SCHEME

This planting plan is styled for a brightly painted farmhouse with an adjacent stone barn, located in northern England. The house is painted aquamarine, with old, gold-coloured window surrounds, a combination which inspires the strong colour scheme of mauves and purples, with creamy gold and white. The planting is designed to be seen both against the house and

the beautiful Lakeland countryside that lies beyond this view, but it could be successfully transferred to an enclosed garden anywhere.

The scheme has a semi-natural feel created by native plants such as holly, ivy, and gorse. The visual forms of giant hogweed (*Heracleum mantegazzianum*) and gorse (*Ulex europaeus*) are strong enough to complement the barn.

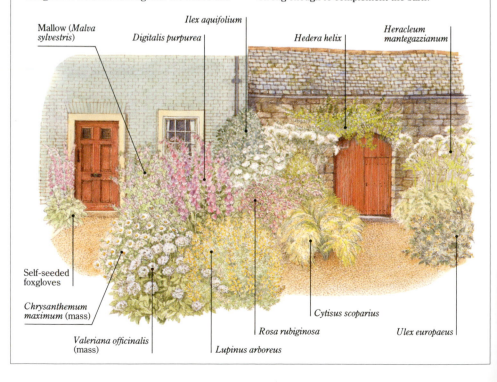

Mallow (*Malva sylvestris*)

Digitalis purpurea

Ilex aquifolium

Hedera helix

Heracleum mantegazzianum

Self-seeded foxgloves

Chrysanthemum maximum (mass)

Valeriana officinalis (mass)

Lupinus arboreus

Rosa rubiginosa

Cytisus scoparius

Ulex europaeus

Beneath the soft plants, however, are the paths, walls, arches, and bold structural planting which make up the framework and prevent the scheme from becoming a jumbled mess. Any bedding scheme of non-structural country planting, which might include love-in-a-mist (*Nigella damascena*), lupins (*Lupinus* sp.), and delphiniums (*Delphinium* sp.), needs to be punctuated with permanent features. Perhaps a bench, a piece of sculpture, or plants with bold form, like the evergreen shrubs Mexican orange blossom (*Choisya ternata*), rosemary (*Rosmarinus officinalis*), and sage (*Salvia officinalis*), to steady and calm the country tapestry when annuals and perennials bloom, and to give it shape during the winter months. One of the charms of the country garden is its fullness, a feeling produced by plants smothering walls and bursting out of their beds. To create this look, allow self-seeders to grow through gravel and between the cracks in paving, and cover walls and fences with climbing plants.

Sentimental artefacts scattered around a garden immediately create a contrived and self-conscious appearance and are best avoided. Rely instead on the colours, scents, and textures of your country plants.

COUNTRY GARDEN PLANTING SCHEME

This country garden scheme is designed for a farm cottage in southern England. The building has dark-stained weatherboarding across the first floor and buff-coloured walls below. It would work well against any similarly neutral walls. There is a strong skeleton of evergreen plants, including yews, viburnums, *Choisya ternata*, and the spectacular golden-leaved *Lonicera nitida* 'Baggesen's Gold'. This year-round plant material provides a strong support for the more traditional perennial and annual cottage-style plants, such as *Helleborus foetidus*.

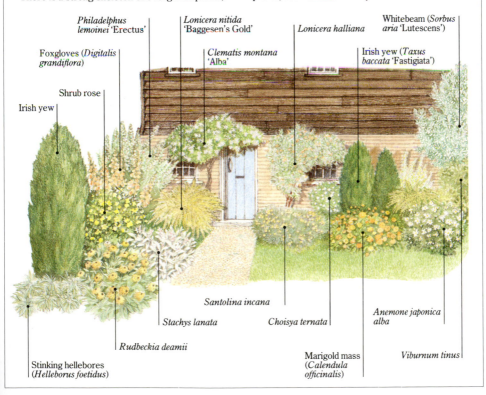

Philadelphus lemoinei 'Erectus'

Lonicera nitida 'Baggesen's Gold'

Lonicera halliana

Whitebeam (*Sorbus aria* 'Lutescens')

Foxgloves (*Digitalis grandiflora*)

Clematis montana 'Alba'

Irish yew (*Taxus baccata* 'Fastigiata')

Shrub rose

Irish yew

Santolina incana

Anemone japonica alba

Stachys lanata

Choisya ternata

Rudbeckia deamii

Stinking hellebores (*Helleborus foetidus*)

Marigold mass (*Calendula officinalis*)

Viburnum tinus

CHOOSING COUNTRY GARDEN PLANTS

For a more comprehensive selection, see p. 210.

Alchemilla mollis
LADY'S MANTLE
Alchemilla is loved for its swathes of bright green flower heads, which produce a relaxed country atmosphere in any garden. After a fall of rain the leaves retain pearly droplets of water. *A. mollis* is a perennial, grows in sun or shade, and in all but boggy soils. Height and spread 50cm (20 in).

Angelica archangelica
ANGELICA
The huge, green heads of this summer-flowering herb are balanced by lush, aromatic foliage. Plant alongside *Foeniculum vulgare*, which flowers into mid-autumn. Angelica is an upright perennial, and grows in sun or shade in well-drained soil. Height to 2m (6½ ft), spread 2.2m (7 ft).

Nigella damascena
LOVE-IN-A-MIST
N. damascena 'Persian Jewel' is grown for its delicate flowers and fine foliage, which create a soft, hazy effect in a country garden. It also has ornamental seed pods that can be cut and dried. This annual grows best in full sun and fertile, well-drained soil. Height 60cm (2 ft), spread 20cm (8 in).

Rosa 'Constance Spry'
SHRUB ROSE
Rosa 'Constance Spry' is a successor to the old-fashioned cabbage rose. It is equally happy growing as a spreading bush or clambering up a wall. It flowers in early summer with spectacular effect. Prefers an open, sunny site and fertile, well-drained soil. Height 2m (6½ ft), spread 1.5m (5 ft).

Rubus 'Benenden'
RUBUS
This deciduous shrub of medium size grows to a height of 3m (10 ft) and has a grace and charm which typifies the country garden look. In late spring/early summer single, eye-catching white flowers appear along its slender branches. Sun or semi-shade. Prefers well-drained soil.

Verbascum 'Gainsborough'
MULLEIN
The spire-like stems of *Verbascum* 'Gainsborough' grow to a height of 1.2m (4 ft) and bear apricot-yellow flowers throughout the summer. Plant alongside the spring-flowering bulb *Narcissus poeticus*, to create a seasonally changing tapestry. Perennial, prefers full sun, well-drained soil.

Wild flowers

Wild flowers have strong romantic associations. They provide food for local fauna and homes for endangered species of insects. With reports of wild flowers being destroyed through agricultural spraying, the appeal of wildflower gardening has never been stronger. Along with the romantic image goes the popular myth that you can quickly and easily transform a spare piece of land into a wonderful wildflower haven.

The reality is something else, however. If you cultivate a piece of ground and leave it, the most invasive of indigenous and locally naturalized plant species will take over, with unimpressive results.

If you don't cut an area of the lawn for a week or two, you will have a wildflower lawn that will look good contrasted with mown lawn. With a planting of naturalized spring bulbs, this is probably the most practical sort of wildflower garden that most of us would aspire to.

The purist who wants a natural wildflower meadow should first consider the work involved. Native grasses in the main grow too vigorously to allow seedling wild flowers to establish themselves. Sprinkling wildflower seeds in the lawn is not the way. First you need to destroy the existing coarse perennial grasses and any other tenacious plant. Here you may have to use the very weedkiller which has destroyed the wild flowers we long to see.

Sow a wildflower and fine grass seed mix suitable for the soil across the prepared ground. This sort of meadow may take up to three years to establish itself.

A rather time-consuming alternative method is to buy seedling wild species from a specialist nursery, or raise them yourself, which you then grow on and plant out among established meadow grass. With maintenance these more mature specimens will be able to compete with the vigour of natives already growing there.

PLANTING SCHEME FOR A WILDFLOWER CORNER

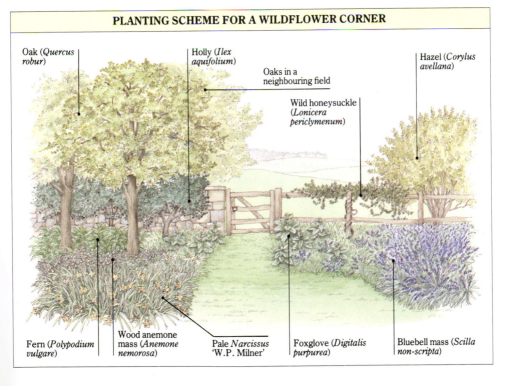

Oak (*Quercus robur*)

Holly (*Ilex aquifolium*)

Oaks in a neighbouring field

Hazel (*Corylus avellana*)

Wild honeysuckle (*Lonicera periclymenum*)

Fern (*Polypodium vulgare*)

Wood anemone mass (*Anemone nemorosa*)

Pale *Narcissus* 'W.P. Milner'

Foxglove (*Digitalis purpurea*)

Bluebell mass (*Scilla non-scripta*)

Planting – the components

Whether you are devising a planting scheme for a single bed or starting a new garden from scratch, consider and select the components by type. Start with trees, the largest elements – consider size now and five years hence, characteristics, and location. Go on to permanent shrub planting. Add in perennials, taking account of how they affect the mood of the garden. Sketch in spring and autumn bulbs and annuals for summer colour.

Trees

The most important characteristic of any tree that is used in garden planning and design is shape. Trees will ultimately be the largest element in the garden, and their positioning is crucial to the overall design. Always consider the size and shape of the mature tree five or ten years hence – well-maintained trees grow quite quickly both upwards and outwards. Think also about where shadow will be cast, whether the tree will impinge on neighbouring gardens, and whether it might undermine any nearby buildings with its invasive root run. Carefully consider the scale of any background trees you propose to plant. Few small gardens can accommodate a forest tree, such as a beech (*Fagus* sp.), an ash (*Fraxinus* sp.), or any of the large conifers. Poplars (*Populus* sp.), which are often planted as screen trees, may be categorized as medium-sized trees, although they can grow to great heights. In hotter climates taller trees are useful for providing shade. Trees with less dense foliage are good here, so that some light gets through.

ROOT SYSTEMS

Some species of tree and shrub have almost as much root below ground level as they have branches above, especially when they are growing in good, loamy soil. Much of such a root system consists of minute feeder roots that penetrate the film of water surrounding each individual granule of soil. Wherever there is a water source, roots will grow towards it. Large trees, therefore, should not be planted too close to any drainage runs. As a general rule, the thinner the foliage the less anchorage is needed and the lighter the root run. When you are planting near existing trees or adding new ones to an established planting, any nutrient held in solution in the ground will be absorbed by the rooting system of the tree to the deprivation of all the surrounding vegetation.

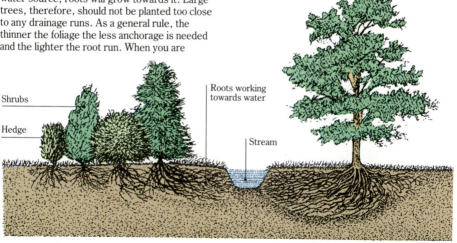

Shrubs

Hedge

Roots working towards water

Stream

PLANTING A TREE

In the past when saplings were sold bare-rooted, it was usual to plant them in autumn, when trees are dormant. Container-grown trees are available today, which can be planted without disturbing the roots more or less throughout the year, as long as there is no frost in the ground.

Dig a hole for the tree approximately 1m (3¼ ft) square. Fork over the ground at the base of the hole before putting in well-rotted organic manure, compost, or hop or farmyard manure, to a depth of 20cm (9 in). Fork this in to the bottom layer of earth. Water the tree well. Position it in the hole. Cut down the side of the container and remove gently, trying not to disturb the roots. Clear any drainage crocks away from the underside of the root ball. Ensure that the finished earth line when the tree is planted in the garden will not be above that of the tree in its pot.

Knock in a sound stake at the side of the root ball, avoiding driving the stake through the young roots. Backfill the hole with organic topsoil, gently shaking the stem up and down to ensure that soil settles between the roots, and firming the soil as you go with your heel.

Examine the young tree regularly. It will need frequent, sometimes daily, watering during dry spells, and particularly so if it was planted out of its dormant period. This will encourage the roots to grow out of the tight ball the container produces and into the prepared earth, quickly allowing them both to feed from the soil around and to support the tree.

Planting a pot-grown sapling, below
Always dig a planting hole big enough to allow plenty of space around the root ball as shown. Backfill with organically enriched topsoil.

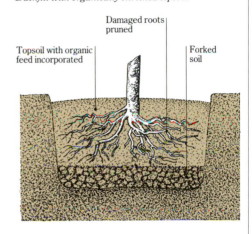

Damaged roots pruned

Topsoil with organic feed incorporated

Forked soil

STAKING TREES

Tie newly planted trees to a stake with plastic cord to give them extra support until the roots establish themselves. Trees in exposed positions should be given a stake set at an angle to the wind and trees with particularly heavy heads may need additional staking and ties.

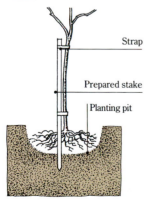

Strap

Prepared stake

Planting pit

Normal standard tree

Stake driven in at 45° against prevailing winds

Exposed position

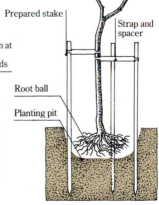

Prepared stake

Strap and spacer

Root ball

Planting pit

Heavy standard tree

Trees needed to screen a bad view may be more profitably sited closer to the house rather than at the garden's perimeter. Not only will you need more trees if they are further away from the viewpoint, but they can all too easily draw the eye to the precise point you are trying to disguise.

Choosing smaller trees

There is an extensive range of smaller trees suitable for the smaller garden. They may either be grouped to provide a screen or become decorative elements in their own right.

Smaller trees tend to have shorter lifespans than forest trees, but they reach maturity more quickly. They grow naturally on higher ground, where wind and cold inhibit growth – a point worth noting for roof gardens.

Various factors will affect what you can grow where. Different locations at the same latitude, for example, might not support the same tree because of contrasted altitudes. Climate will also affect your choice. The long, cold winters and hot summers of the European continent will not support the same trees as the less extreme conditions of the British Isles.

PLANTING A SPINNEY

A spinney is a small clump of trees, a sparse planting of standards with open glades of younger shrubby plants beneath. New spinneys may be planted with any number of trees, although for relatively quick decorative effect, stick to forest-scale trees and avoid mixing the species too wildly. In the traditional spinney flowering trees are planted at the edge of the grouping and trees with autumn colour and/or fruit are used to extend visual interest towards winter.

Where a wooded boundary is becoming too tall, with an undesirable view beginning to appear beneath the tree canopy, you might consider planting a younger spinney, both as a foreground feature and to increase the effectiveness of the boundary screen.

In this case, below, the existing planting was of silver birch and pine and, on the perimeter, *Amelanchier lamarckii*, all of which are used in the new foreground planting.

Silver birch (*Betula pendula*)

New spinney planted in a circle for ease of fencing against stock, deer, and rabbits, and easier mowing

Scots pine (*Pinus sylvestris*)

Silver birch

Scots pine

Snowy mespilus (*Amelanchier lamarckii*)

Rough mown grass

Snowy mespilus

Decorative trees and conifers

Decorative trees include the genera *Prunus* (cherry and plum), *Malus* (crab apple), and *Crataegus* (thorn), which all flower, fruit, and have a degree of autumn colour. They have no sculptural quality, however, and you will look at a bare tree for half the year.

Conifers, on the other hand, have their full shape the whole year round, but when used *en masse* provide a shape that is too demanding to fit most planting plans and too boring to view. A uniform conifer planting cannot match the diversity of broad-leaved trees.

And conifers have been responsible for the loss of too many acres of open moorland, particularly in northern England. The original rigid patterns of conifer afforestation have more recently been tempered by contour planting and the inclusion of some hardwoods, but the damage has largely been done.

Certain conifers, however, have a place within the garden layout if carefully used. Their strong forms can successfully emphasize a point. Many of the dark, matt green conifers make admirable background and shelter.

Feature trees

Preferable alternatives to conifers include the smaller variety of silver birch or the thin weeping head of the willow-leaved pear (*Pyrus salicifolia*), and gnarled old apple trees, whether alive or dead. More exotic, good value small trees include many of the maples (*Acer* sp.), admired for their leaves, branches, and autumn colour. Magnolias are grown for their magnificent flowers, but also have a good shape. The golden catalpa (*Catalpa bignonioides*) is spectacular when in flower, but is most memorable for its huge, heart-shaped leaves. The showering sprays of golden *Genista aethnensis*, and the mid-summer gold of *Koelreuteria paniculata* followed by bronze bladder fruits, are also attractive. *Amelanchier lamarckii*, the snowy mespilus, is a charming white-blossomed spring alternative to the cherry and has the advantage of distinctive sculptural qualities. Trees for the wild garden include whitebeam (*Sorbus aria* 'Lutescens') and the autumn-fruiting rowan (*Sorbus aucuparia*). Also alders (*Alnus* sp.), hornbeam (*Carpinus* sp.), and hazels (*Corylus* sp.).

Topiary

The concept of topiary, or clipping plants to shape, conjures images of seventeenth-century country gardens decorated with grand pyramids of yew and peacocks of box. Scaled down, however, the neatly tailored shapes of clipped plants suit the strong lines and hard shapes of the modern garden, and contrast well with the natural, loose shapes of other plants.

Many topiary plants are naturally voracious feeders, and their demands increase the more they are clipped and attempt to put out new shoots. Use a rich compost, and feed and water regularly. Grow in full sun and protect from strong winds. For a list of plants suitable for topiary, see p. 214

Traditional archway
*Yew (*Taxus baccata*) is here clipped to form a dramatic archway, right, with other clipped yews glimpsed beyond. Topiary has great architectural potential for modern garden design, too.*

Shrubs

Background shrubs may not be the star features of the garden but they do most of the hard work. They provide a backdrop for other garden elements, winter form, foliage for cutting, and food and shelter for wildlife. Most of them come into their own at some point during the year, whether with early spring colour, deep coloured berries, or striking winter stems. As a general rule, groupings of shrubs should be bold and simple.

Evergreen shrubs
For an introduction to the diversity of size, form, and colour in shrubs, compare the genera *Cotoneaster, Viburnum,* and

PLANTING DISTANCES FOR SHRUBS

Spacing between shrubs really depends on how quickly you want to achieve an interlocking mass of plants. Different plants grow at different rates. Rhododendrons, for example, grow to 5m (16½ ft) across, so you might plant them at 2m (6½ ft) distances. Five years is the longest you will have to wait for shrubs to mature, and during that time many shrubs will need to be cut right back or thinned drastically. Use the box below right as a rough guide to planting distances, placing shrubs not listed in the appropriate category yourself. Avoid the common mistake of planting young shrubs, which may be no more than twigs, too close together.

While waiting for shrubs to knit together, cultivate the ground between them. Cover the soil with a mulch or plant perennial bulbs or annuals. Try sunflowers (*Helianthus* sp.) or *Nicotiana* sp. for bulk in tall shrub areas during the first few years.

Shrub planning, left
Draw your shrub planting area to scale and plan a planting scheme by plotting the mature size of shrubs as circles. The grouping of shrubs here depends on the siting of the central small tree. Large, medium-sized, and small shrubs have been added, bearing in mind the positions of both evergreen and deciduous subjects.

Cotoneaster franchetii sternianus (tall shrub)

Rosa moyesii 'Geranium' (medium-sized shrub)

1m (3¼ ft)

1.5m (5 ft)

2m (6½ ft)

Hebe pinguifolia 'Pagei' (small shrub)

Hydrangea 'Hortensis' (medium-sized shrub)

Buddleia davidii 'Empire Blue' (tall shrub)

PLANTING DISTANCE GUIDE

Tall shrubs
Plant 2 m (6½ ft) apart
Buddleia
Cotoneaster
Philadelphus
Viburnum
Medium-sized shrubs
Plant 1.5m (5 ft) apart
Berberis
Cytisus
Hydrangea 'Hortensis'
Viburnum davidii
Small shrubs
Plant 1m (3¼ ft) apart
Rosmarinus officinalis
Skimmia japonica
Senecio laxifolius
Hebe pinguifolia 'Pagei'

Pyracantha. Next look at bamboos (*Arundinaria* sp.), privets (*Ligustrum* sp.), laurels (especially *Prunus laurocerasus* and *P. lusitanica*), *Berberis, Mahonia, Elaeagnus, Escallonia,* and *Griselinia* sp., yew (*Taxus* sp.), box (*Buxus* sp.), and bay (*Laurus nobilis*). Find out which suit your soil, location, and climate. Camellias can be included in a sheltered town garden. Rhododendrons need an acid soil and are slow growing. They can be magnificent in flower, but dull out of flower. Select hardy species for gardens exposed to wind or sea spray.

Deciduous shrubs

Amongst and in front of this evergreen background come the large deciduous shrubs, which will generally be faster growing but offer little or no winter protection. Consider azaleas for late spring scent and flower, blackthorn (*Prunus spinosa*) for a wild effect, or grey-leaved sea buckthorn (*Hippophäe rhamnoides*). Buddleia and Spanish broom (*Spartium junceum*) are quick growing, good flowering, but short-lived shrubs, ideal for interplanting with slower evergreens and then rooting out in five years' time. Look at *Chaenomeles* sp. for early season and autumnal interest and *Cornus* sp. for foliage, stem colour, or flowers. The flowering currants (*Ribes* sp.) are useful shrubs if you can stand their smell. After early-flowering forsythia comes philadelphus, with

Bold grouping
*Careful thought has been given to leaf shape in this bold composition, above. Although the foreground hosta (*Hosta sieboldiana 'Royal Standard'*) has distinctive form itself, it is made more dramatic by the background of* Phormium tenax *and* Lonicera nitida *'Baggesen's Gold'.*

PLANTING SHRUBS

Ideally shrubs should be planted in their dormant period. Container-grown shrubs can be transplanted at other times if care is taken not to disturb the root ball. Autumn, or spring for less hardy subjects, is still the best time for planting when you are working on a large scale and planting out whole beds of shrubs.

Dig a hole large enough to accommodate the bare roots or the root ball. Thoroughly turn the soil and work in some compost. Trim any damaged roots. Spread the roots of a bare-rooted shrub but leave the root ball of a container-grown shrub, place in the hole, backfill with soil, and firm down with your heel.

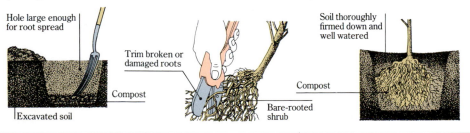

Hole large enough for root spread

Excavated soil

Compost

Trim broken or damaged roots

Compost

Bare-rooted shrub

Soil thoroughly firmed down and well watered

its delicious, evocative scent. The larger and more rampant forms of shrub rose make excellent background material. Look at the deciduous viburnums and lilacs (*Syringa* sp.).

The larger summer-flowering shrubs, such as species of the genera *Hebe* and *Cistus*, can be more spectacular and warrant a prominent site. Shrubs can be spot planted – on their own, perhaps in gravel or grass – or more usually planted in a prepared bed as part of the garden ground pattern.

Feature shrubs

The plants recommended so far have been for their serviceability and bulk. Against this mass go the star decorative items, which will maintain sculptural and colour interest throughout the year. These might be called architectural shrubs.

Start with plants that would become trees if left to their own devices. *Aralia elata* and *Eucalyptus gunnii* are examples. Spiky cordylines will articulate your border, although their heads need tying up through cold winters. *Rhus typhina* is a good choice, particularly for its lovely skeletal shape in winter. *Fatsia japonica* and *Fatshedera lizei* provide handsome evergreen foliage, while *Magnolia grandiflora* bears magnificent spring flowers, once established. The fig (*Ficus carica*) grows well against a wall, but it is not evergreen.

Shrubs with statuesque qualities include tree peonies, viburnums, including *Viburnum rhytidophyllum*. Coming down in size, use handsome yuccas grouped together in your composition, and New Zealand flax (*Phormium* sp.) in sites where the wind is not too strong. Consider the small *Viburnum davidii, Skimmia* sp., and *Choisya ternata*.

Between these architectural species, start to blend and contrast other decorative shrubs in simple groupings. Keep the interest dispersed throughout the season. Work towards a positive arrangement rather than a jumble of plants, using two to four individual plants from the larger scale species and eight or nine from the smaller.

Herbs have summer-flowering value and some, like the little herb *Ruta* sp., have the added attraction of being evergreen or evergrey. Hydrangeas, too, give good summer colour. The lacecaps have more subtle flower colour than the more blatant blue or pink, mop-headed *Hydrangea* 'Hortensis'. Consider also tree lupins, potentilla cultivars, and the *Romneya coulteri* white Californian tree poppy, which is exquisite but difficult to establish. And of course the rose, particularly old-fashioned smaller roses. Some floribunda roses mix well with decorative shrubs too, perhaps with lavender and sage for a charming effect and delicious scents on a warm evening.

Graded shrub border
Mound-forming shrubs are graded in a pleasing arrangement in this border, right. Planting includes Hypericum *sp., bushes of lavender* (Lavandula *sp.), with* Stachys lanata *and* Senecio laxifolius *behind.*

CHOOSING SHRUBS

For a more comprehensive selection, see p. 215.

Eucalyptus gunnii
CIDER GUM
If left unchecked, *Eucalyptus gunnii* will grow into a tree. Pruning back each autumn ensures beautiful, fine grey leaves that make a good foil to many colours. Full sun, fertile, well-drained soil. Shelter from strong winds. Maximum height 20m (70 ft), spread to 9m (27 ft).

Fatsia japonica 'Variegata'
JAPANESE ARALIA
Well known to urban gardeners for its handsome, evergreen, fig-like leaves, *Fatsia japonica* has globular, cream flowers on stalks in October. Tolerates sun or shade and requires fertile, well-drained soil. Shelter from strong winds. Height 2.8m (9 ft), spread 3m (10 ft).

Forsythia suspensa
FORSYTHIA
Some forms of forsythia have a strong yellow flower and an ugly upright stance. The lemon-flowered *F. suspensa atrocaulis* is a much more graceful shrub with slender shoots. Flowers on bare branches in early spring. Prefers full sun and fertile, well-drained soil. Height and spread 2m (6½ ft).

Garrya elliptica
SILK-TASSEL BUSH
The beautiful grey-green catkins of *G. elliptica* bring winter and early spring colour and interest to the garden. This evergreen shrub has leathery, dark green leaves, which provide a good backdrop to foreground colour. Tolerates any poor soil and needs a sunny, sheltered site. Height and spread 4m (12 ft).

Paeonia delavayi
TREE PEONY
Tree peonies have a wonderful statuesque quality, with ravishing flowers in spring. They take a while to establish but are well worth it. *P. delavayi* has rich, dark red flowers in late spring. Sun or light shade, rich, well-drained soil. Height to 2m (6½ ft), spread to 1.2m (4 ft).

Viburnum opulus 'Compactum'
GUELDER ROSE
A good background shrub for a mixed border, *V. opulus* is vigorous, bushy, and deciduous. It bears white flowers in summer, large bunches of red fruits in autumn. It needs sun and fertile, well-drained soil. *V. o.* 'Compactum' is a small variety. Height and spread 1.5m (5 ft).

Perennials

Perennials are the group of plants whose flowers give permanent summer colour. Few are evergreen but most are fairly easy to grow. There are types of perennial suitable for every location and condition. You may find clues to their needs in the climate and soil types of their country of origin. Many of the grey-foliaged perennials, for example, grew first in New Zealand, while many of the plants with brilliantly coloured daisy-type flowers came from South Africa. Perennials indigenous to northern Europe tend to have flowers of softer hue, even though *en masse* they will provide a vivid spectacle.

The difference between a pure herbaceous border and a mixed one is that a mixed border includes shrubs as well as perennials, which contribute interest in the months when the perennials are dormant, and physically support the arrangement. A mixed border is easier to maintain, because much freestanding, perennial material needs staking to support it throughout the summer months. This may be because we provide them with over-rich soil. Many of the parents of our hybrid garden subjects survive in the most arid conditions, for example in the high desert areas of Iran.

When you are choosing perennials, look at size and shape first and then colour. The flowers after all may last no longer than a week, but the foliage will be there for a whole season. Peonies, for instance, are in perfect bloom for only a few days – conditions rarely allow their delicate flowers to survive. Site peonies in front of a bold and later-flowering plant to make a virtue of their foliage.

The range of architectural perennials includes euphorbias for year-round interest and different species of hellebore. Grey verbascum, with its towering lemon spikes, enhances any border, as do the huge leaves of the globe artichoke (*Cynara scolymus*).

The colours of summer flowers are bewildering in their variety, but one way of mastering this abundance is to plan your border and make your selection in a particular colour range. Alternatively, stick to grasses in one area and plants with daisy flowers in another. Try to avoid too many varieties in one bed.

Plant in bold clumps and drift one mass into another. If you are buying from a garden centre, you will often find that one good young plant can be separated into two or three. While the group will be thin in its first year, perennials grow rapidly.

Once established, perennials, and particularly grasses, will need to be divided almost every year. Perennials grow out from the centre and eventually leave a hole in the middle of the plant. It may be worth labelling the plants as they die down in the autumn and drawing a plan of what is where, so that you can recognize them when dividing them in the spring.

REJUVENATING PERENNIALS

Perennials need a certain amount of maintenance. If left to grow untended for many seasons, they become large and untidy and their quality of growth becomes poorer and poorer, until eventually they die. Rejuvenate perennials by dividing them after flowering, using a spade for tuberous perennials and two forks for fibrous ones as illustrated.

Step 1
Use forks to divide fibrous-rooted perennials.

Step 2
Replant the two new plants for healthy growth.

PLANTING DISTANCES FOR PERENNIALS

It is impossible to be precise about planting distances for perennials. Some such as globe artichokes (*Cynara scolymus*) grow to about 1m (3¼ ft) across, while others hardly spread at all. As a general guideline to how many of each plant you need in a border, however, calculate five to every square metre/yard. Make your selection by shape as well as colour. In the bed shown here tall blue lupins are grouped with the blue heads of *Erigeron* sp. in front.

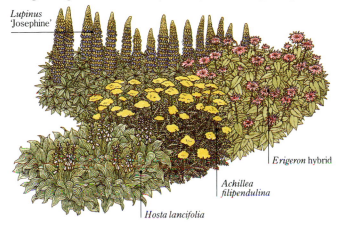

Lupinus 'Josephine'

Erigeron hybrid

Achillea filipendulina

Hosta lancifolia

A perennial scheme
Always plant perennials in bold masses, allowing for a drift and flow effect as one plant comes into full bloom and then recedes. This scheme, left, avoids the danger of jumbling too many species together, and limits itself to just four different plants. Perennials spread at varied rates and many need thinning after flowering. As a general rule, plant five plants to every square metre/yard.

CHOOSING PERENNIALS

For a more comprehensive selection, see p. 218.

Euphorbia characias wulfenii
SPURGE
Euphorbias are very useful for their architectural qualities and greenish-yellow flowering heads. *E. wulfenii* is a biennial, producing clustered grey-green leaves one year and spikes of yellow-green blooms the following spring. Sun or partial shade, well-drained soil. Height and spread to 1m (3 ft).

Helleborus orientalis
LENTEN ROSE
A fascinating family of winter to early spring-flowering plants with attractive foliage. *H. orientalis* has white-pink-purple flowers from November to March (white form shown here). *H. corsicus* has delicate, pale green flowers in February. Semi-shade, well-drained soil. Height and spread 45cm (18 in).

Phlox maculata
PHLOX
Broad panicles of bright flowers are produced all summer. Use plenty of white forms to cool other bright colours of high summer. *P. maculata* has pointed leaves and fragrant, lilac flowers. Sun or semi-shade. Prefers fertile, moist, well-drained soil. Height 1m (3ft), spread 45cm (18 in).

Bulbs

Bulbs look best if they are planted naturally, scattered in drifts in grass, or incorporated with mixed planting, where their dying leaves will be less obvious. Look at their natural habitat, how they grow there, and at their shape. Some bulbs such as hyacinths and *Galtonia* sp. have a formality that needs to be offset by other plants, while others such as *Narcissus* sp. and snowdrops are never successful within a border and need to be planted in a more natural way.

The annual bulb cycle

Winter and spring-flowering bulbs dominate planting areas during their flowering season, when they herald the end of winter. In the British Isles, for example, the winter aconite (*Eranthis hyemalis*) and snowdrop appear as early as December. Crocuses follow, then early narcissus such as the cultivar 'February Gold'. Anemones begin to show soon afterwards and are followed by other daffodils, *Chionodoxa luciliae* and grape hyacinths (*Muscari* sp.). Hyacinths and tulips do well in tubs and formal beds. In early summer come the bright coloured forms of Dutch iris, followed by the architectural forms of *Allium* sp. and *Ixia* sp. Majestic crown imperials

(*Fritillaria imperialis*) are also magnificent. In high summer there are the white hyacinths (*Galtonia candicans*), all the lilies, and the simple butterfly gladioli. Forms of autumn crocus then brighten the dying garden and continue throughout winter, and the cycle begins again.

Bulbs in a country setting

While flowers from bulbs provide the predominant colours in the cultivated spring garden, in the natural country garden they should simply complement native species. Narcissus, for example, combines well with dandelions (*Taraxacum officinale*).

Unfortunately, hybridization has led to the development of showy plant forms that bear little resemblance to their natural parents. The natural colours of the spring garden are quite subtle – the new greens of tree and grass foliage, for example – and it is all too easy to allow strident, cultivated colours to overpower them. Strong pink, for example, is not a spring colour in the wild, where lemon and yellow predominate. Strong blues are usually diffused in a mass of greenery. In a rural garden, plant strongly coloured bulbs near to the house and terrace, where they will be seen against buildings and hard surfacing or gravel, rather than in the wilder zones among the subtle greens of Nature.

SCATTER PLANTING WITH BULBS

Mentally outline the area you want to plant. Within that area scatter the bulbs casually and plant them where they fall. This will achieve a pleasantly natural effect when they later appear and flower. Plant bulbs to the correct depth either with a bulb planter or spade. Dig the spade in and lever up a section of turf. Place the bulb under the turf and firm it back down.

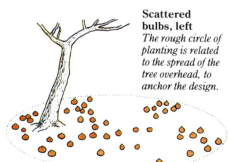

Scattered bulbs, left
The rough circle of planting is related to the spread of the tree overhead, to anchor the design.

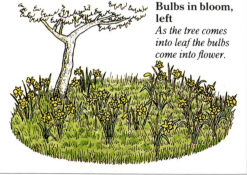

Bulbs in bloom, left
As the tree comes into leaf the bulbs come into flower.

PATTERNS IN GRASS WITH BULBS

Some bulbs, such as the later narcissi, will not have finished flowering when you need to begin mowing your lawn. Until the leaves have dried out, bulbs are making their growth for the next year, so you will need to allow a further six weeks after flowering before cutting the grass over them. This means you will have an area of longer, rougher grass containing, but also disguising, dying bulbous plant leaves within your lawn. By giving this area of uncut grass a definite pattern and making it part of the overall design of your garden, you can make a virtue of necessity.

Integrated design, right
Lawn, trees, and bulbs are integrated in a design of intersecting circles and curves, with the planted bulbs arranged in a distinctive yin/yang pattern.

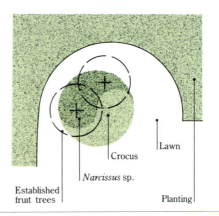

Lawn

Crocus

Narcissus sp.

Established
fruit trees

Planting

SPRING-FLOWERING PLANTING SCHEME

This birch grove makes a wonderful transition from garden to countryside beyond, and is the perfect location for naturalized, spring-flowering bulbs. The planting scheme is made up of bulb masses planted between silver birches on either side of a meandering gravel path.

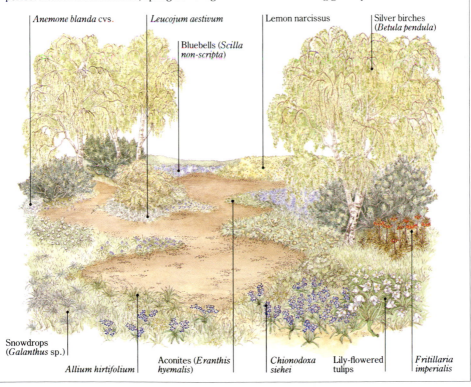

Anemone blanda cvs.

Leucojum aestivum

Bluebells (*Scilla non-scripta*)

Lemon narcissus

Silver birches (*Betula pendula*)

Snowdrops (*Galanthus* sp.)

Allium hirtifolium

Aconites (*Eranthis hyemalis*)

Chionodoxa siehei

Lily-flowered tulips

Fritillaria imperialis

CHOOSING BULBS

For a more comprehensive selection, see p. 217.

Anemone blanda
ANEMONE
Anemones are excellent for the semi-wild look. *A. blanda* does well in sun or light shade, and will increase and ramble in light woodland. It prefers humus-rich, well-drained soil. Height to 10cm (4 in), spread to 15cm (6 in). The true woodland anemone is *A. nemorosa*, which prefers a damp situation.

Chionodoxa siehei
GLORY-OF-THE-SNOW
Glory-of-the-snow has charming, clear blue flowers, so named because it blooms as the snow melts in the mountains of Turkey. It is good for rock gardens or naturalizing under shrubs. It likes the sun and good drainage and is an ideal gravel bulb. Height to 25cm (10 in), spread to 5cm (2 in).

Eranthis hyemalis
WINTER ACONITE
Charming, yellow-flowered perennial, among the first of the spring-flowering bulbs to appear. *Eranthis* has pretty, stalkless, cup-shaped flowers surrounded by leaf-like ruffs of bracts. It prefers partial shade and humus-rich, well-drained soil. Plant in drifts. Height and spread to 10cm (4 in).

Fritillaria meleagris
SNAKE'S HEAD FRITILLARY
Fritillaria meleagris has a gentle appeal. It can take two or three seasons to establish, but its beautiful, pendulous flowers are ample reward. It does best in semi-shaded conditions. It likes well-drained soil that dries out slightly in summer. Good for naturalizing. Height to 30cm (1 ft), spread 8cm (3 in).

Lilium regale
REGAL LILY
The graceful lily brings elegance to the summer border. It is also excellent for growing in containers. *L. regale* has large, white flowers in mid-summer and a fabulous scent. It needs sun and any well-drained soil. Produces up to 25 funnel-shaped flowers. Height to 2m (6 ft).

Scilla non-scripta
ENGLISH BLUEBELL
An English bluebell wood in May is a classic model for the natural gardener. The bluebell likes partial shade and plenty of moisture, and is ideal for naturalizing in grass beneath trees and shrubs. Prefers heavy soil. Plant bulbs in autumn. Height to 40cm (16 in), spread to 10cm (4 in).

Annuals

Annuals are plants that develop from seed and then flower, produce seeds, and die off in one year. Many of their flowers are extremely bright and provide most of the colourful splashes in the garden. The majority of annuals have a very short flowering period, so successive sowing of seeds or planting of seedlings is often necessary to maintain the display. There are some annuals that self-seed, such as marigolds (*Calendula*), tobacco plants (*Nicotiana*), and poppies (*Papaver*), which will appear at random year after year.

Annuals are hardy or half hardy. Hardy annuals, such as alyssum, antirrhinums, species of chrysanthemum, and dianthus, can be sown directly into the ground in spring or early summer. Half-hardy species, such as blue *Ageratum conyzoides*, Busy Lizzies (*Impatiens* sp.), lobelias, and stocks (*Matthiola* sp.), must be brought on in gentle heat, pricked out into a temporary bed, and later moved to their flowering position.

There are many uses for annuals in the garden, among them to thicken out young shrub planting schemes, for quick height, or to enliven the front of a mixed planting scheme. Annual colour can be used in bold splashes or intermingled for a cottage garden feel.

As soon as your annuals die down, be decisive and either cut them back to get another flowering if the season is young, or take them out and seed a quickly maturing alternative for a late summer show of colour.

USING WHITE AND CREAM ANNUALS

White flowers used entirely on their own will tend to have a cold feel but enriched with the green shades of herbaceous plant material they can look superb. While the justly famed white gardens of England rely on perennials for their effect, they are always supported by annual planting. Solid white planting in windowboxes over a building façade will look crisp, sharp, and sometimes spectacular. White can be mixed with other, bright flower colours to soften their effect. Cream should not be used as a substitute for white, but as a colour in its own right. It has a warmth and quality that white cannot match. Use cream to soften strong, hot colours, or with green or gold flowers or foliage. Cream also looks good alongside the vivid green of grass.

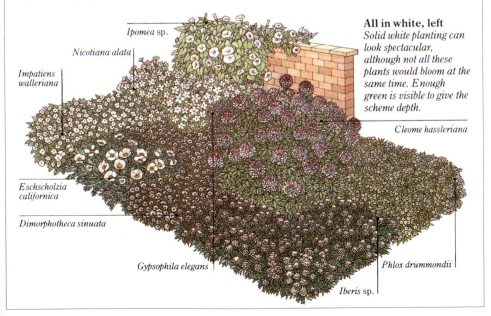

Ipomea sp.

Nicotiana alata

Impatiens walleriana

All in white, left
Solid white planting can look spectacular, although not all these plants would bloom at the same time. Enough green is visible to give the scheme depth.

Cleome hassleriana

Eschscholzia californica

Dimorphotheca sinuata

Gypsophila elegans

Phlox drummondii

Iberis sp.

USING YELLOW, ORANGE, AND RED ANNUALS

Annual flower colour in summer in the northern hemisphere is predominantly yellow, orange, and red, colours that can be harsh and strident. Used sensitively, however, warm sun colours can be extremely effective, particularly when muted by lighter colours, such as lemon, alongside.

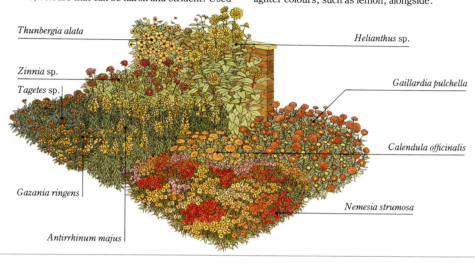

Thunbergia alata

Helianthus sp.

Zinnia sp.

Gaillardia pulchella

Tagetes sp.

Calendula officinalis

Gazania ringens

Nemesia strumosa

Antirrhinum majus

CHOOSING ANNUALS

For a more comprehensive selection, see p. 219.

Eschscholzia caespitosa
POPPY
E. caespitosa, with its bright, poppy-like flowers, is a good choice for rock gardens and gaps in paving. It grows fast and has delicate, yellow flowers in summer and early autumn. Regular deadheading ensures continued flowering. Grows well in poor soil. Full sun. Height and spread 15cm (6 in).

Lobularia maritima
SWEET ALYSSUM
Sweet alyssum, though actually a perennial, is often grown as an annual and is a popular garden plant. It has small leaves, a dense, mounded growth, and a profusion of flowers which last right through from early spring until autumn. Sun and well-drained soil. Height to 15cm (6 in), spread to 30 cm (1 ft).

Tropaeolum majus
NASTURTIUM
Trailing, sometimes climbing, hardy annual, with bright orange, tubular flowers. Its pretty, round leaves are edible in salads. Prefers sun and poor soil. *T. majus* offers a variety of shades of yellow and red. *T.m.* 'Alaska' shown here has variegated leaves. Height and spread 30cm (1 ft).

Herbs

Herbs may be shrubby, perennial, or annual, and can be grown in a herb garden or as decorative additions to a mixed planting. Some herbs, such as bay (*Laurus nobilis*), myrtle (*Myrtus communis*), and witch hazel (*Hamamelis* sp.), grow into good-sized trees. For a small area in an open and sunny position, herbs are ideal. They are not fussy about soil quality, they have decorative foliage, and they are fragrant. Those that are not hardy, such as sweet basil (*Ocimum basilicum*) and sunflowers (*Helianthus annuus*), can be planted annually and grown as summer additions.

Perhaps more important than the decorative value of herbs are their culinary and medicinal properties. Their place in cooking is becoming increasingly appreciated in these times of tasteless packaged food. In the East and increasingly in the West, spices are used for their medicinal properties – in homeopathy and aromatherapy. Herbs are used in tisanes for a variety of different purposes, among them inducing sleep, tranquillizing, or painkilling. They have other domestic uses – their dried leaves are an essential ingredient of pot pourri, their essential oils are extracted to produce scents and body oils.

Choosing plants

Many of the plants we commonly include in mixed planting are in fact herbs. For example, *Gaultheria procumbens*, St. John's wort (*Hypericum perforatum*), *Rosa damascena*, *Rosa gallica*, hollyhock (*Alcea rosea*), sunflower (*Helianthus annuus*), juniper (*Juniperus communis*), *Cytisus scoparius*, mullein (*Verbascum thapsus*), and houseleek (*Sempervivum tectorum*).

Most herbs prefer an open, sunny position, with moderately good, neutral soil. Mint (*Mentha* sp.), chives (*Allium schoenoprasum*), parsley (*Petroselinum crispum*), and wild strawberry (*Fragaria vesca*), however, will grow perfectly well in partial shade. In lighter, dappled shade you can grow angelica, celery (*Apium graveolens dulce*), chervil (*Anthriscus cerefolium*), *Aloe vera*, and sweet rocket (*Hesperis matronalis*).

HERB CARE AND MAINTENANCE

Your herb garden will need regular attention. Maintenance includes cutting back annual growth and dead-heading, and generally shaping bushes in autumn. Sage, for example, becomes very straggly after two or three years and will need to be cut back to the main stem or dug up and replaced with new stock. Some clumping herbs, such as sorrel, will need to be lifted and divided or they will swamp the area. Mints planted in open ground need dramatic restraint, or their rampant underground and aerial rooting systems will carry the plant to all corners of the garden.

Many herbs, especially those like lovage with umbelliferous flowers, seed extensively and must be pulled out each year. If the ripe seeds fall into the soil and germinate, they grow through other species and can be difficult to remove.

Collecting seeds

If you wish to collect herb seeds, remove the entire plant with its seed heads before they have dried out, tie the heads in bundles and hang upside-down from a stake over a prepared bed into which the seeds will drop. This method of collecting seeds is especially successful with chervil, angelica, fennel, and dill.

Lifting and dividing

Remove annual herbs such as dill and sweet basil at the end of the season. They will not reappear the following year and you will need the space for new planting. Chives have a habit of hosting grass roots, so lift the clumps when necessary, divide them, remove any entwined foreign roots, and replant.

The leaves of some herbs, such as basil and marjoram, may be harvested for immediate use. Remove the centre tip to promote bushy side growth. With herbs such as parsley and lovage, take the outside leaves and their stalks.

Drying and storing

Other herbs need to be dried and stored after harvesting. Take only as much as you can manage to dry at one time – delay after cutting reduces the strength of their essential oils.

Herb bed designs

Many books on herbs will suggest growing herbs within strict, formalized patterns edged with box, as was the practice in medieval times. Anyone who has grown herbs, however, will realize how invasive they can be, and it seems a misplaced effort to be constantly restraining them to conform to a rigid design. The glory of a herb garden is its profusion, alive with the hum of bees on a hot summer day. Build up your herb planting plan along the lines of your general garden planting. Consider first whether herbs are deciduous or evergreen; next find out their height, foliage colour, and form of growth.

Colour in herb planting

Foliage colour will dominate a herb planting. Consider the contrasting colours that you can work with. There are the golds of varieties of

---

A HERBAL PLANTING SCHEME

This herbal planting scheme can either be planted on its own or merged into general garden planting. On a south-facing site for full sun, it might double up as a terrace. Three small beds, 2–3m (6½–10 ft) square, make up the pattern. One of the beds is raised 45cm (18 in) within a brick surround to add height to the design.

The overall pattern is dominated by woody herbs. The largest bed, on the lower level of the garden, has stepping stones within it to match the main paving. These support a pot with a bold, simple form that contrasts with the tall lovage (*Levisticum officinale*) behind, and the feathery leaves of fennel (*Foeniculum vulgare*).

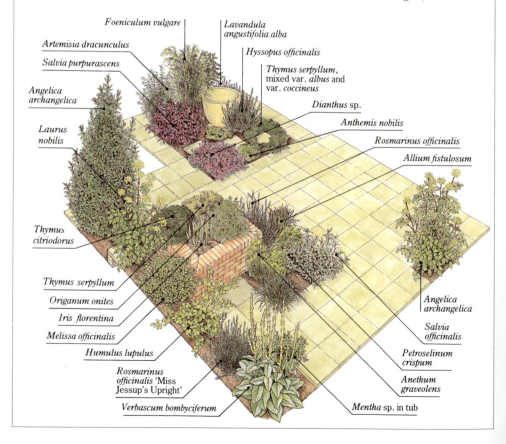

- Foeniculum vulgare
- Artemisia dracunculus
- Salvia purpurascens
- Angelica archangelica
- Laurus nobilis
- Thymus citriodorus
- Thymus serpyllum
- Origanum onites
- Iris florentina
- Melissa officinalis
- Humulus lupulus
- Rosmarinus officinalis 'Miss Jessup's Upright'
- Verbascum bombyciferum
- Lavandula angustifolia alba
- Hyssopus officinalis
- Thymus serpyllum, mixed var. *albus* and var. *coccineus*
- Dianthus sp.
- Anthemis nobilis
- Rosmarinus officinalis
- Allium fistulosum
- Angelica archangelica
- Salvia officinalis
- Petroselinum crispum
- Anethum graveolens
- Mentha sp. in tub

marjoram, feverfew, thyme, and sage, and then the much larger range of silver and grey-leaved plants, the artemisias, lavenders, and mints, and also sage, rue, and santolina. The final element of the palette will be tones of purple, choosing from bronze fennel, purple sage, black peppermint, and purple basil.

Incorporating features

Eye-catching features can be useful in a herb garden. Changes of level, raised beds, and steps will all help to set herbs, many of which are low growing, at different heights. Attractive containers, simple sculpture, or even, if you are a bee-keeper, a live bee-hive. You will need hard-surfaced access to your herbs as they need regular clipping, dividing, and picking. This surfacing can of course be interspersed or bordered with low-growing thymes or chamomile to scent your way. Alternatively devote a narrow border to herbs giving you access along its length. For very

invasive herbs such as mints (*Mentha* sp.), horse radish (*Armoracia rusticana*), and comfrey (*Symphytum officinale*), make a separate collection in individual tubs. Their foliage and flower colour are well worthwhile.

Herbs for pest control

Herbs growing as companion plants to other food crops may well have a beneficial effect while they are growing. One theory suggests that certain herbal scents, root excretions, and other plant exhalations will deter insect pests. It is certainly true that herbs themselves are seldom attacked by them. Nasturtiums (*Tropaeolum majus*), for instance, are said to deter aphids, while tansy (*Tanacetum vulgare*) and southernwood (*Artemisia abrotanum*) ward off fruit moth, and garlic and other alliums protect most garden plants from a variety of pests. Wormwood (*Artemisia absinthium*) and rue (*Ruta graveolens*) are said to discourage animal pests such as slugs and moles.

CHOOSING HERBS

For a more comprehensive selection, see p. 220.

Myrrhis odorata
SWEET CICELY
The attractive fern-like leaves of sweet cicely are among the first to appear in spring and the last to depart in autumn. The stems can be chopped up and stewed with fruit as a sugar substitute, and the seeds taste of liquorice. Prefers shade, tolerates sun. Humus-rich soil. Height to 1m (3 ft).

Ocimum basilicum
'Purpurascens'
SWEET BASIL
The dark opal form of sweet basil is best grown in a separate pot. It likes a very hot position, is annual, and can be kept quite dry. Protect from wind, frost, and scorching sun. Prefers moist, well-drained soil. Its leaves have a good medium flavour. Height to 45cm (18 in).

Salvia officinalis
SAGE
Sage likes full sun and an alkaline and well-drained soil. It tends to be over-used with fatty foods, but is excellent with sausage meat and as a flavouring for cheeses. An infusion makes a good gargle for a sore throat. *S.o.* 'Icterina' has pretty, gold, variegated leaves. Height to 75cm (2½ ft).

Vegetables

Vegetable gardens are often hidden from the house because they are not considered decorative. In fact, well-organized rows of healthy, green plants can make a fine display. If there is a sunny open site close to the kitchen door, the vegetable patch is more conveniently sited there, rather than at the end of a long tramp across the garden.

For those with small gardens, a rented allotment at the edge of town may be the next best thing. In the United Kingdom there is a move towards self-sufficiency, and allotments are now associated with growing pure food as well as saving money. On the continent of Europe, an allotment has never been a place just to produce food crops. Individual plots usually incorporate a small, well-designed building. In parts of Germany, for example, the allotment is a private garden and the tool shed also acts as a weekend retreat in summer. The areas surrounding these "chalets" are usually given over to a combination of vegetables, flowers for cutting, and herbs. Such a combination has much to recommend it, being both useful and decorative.

Even a small garden can have a productive corner, perhaps for dwarf beans, tomatoes, and herbs. Or vegetables can be included in general mixed plantings of perennials and shrubs. Decorative vegetables include maize, ornamental cabbages for wonderful winter colour and form, and *Rubus* (blackberry).

Vegetables with strong form and colour, below
Both flower colour and plant shape contribute to this pleasing and highly productive plot.

The full-scale vegetable garden

Consider what is involved before embarking on a full-scale vegetable garden, however. If you are aiming at self-sufficiency, the planting, care, and harvesting of food crops will dominate the time you spend outside.

Providing enough vegetables for a whole family throughout the year needs more land than most gardeners have. The labour is heavy, considerable time is needed to keep the garden fully productive and in good order, and to be truly organic you will need space and time to maintain a compost cycle. The vegetables you produce will therefore not be cheap.

Home-grown vegetables, however, are more wholesome than shop-bought ones, especially when eaten straight from the ground. And a deep freeze will help you to deal with gluts and regulate your supply throughout the year. Other vegetables, such as potatoes, onions, and apples, can be dry-stored.

The location of the garden will determine what plants grow best. The balmier the climate, the greater the yield. Production should increase over the years as you gain expertise, learn from your mistakes, and enrich the ground. Always look at what other gardeners in your area are achieving and learn from their experience, as well as carrying out your own experiments with new crops.

Planning the garden

Ensure that the shape of your proposed vegetable garden is strong and simple. It must be able to retain its character despite the constant change from bare soil to mature crop that occurs as you prepare the soil, grow the crop, and harvest it. The traditional growing rows for crops must be served by hard paths throughout the year, and these practicalities will determine the design of the garden to a large extent. The garden should also be divided

---

CROP ROTATION

The object of rotating your vegetables is both to deter soil-borne pests and to maintain a balance of nutrients in the soil. The two main enemies are clubroot disease in the cabbage family and eel worm in potatoes, for these will rapidly infest the soil if the *Brassica* crops and potatoes are planted in the same position in consecutive years. You must always ensure that when a crop is lifted, the soil is suitable for the next growth. Dividing your garden into four sections is ideal. Here Plot A is planted with semi-permanent asparagus and sea kale, and a fruit cage might be introduced as well. Plot B contains leguminous vegetables and salad crops; Plot C contains *Brassica* crops, while Plot D contains root crops.

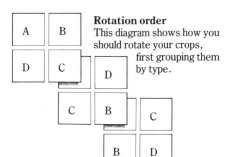

Rotation order
This diagram shows how you should rotate your crops, first grouping them by type.

Plot A
Soft fruit, asparagus, sea kale, and herbs

Plot B
Peas, beans, onions, shallots, leeks, lettuce, celery, and radish

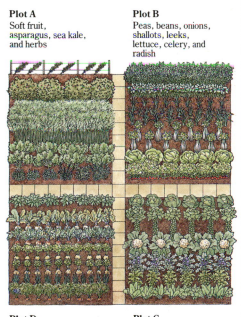

Plot D
Potatoes, turnips, swedes, parsnips, salsify, celeriac, and carrots

Plot C
Cabbages, Brussels sprouts, cauliflowers, kale, broccoli, and spinach

into portions, so that different types of vegetable can be grown in different areas each year in rotation, as shown in the crop rotation scheme illustrated on p. 191.

The vegetable area may be encompassed, and perhaps sub-divided, by some form of low surround. Edging box, a traditional garden surround, will harbour slugs that feed on *Brassica* leaves, so it is better to use herbs such as sage or rosemary for hedging. Some herbs have the beneficial side-effect of discouraging particular pests (see p. 189).

Traditional crop rotation

Traditionally the vegetable garden was walled to keep out pests, and divided into four sections by wide paths, bordered with flowers for cutting, or with herbs or trained fruit trees, while other trained fruit trees lined the walls. There would be an adjacent potting shed, a greenhouse, some frames, places for storing sand and mixed soil, both for propagation and making compost. One of the four working sections contained soft fruit, an asparagus bed, or sea kale (*Beta vulgaris*), and possibly herbs,

DECORATIVE VEGETABLE GARDEN DESIGN

These two decorative borders are shown in their early autumn prime. The areas will certainly look bleak in spring but no amount of planning and selection can make a vegetable arrangement look well throughout the whole year. Some preliminary thought, however, will reduce dull periods to a minimum.

An arrangement such as this is quite possible in a small garden, as long as it is open and sunny in aspect and you don't require too many vegetables. Some of the more usual herbs are included, although angelica is among them solely for its appearance. The borders of the central gravel path are of brick but could equally well be of grass.

Globe artichoke (*Cynara scolymus*)

Ruby chard

Hyssop (*Hyssopus officinalis*)

Beetroot (*Beta vulgaris conditiva*)

Fennel (*Foeniculum vulgare*)

Angelica archangelica

Runner beans (*Phaseolus coccineus*)

Sorrel (*Rumex acetosa*)

Ornamental kale

Parsley (*Petroselinum crispum*)

for its crops were semi-permanent. The other three cultivated areas housed crops that were rotated annually, both to deter soil-borne pests and to maintain a balance of nutrients in different parts of the garden.

The modern version

The way this traditional rotation works today is as follows. Planted in the first bed are leguminous crops (peas and beans) with onions, shallots, leeks, lettuce, celery, and radish, which all need well-dug soil and plenty of manure or organic compost incorporated. In the next quarter are mainly *Brassica* plants (cabbage, Brussels sprouts, cauliflower, kale, spinach, and broccoli) which might need an inorganic feed to replace used minerals and possibly an application of lime if the ground is too acid. The third quarter, in which the root crops are grown (potatoes, turnips, swedes, parsnips, salsify, celeriac, and carrots) might need an initial application of inorganic fertilizer. Once the rotation is established, however, inorganic feed will not be necessary as the

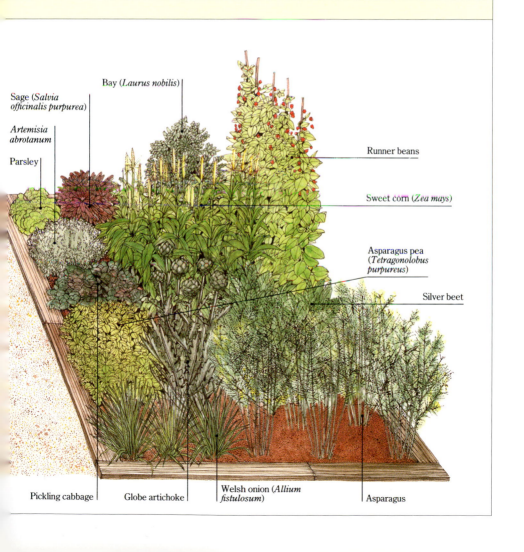

Bay (*Laurus nobilis*)

Sage (*Salvia officinalis purpurea*)

Artemisia abrotanum

Parsley

Runner beans

Sweet corn (*Zea mays*)

Asparagus pea (*Tetragonolobus purpureus*)

Silver beet

Pickling cabbage

Globe artichoke

Welsh onion (*Allium fistulosum*)

Asparagus

plots will remain in good health from the manure or organic compost they receive every third year.

This traditional system of rotating the crops of the kitchen garden is as applicable now as it was in the old walled vegetable gardens that existed until fifty years ago, though few of us can practise the system on the large scale of a traditional fruit and vegetable garden.

The smaller vegetable plot

Scale the system down and adapt it to your available space, to more intensive ways of inter-cropping vegetables. Start by selecting varieties of vegetable that are of small growth, though not necessarily small cropping, which can be planted closer within the individual row. Between rows of slower, taller growing vegetables, plant fast-growing "catch" crops. You will need to judge the different times of

planting, rates of growth, and size at maturity of your main crop vegetables, and then put in a fast-maturing crop before all the ground and light are used up. Fast-growing vegetables include radish, which reaches maturity within six weeks, kohlrabi and beetroot, which grow in eight weeks, and Chinese cabbage and carrots, which take nine or ten weeks. These are also useful as succession crops to exploit fully the well-prepared ground once the main crop for the year has been harvested. Succession crops are not the same as successional sowings, which are sowings of the same vegetable at intervals to avoid a glut.

During the growing season be ready to fill any ground vacated by a previous crop. If you do not, Nature will. It is usually wise to abandon a row of seedlings where germination has been poor in a small area and start again with a freshly planted crop.

CHOOSING VEGETABLES

If you have space for a vegetable garden, and the time and enthusiasm to cultivate it, give careful thought to your choice of crops and the growing area each will need.

Make a series of plans showing the garden at different times of the year, taking account of sowing times and how long each crop needs to be in the ground before harvesting.

	Sowing time	Months to harvest		Sowing time	Months to harvest
CHENOPODIACEAE			Savoy cabbage (plant June)	Apr, May	From 6
Beetroot	Mar–Jun	2			
Spinach	Mar–Jul	From 2½	Brussels sprouts (plant May, June)	Mar, Apr	6
COMPOSITAE					
Lettuce	Mar–Jul	2	Kale (plant June, July)	Apr, May	8
CRUCIFERAE					
Cabbage (plant 2 months after sowing)	Mar–Jul	4½	Broccoli (Sprouting) (plant May, June)	Apr, May	4

CHOOSING VEGETABLES

	Sowing time	Months to harvest		Sowing time	Months to harvest
Cauliflower (plant June, July)	Apr	From 11	**LILIACEAE**		
			Onion (from seed)	Mar–Apr	6½
Swede	May, Jun	From 7½	Onion (from sets)	Plant Mar, Apr	5½
Turnip	Feb–Jul	5	Shallot	Plant Feb–Mar	6
Radish	Mar–Aug	1½	Leek	Jan–Mar	10
GRAMINEAE			**SOLANACEAE**		
Sweet corn (plant May, June)	Apr–May under glass	3	Potato	Plant late Feb–May	From 3½
LEGUMINOSAE			Tomato (plant May, June)	Feb–Mar under glass	5
Broad beans	Feb–Apr Jul	3½	**UMBELLIFERAE**		
French beans	Apr–Jun	From 3	Carrot	Mar–Jul	From 5½
Runner beans	May–Jun	From 4	Parsnip	Feb–Apr	From 7½
Peas	Mar, Jun	From 3½	Celery (plant June)	Feb–Apr under glass	From 7

CHAPTER FIVE

PLANT SELECTION GUIDE

The lists in this section offer a wide choice
of plants to consider within each of the
categories covered in Chapter four,
Plants and planting, pp. 136–195. Some
plants are listed under more than one
category. The Latin name is given for
each plant, together with the common
name where there is one, bearing in mind
that usage of common names varies from
one region to another. Details of soil
preference and sun/shade tolerance are
given, together with the dominant
characteristic of the plant – for example,
whether it is grown for its fragrant flowers
or its autumn foliage colour. The height
and spread of the mature plant are noted,
except where a whole genus is referred
to, and heights vary from one species to
another. Where a whole genus is referred
to, such as *Dianthus* (Carnation, Pink),
note that different species within that
genus may have varying characteristics –
for example, one species will be an
evergreen perennial, another will be a
deciduous shrub.

Charming spring border
*White, lily-flowered tulips look well in spring with
forget-me-nots* (Myosotis sp.), *emergent* Alchemilla
mollis, *cranesbill* (Geranium macrorrhizum), *and
the coarse foliage of* Crambe cordifolia.

Plants for colour

TREES AND SHRUBS FOR AUTUMN LEAF COLOUR

Acer palmatum
Japanese maple
Well-drained, acid soil, full sun or semi-shade, deciduous, height and spread 6m (20 ft).

Amelanchier lamarckii
Snowy mespilus
Damp, neutral to acid soil, full sun or semi-shade, deciduous, height 6m (20 ft), spread 3.5m (12 ft).

Cercidiphyllum japonicum
Any well-drained soil, full sun or semi-shade, deciduous, height 20m (70 ft), spread 15m (50 ft).

Koelreuteria paniculata
Pride of India
Well-drained, alkaline soil, full sun or semi-shade, deciduous, height and spread 10m (30 ft).

Prunus padus **Bird cherry**
Any well-drained soil, full sun or semi-shade, deciduous, height 15m (50 ft), spread 10m (30 ft).

Sorbus aucuparia **Rowan**
Any well-drained soil, full sun or semi-shade, deciduous, height 15m (50 ft), spread 8m (25 ft).

TREES AND SHRUBS FOR WINTER INTEREST

Camellia sasanqua
Prefers damp, acid soil, semi to full shade, evergreen, height 3m (10 ft), spread 1.5m (5 ft).

Chimonanthus praecox
Wintersweet
Well-drained, alkaline soil, full sun, slightly tender when young, deciduous, height 2.5m (8 ft), spread 3m (10 ft).

Cornus alba
Red-barked dogwood
Any soil, semi to full shade, deciduous, grown for stems, height and spread 3m (10 ft).

Corylus avellana **Hazel**
Any well-drained soil, sun or semi-shade, deciduous, grown for catkins, height and spread 5m (16½ ft).

Erica carnea **Winter heath**
Tolerates alkaline soil, full sun or semi-shade, evergreen, height to 30cm (1 ft), spread to 45cm (18 in).

Garrya elliptica
Silk-tassel bush
Any soil, full sun or semi-shade, evergreen, grown for catkins, height and spread 4m (12 ft).

Hamamelis japonica
Japanese witch hazel
Prefers acid soil, full sun or semi-shade, deciduous, height and spread 4m (12 ft).

Lonicera x *purpusii*
Any well-drained soil, full sun, semi-evergreen, height and spread 1.5m (5 ft).

Mahonia japonica
Any well-drained soil, full sun or semi-shade, evergreen, height 2m (6½ ft), spread 3m (10 ft).

Parrotia persica
Persian ironwood
Prefers alkaline soil, full sun or semi-shade, deciduous, height 8m (25 ft), spread 10m (30 ft).

Prunus subhirtella
'Autumnalis' **Spring cherry**
Any well-drained soil, full sun, deciduous, height and spread 8m (25 ft).

Sycopsis sinensis
Peaty soil, not too dry, full sun or semi-shade, evergreen, height 5m (15 ft), spread 4m (12 ft).

Viburnum farreri
Any soil, full sun to full shade, deciduous, height 3m (10 ft), spread 2m (6 ft).

Viburnum tinus
Laurustinus
Any soil, full sun to full shade, evergreen, height and spread 3m (10 ft).

COLOURFUL PERENNIALS

Blue flowers

Agapanthus africanus
African lily
Any well-drained soil, full sun, needs frost protection, height 1m (3 ft), spread 50cm (20 in).

Aster frikartii
Michaelmas daisy
Any well-drained soil, full sun, height 75cm (30 in), spread 45cm (18 in).

Brunnera macrophylla
Siberian bugloss
Any well-drained soil, accepts shade, height 45cm (18 in), spread 60cm (2 ft).

Campanula persicifolia
Bellflower
Prefers damp soil, full sun to full shade, height 1m (3 ft), spread 30cm (1 ft).

Echinops ritro
Globe thistle
Any soil, full sun, height 1.2m (4 ft), spread 75cm (2½ ft).

Geranium 'Johnson's Blue'
Cranesbill
Any soil, full sun to full shade, height 30cm (1 ft), spread 60cm (2 ft).

Iris pallida 'Aurea Variegata'
Dalmation Iris
Any soil, full sun to full shade, height to 1m (3 ft), spread indefinite.

Omphalodes cappadocica
Any well-drained soil, semi to full shade, height to 20cm (8 in), spread 25cm (10 in).

Green flowers

Alchemilla mollis
Lady's mantle
Prefers damp soil, accepts shade, height and spread 50cm (20 in).

Euphorbia characias **Spurge**
Any soil, full sun to full shade, height 1.2m (4 ft), spread 1m (3 ft).

Galtonia viridiflora
Any well-drained soil, full sun, height to 1.2m (4 ft), spread to 23cm (9 in).

Helleborus lividus corsicus
Corsican hellebore
Prefers damp soil, accepts shade, height and spread 45cm (18 in).

Zantedeschia aethiopica
'Green Goddess'
Arum lily
Prefers damp soil, full sun to full shade, height to 1m (3 ft), spread to 45cm (18 in).

Red flowers

Bergenia 'Evening Glow'
Elephant's ears
Any well-drained soil, accepts shade, height 23cm (9 in), spread 30cm (1 ft).

Helenium 'Moerheim Beauty'
Sneezewort
Any well-drained soil, full sun, height 1m (3 ft), spread 60cm (2 ft).

Hemerocallis fulva
Tawny daylily
Any soil, accepts shade, height 1m (3 ft), spread 75cm (2½ ft).

Papaver commutatum
Poppy
Any well-drained soil, full sun, height and spread 45cm (18 in).

Phlox paniculata 'Brigadier'
Prefers damp soil, accepts shade, height 1.2m (4 ft), spread 60cm (2 ft).

White flowers

Achillea ptarmica 'The Pearl'
Yarrow
Any well-drained soil, full sun, height and spread 75cm (2½ ft).

Agapanthus campanulatus
African lily
Any well-drained soil, full sun, height to 1.4m (2 ft), spread 50cm (20 in).

Bergenia 'Silver Light'
Elephant's ears
Any well-drained soil, accepts shade, height 30cm (1 ft), spread 50cm (20 in).

Chrysanthemum maximum
Any well-drained soil, full sun, height 1m (3 ft), spread 60cm (2 ft).

Dianthus 'White Ladies'
Pink
Any well-drained soil, full sun, height to 45cm (18 in), spread to 30cm (1 ft).

Helleborus niger
Christmas rose
Prefers damp soil, accepts shade, height and spread 30cm (1 ft).

Hosta plantaginea
Plantain lily
Prefers damp soil, accepts shade, height 60cm (2 ft), spread 1.2m (4 ft).

Yellow flowers

Achillea 'Moonshine'
Yarrow
Any well-drained soil, full sun, height 60cm (2 ft), spread 50cm (20 in).

Digitalis grandiflora
Foxglove
Any soil, full sun to full shade, height 75cm (30 in), spread 30cm (1 ft).

Euphorbia characias wulfenii
Spurge
Any soil, full sun to full shade, height 1m (3 ft), spread 80cm (32 in).

Lysimachia punctata
Garden loosestrife
Well-drained soil, full sun or semi-shade, height to 75cm (2½ ft), spread 60cm (2 ft).

Paeonia mlokosewitschii
Peony
Prefers damp soil, full sun to full shade, height and spread to 75cm (2½ ft).

Sisyrinchium striatum
Any well-drained soil, full sun, height to 60cm (2 ft), spread 30cm (1 ft).

Verbascum olympicum
Mullein
Well-drained soil, full sun, tolerates shade, height 2m (6 ft), spread 1m (3 ft).

Vertical climbers

CLINGERS AND TWINERS

Akebia quinata
Chocolate vine
Any soil, full sun or semi-shade, fast growing, semi-evergreen, grown for flowers, height to 10m (30 ft).

Aristolochia grandiflora
Swan flower
Any soil, full sun, evergreen,
grown for foliage and flowers,
height 7m (22 ft).

Campsis radicans
Trumpet vine
Any soil, full sun, deciduous,
fast growing, grown for
flowers, height to 12m (40 ft).

Hedera colchica **Persian ivy**
Any soil, semi or full shade,
evergreen, fast growing,
grown for foliage, height 10m
(30 ft), spread 5m (15 ft).

Humulus lupulus **Hop**
Any well-drained soil, full sun
or semi-shade, herbaceous,
fast growing, grown for foliage,
height to 6m (20 ft).

Hydrangea petiolaris
Any soil, full sun or semi-
shade, deciduous, grown for
flower heads, height to
15m (50 ft).

Jasminum officinale
Common white jasmine
Any soil, full sun, semi-
evergreen or deciduous, fast
growing, grown for foliage and
fragrant flowers, height to 12m
(40 ft).

Lonicera periclymenum
Common honeysuckle
Any well-drained soil, full sun
or semi-shade, deciduous,
grown for foliage and flowers,
height to 7m (22 ft).

Parthenocissus quinquefolia
Virginia creeper
Any soil, full sun or semi-
shade, deciduous, grown for
foliage, height 15m (50 ft).

Passiflora caerulea
Passion flower
Well-drained soil, full sun or
semi-shade, semi-evergreen,
fast growing, grown for
flowers, height 10m (30 ft).

Polygonum baldschuanicum
Russian vine
Prefers damp soil, any location,
deciduous, fast growing,
vigorous, height 12m (40 ft) or
more.

Solanum jasminoides
Jasmine nightshade
Well-drained or damp, alkaline
soil, full sun, semi-evergreen,
grown for flowers and
ornamental fruits, height to
6m (20 ft).

Wisteria
Any soil, full sun, deciduous,
fast growing, grown for
spectacular flowers, height to
9m (28 ft).

WALL SHRUBS

Abutilon x *suntense*
Well-drained, alkaline soil, full
sun, deciduous, fast growing,
grown for flowers and foliage,
height 5m (15 ft), spread
3m (10 ft).

Ceanothus thyrsiflorus
Well-drained, alkaline soil, full
sun, grown for flowers, height
and spread 6m (20 ft).

Chaenomeles speciosa
Flowering quince
Any well-drained soil, full sun
or semi-shade, deciduous,
grown for fragrant flowers and
showy fruits, height 2.5m
(8 ft), spread 5m (15 ft).

Eccremocarpus scaber
Glory vine
Any well-drained soil, full sun,
tender, grown for attractive
flowers, height to 3m (10 ft).

Garrya elliptica
Silk-tassel bush
Any soil, semi or full shade,
evergreen, grown for catkins in
winter and spring, height and
spread 4m (12 ft).

RAMBLERS

Clematis
Any well-drained soil, different
varieties for sun and shade,
grown for foliage and flowers,
many species.

Rosa **Rambler rose**
Any well-drained soil, full sun
or semi-shade, many species.

Ground cover plants (low-growing)

Ajuga reptans 'Atropurpurea'
Bugle
Any soil, full sun or semi-
shade, perennial, grown for
foliage and flowers, height
38cm (15 in), spread
60cm (2 ft).

Alchemilla alpina
Lady's mantle
Prefers damp soil, semi-
shade, perennial, grown for
greenish-yellow flowers,
height 15cm (6 in), spread
60cm (2 ft).

Aubrieta 'Gurgedyke'
Any well-drained soil, full sun,
evergreen perennial, grown
for spring flowers, height
10cm (4 in), spread
20cm (8 in).

Bergenia 'Evening Glow'
Elephant's ears
Any well-drained soil, semi to
full shade, evergreen
perennial, grown for foliage
and flowers, height 23cm
(9 in), spread 30cm (1 ft).

Epimedium alpinum
Barrenwort
Any well-drained soil, full sun
to full shade, evergreen
perennial, grown for flowers,
height 23cm (9 in), spread to
30cm (1 ft).

Erica **Heath**
Most species prefer well-drained, acid soil, full sun, evergreen, grown for flowers and spreading habit.

Festuca glauca **Blue fescue**
Any well-drained soil, full sun, evergreen perennial, grown for foliage, height and spread 10cm (4 in).

Geranium **Cranesbill**
Any soil, full sun or semi-shade, perennial, grown for foliage and flowers, many species.

Helianthemum nummularium **Rock rose**
Well-drained, alkaline soil, full sun, evergreen, grown for flowers, height to 15cm (6 in), spread 60cm (2 ft).

Helleborus purpurascens **Christmas rose**
Prefers damp soil, semi to full shade, perennial, grown for early spring flowers, height and spread 30cm (1 ft).

Lamium maculatum 'Beacon Silver' **Dead nettle**
Prefers moist, but well-drained soil, full sun to full shade, perennial, grown for flowers and foliage, height 20cm (8 in), spread 1m (3 ft).

Liriope muscari **Lilyturf**
Any well-drained soil, full to semi-shade, evergreen perennial, grown for flowers and foliage, height 30cm (1 ft), spread 45cm (18 in).

Ruta graveolens **Garden rue**
Well-drained, alkaline soil, full sun, evergreen, grown for aromatic foliage and flowers, height to 60cm (2 ft).

Santolina pinnata **Cotton lavender**
Well-drained, alkaline soil, full

sun, evergreen, grown for aromatic foliage and button-like flower heads, height 75cm (2½ ft), spread 1m (3 ft).

Sarcococca humilis **Sweet box**
Any well-drained soil, but not too dry, full sun to full shade, evergreen, grown for foliage, fragrant winter flowers, and fruits, height and spread 1.5m (5 ft).

Saxifraga **Saxifrage**
Any well-drained soil, semi to full shade, perennial, many species.

Sedum **Stonecrop**
Any well-drained soil, full sun to semi-shade, perennial, annual, or biennial, many species.

Stachys lanata **Lamb's ears**
Any well-drained soil, tolerates poor soil, full sun to semi-shade, evergreen, grown for woolly foliage, height 15cm (6 in), spread 60cm (2 ft).

Teucrium aroanium
Well-drained, alkaline soil, full sun, evergreen, grown for flowers and foliage, height 2.5cm (1 in), spread 15cm (6 in).

Thymus praecox **Thyme**
Moist, well-drained soil, full sun, evergreen, grown for aromatic foliage, height 1cm (½ in), spread indefinite.

Tiarella wherryi **Foamflower**
Any soil, semi to full shade, perennial, grown for foliage and tiny flowers, height 10cm (4 in), spread 15cm (6 in).

Vinca **Periwinkle**
Any well-drained soil, semi to full shade, evergreen, grown for foliage and flowers, height 15cm (6 in), spread indefinite.

Plants for shade

PLANTS FOR MOIST SHADE

Trees

Acer japonicum **Full-moon maple**
Well-drained, acid soil, deciduous, grown for autumn colour, height and spread 10m (30 ft).

Acer pseudoplatanus **Sycamore**
Any soil, deciduous, grown for foliage, height 30m (100 ft), spread 15m (50 ft).

Betula pendula **Silver birch**
Any well-drained soil, deciduous, grown for bark and autumn colour, height 20m (70 ft), spread 10m (30 ft).

Crataegus **Hawthorn**
Prefers damp, but not wet, soil, deciduous, grown for flowers, ornamental fruits, and autumn colour, height 10m (30 ft), spread 8m (25 ft).

Davidia involucrata **Dove tree**
Well-drained, moist soil, deciduous, grown for showy white flower bracts, height 12m (40 ft), spread 7m (22 ft).

Fraxinus **Ash**
Any well-drained soil, deciduous, grown for foliage, height 30m (100 ft), spread 20m (70 ft).

Populus canescens **Poplar**
Well-drained, moist soil, deciduous, grown for foliage and quick growth, height 25m (80 ft), spread 15m (50 ft).

Pterocarya fraxinifolia **Caucasian wing nut**
Well-drained, moist soil,

deciduous, grown for foliage and catkins, height 25m (80 ft), spread 20m (70 ft).

Quercus **Oak**
(smaller forms)
Prefers damp soil, deciduous or evergreen, grown for foliage and autumn colour, many species.

Salix babylonica
Weeping willow
Prefers damp soil, deciduous, grown for foliage and catkins, height and spread 12m (40 ft).

Shrubs and perennials

Alchemilla mollis
Lady's mantle
Prefers damp soil, perennial, grown for greenish-yellow flowers, height and spread 50cm (20 in).

Astilbe chinensis
False goat's beard
Moist soil, perennial, grown for panicles of flowers, height 30cm (1 ft), spread 20cm (8 in).

Aucuba japonica 'Gold Dust'
Well-drained, alkaline soil, evergreen shrub, grown for foliage and fruits, height and spread 2.5m (8 ft).

Camellia
Prefers damp, acid soil, evergreen shrub, grown for flowers and foliage, many species.

Clerodendrum trichotomum
Well-drained soil, deciduous, grown for showy flowers and decorative berries, height and spread 3m (10 ft).

Elaeagnus x *ebbingei*
Any well-drained soil, evergreen, grown for foliage and fragrant flowers, height and spread 5m (15 ft).

Fatsia japonica
Japanese aralia
Any well-drained soil, evergreen, grown for foliage, flowers, and fruits, height and spread 3m (10 ft).

Filipendula ulmaria
'Aurea' **Meadowsweet**
Prefers moist soil, perennial, grown for bright golden-yellow foliage, height and spread 30cm (1 ft).

Gaultheria procumbens
Moist, acid soil, evergreen shrub, grown for foliage, flowers, and fruits, height to 15cm (6 in), spread indefinite.

Hamamelis japonica
Japanese witch hazel
Prefers well-drained, acid soil, deciduous shrub, grown for autumn colour and flowers, height and spread 4m (12 ft).

Hedera colchica
Persian ivy
Any soil, evergreen perennial, grown for foliage, height 10m (30 ft), spread 5m (15 ft).

Helleborus lividus
Christmas rose
Prefers damp soil, perennial, evergreen, grown for late winter flowers, height and spread 45cm (18 in).

Hosta **Plantain lily**
Prefers damp soil, perennial, grown for foliage, many species.

Lythrum virgatum
Purple loosestrife
Moist or wet soil, perennial, grown for flowers and foliage, height 1m (3 ft), spread 60cm (2 ft).

Osmanthus decorus
Well-drained soil, evergreen shrub, grown for foliage and small fragrant flowers, height 3m (10 ft), spread 5m (15 ft).

Pachysandra terminalis
Prefers damp soil, evergreen perennial, grown for tufted foliage, useful for ground cover, height 10cm (4 in), spread 20cm (8 in).

Pieris formosa
Prefers damp, acid soil, evergreen shrub, grown for leaves that are bronze when young and profuse flowers, height and spread 4m (12 ft).

Rheum palmatum
Ornamental rhubarb
Well-drained soil, perennial, grown for foliage and striking appearance, height and spread 2m (6½ ft).

Sarcococca humilis
Sweet box
Any well-drained soil, evergreen shrub, grown for foliage, fragrant winter flowers, and fruits, height and spread 1.5m (5 ft).

Stachyurus praecox
Prefers acid soil, deciduous shrub, grown for flowers borne before leaves, height 2.5m (8 ft), spread 3m (10 ft).

Symphoricarpos albus
Snowberry
Any soil, deciduous shrub, grown for clusters of showy fruit, height and spread 2m (6½ ft).

Viburnum opulus
Guelder rose
Any not too dry soil, evergreen or deciduous shrub, grown for foliage, autumn colour, flowers, and fruits, height and spread 4m (12 ft).

Vinca major
Greater periwinkle
Any well-drained soil, evergreen shrub, grown for foliage and flowers, height 45cm (18 in), spread indefinite.

PLANTS FOR DRY SHADE

Trees

Acer palmatum
Japanese maple
Well-drained, acid soil,
deciduous, grown for autumn
colour, height and spread
6m (20 ft).

Betula pendula **Silver birch**
Any well-drained soil,
deciduous, grown for bark and
autumn colour, height 20m
(70 ft), spread 10m (30 ft).

Carpinus betulus
Common hornbeam
Prefers damp soil, deciduous,
grown for foliage, autumn
colour, and clusters of winged
nuts, height 25m (80 ft),
spread 20m (70 ft).

Gleditsia triacanthos
Honey locust
Any well-drained soil,
deciduous, grown for foliage,
height 20m (70 ft), spread
15m (50 ft).

Ilex **Holly**
Any well-drained soil,
deciduous or evergreen,
grown for foliage and berries,
many species.

Quercus **Oak**
Prefers damp soil, deciduous
or evergreen, grown for
foliage, many species.

Robinia x *ambigua*
'Decaisneana'
Any soil, accepts poor, dry
soil, deciduous, grown for
foliage and clusters of pea-like
flowers, height 15m (50 ft),
spread 10m (30 ft).

Sorbus aria **Whitebeam**
Any well-drained soil,
deciduous, grown for foliage,
flowers, fruits, and autumn
colour, height 15m (50 ft),
spread 10m (30 ft).

Shrubs and perennials

Ajuga reptans **Bugle**
Any soil, perennial, grown for
foliage and flowers, height
38cm (15 in), spread
60cm (2 ft).

Aucuba japonica
Well-drained, alkaline soil,
evergreen shrub, grown for
foliage and fruits, height and
spread 2.5m (8 ft).

Bergenia 'Silver Light'
Elephant's ears
Any well-drained soil,
evergreen perennial, grown
for foliage and flowers, height
30cm (1 ft), spread
50cm (20 in).

Brunnera macrophylla
Siberian bugloss
Any well-drained soil, grown
for flowers and foliage, height
45cm (18 in), spread
60cm (2 ft).

Buxus sempervirens
Common box
Any soil, evergreen shrub,
grown for foliage, height and
spread 5m (15 ft).

Cyclamen coum
Well-drained soil, tuberous
perennial, grown for flowers,
height and spread to
10cm (4 in).

Epimedium perralderianum
Well-drained, moist soil, semi-
evergreen perennial, grown
for flowers, height 45cm
(18 in), spread 30cm (1 ft).

Euphorbia palustris
Spurge
Well-drained soil, evergreen
perennial, grown for foliage
and flowers, height and spread
1m (3 ft).

Garrya elliptica
Silk-tassel bush
Any soil, evergreen shrub,
grown for catkins in winter and
spring, height and spread
4m (12 ft).

Geranium **Cranesbill**
Any soil, perennial, grown for
foliage and flowers, many
species.

Helleborus foetidus
Stinking hellebore
Prefers damp soil, perennial,
grown for winter and spring
flowers, height and spread
45cm (18 in).

Iris foetidissima
Stinking iris
Any soil, thrives in bog or
water garden, rhizomatous
evergreen, grown for foliage
and flowers, height to 1m
(3 ft), spread indefinite.

Lamium maculatum 'Beacon
Silver' **Dead nettle**
Moist, well-drained soil,
evergreen perennial, grown
for flowers and foliage, height
20cm (8 in), spread 1m (3 ft).

Liriope muscari
Lilyturf
Any well-drained soil,
evergreen perennial, grown
for flowers, height 30cm (1 ft),
spread 45cm (18 in).

Lonicera pileata
Honeysuckle
Any well-drained soil,
evergreen shrub, grown for
fragrant flowers, height 60cm
(2 ft), spread 2.5m (8 ft).

Lunaria annua **Honesty**
Any well-drained soil, biennial
or perennial, grown for
flowers and silvery seed pods,
height 75cm (2½ ft), spread
30cm (1 ft).

Osmanthus decorus
Well-drained soil, evergreen
shrub, grown for foliage and
fragrant flowers, height 3m
(10 ft), spread 5m (15 ft).

Polygonatum commutatum
Solomon's seal
Well-drained soil, rhizomatous perennial, grown for bell-shaped, white flowers, height 1.5m (5 ft), spread 60cm (2 ft).

Prunus laurocerasus
Common laurel
Any soil, evergreen shrub, grown for flowers and fruits, height 6m (20 ft), spread 10m (30 ft).

Pulmonaria angustifolia
Lungwort
Moist, well-drained soil, perennial, grown for flowers, height 23cm (9 in), spread to 30cm (1 ft).

Rhus typhina
Stag's horn sumach
Any well-drained soil, deciduous shrub, grown for foliage, autumn colour, and fruits, height 5m (16½ ft), spread 6m (20 ft).

Ruscus aculeatus
Butcher's broom
Any soil, evergreen shrub, grown for foliage and fruits, height 75cm (2½ ft), spread 1m (3 ft).

Sambucus racemosa
Red-berried elder
Moist soil, deciduous shrub, grown for foliage, flowers, and fruits, height and spread 3m (10 ft).

Skimmia japonica
Well-drained, moist soil, evergreen shrub, grown for flowers, aromatic foliage, and fruits, height and spread 1.5m (5 ft).

Tellima grandiflora
Fringecups
Any well-drained soil, semi-evergreen perennial, grown for foliage, height and spread 60cm (2 ft).

Tiarella cordifolia
Foamflower
Moist, well-drained soil, evergreen perennial, grown for profuse white flowers, height to 20cm (8 in), spread to 30cm (1 ft).

Vinca major
Greater periwinkle
Any well-drained soil, evergreen shrub, grown for flowers and foliage, height 45cm (18 in), spread indefinite.

Viola labradorica **Violet**
Well-drained soil, perennial, grown for distinctive flowers, height to 5cm (2 in), spread indefinite.

Waldsteinia fragarioides
Well-drained soil, semi-evergreen perennial, grown for foliage and flowers, height to 15cm (6 in), spread indefinite.

Plants for exposed sites

HOT, DRY, WINDY CONDITIONS

Berberis thunbergii 'Aurea'
Golden barberry
Any well-drained soil, full sun to semi-shade, deciduous shrub, grown for flowers and fruits, height 2m (6 ft), spread 3m (10 ft).

Chamaecyparis lawsoniana
Lawson cypress
Any soil, full sun or semi-shade, conifer, height to 25m (80 ft), spread to 4m (12 ft).

Chamaecyparis obtusa
Hinoki cypress
Any soil, full sun or semi-shade, conifer, height to 20m (70 ft), spread 5m (15 ft).

Cistus x *lusitanicus*
Rock rose
Light, well-drained soil, full sun, evergreen shrub, grown for showy flowers, height and spread 1m (3 ft).

Cytisus albus
Broom
Any well-drained soil, full sun, deciduous shrub, height 30cm (1 ft), spread 1m (3 ft).

Gaultheria procumbens
Prefers moist, acid soil, semi to full shade, evergreen shrub, grown for foliage, flowers, and fruits, height to 15cm (6 in), spread indefinite.

Genista hispanica **Spanish broom,** *G. lydia* **Bulgarian broom,** *G. pilosa* **Broom,** *G. tinctoria* **Dyer's greenwood**
Well-drained soil, full sun, deciduous shrub, grown for mass of pea-like flowers.

Lavandula angustifolia
Lavender
Well-drained, alkaline soil, full sun, evergreen shrub, grown for aromatic flowers and foliage, height and spread 60cm (2 ft).

Philadelphus 'Manteau d'Hermine' **Mock orange**
Any well-drained soil, full sun or semi-shade, deciduous shrub, grown for fragrant flowers, height 75cm (2½ ft), spread 1.5m (5 ft).

Pinus mugo
Mountain pine
Any well-drained soil, semi to full shade, conifer, height to 5m (15 ft), spread to 8m (25 ft).

Rosmarinus officinalis
Rosemary
Well-drained, alkaline soil, full sun, evergreen shrub, grown for flowers and aromatic foliage, height and spread 2m (6½ ft).

Spartium junceum
Spanish broom
Any well-drained soil, full sun, deciduous shrub, grown for green shoots and showy flowers, height and spread 3m (10 ft).

Syringa x *chinensis*
Rouen lilac
Well-drained alkaline soil, full sun, deciduous shrub, grown for fragrant flowers, height and spread 4m (12 ft).

Taxus baccata **Yew**
Any well-drained soil, full sun to full shade, conifer, height to 15m (50 ft), spread to 10m (30 ft).

Thuja occidentalis
'Rheingold' **White cedar**
Any soil, full sun or semi-shade, conifer, height and spread to 4m (12 ft).

Ulex europaeus **Gorse**
Well-drained, alkaline soil, full sun or semi-shade, almost leafless shrub, grown for flowers, height 1m (3 ft), spread 1.2m (4 ft).

Viburnum davidii
Any soil, semi to full shade, evergreen shrub, grown for foliage, autumn colour, flowers, and fruit, height 1m (3 ft), spread 1.5m (5 ft).

COLD, DRY, WINDY CONDITIONS

Acer negundo
Ash-leaved maple
Any well-drained soil, full sun or semi-shade, deciduous tree, grown for foliage and flowers, height 15m (50 ft), spread 8m (25 ft).

Berberis **Barberry**
Any well-drained soil, full sun or semi-shade, deciduous or evergreen shrub, grown for flowers and fruits, many species.

Betula pendula **Silver birch**
Any well-drained soil, full sun or semi-shade, deciduous tree, height to 20m (70 ft), spread 10m (30 ft).

Buddleia davidii
Butterfly bush
Any well-drained soil, full sun or semi-shade, deciduous shrub, grown for fragrant flowers, height and spread 5m (15 ft).

Chaenomeles speciosa
Flowering quince
Any well-drained soil, full sun or semi-shade, deciduous shrub, grown for showy flowers and fruits, height 2.5m (8 ft), spread 5m (15 ft).

Cornus alba
Red-barked dogwood
Any soil, semi to full shade, deciduous, grown for foliage and winter stems, height and spread 3m (10 ft).

Crataegus
Ornamental thorn
Prefers damp soil, full sun or semi-shade, deciduous tree, grown for flowers and fruits, height 10m (30 ft), spread 8m (25 ft).

Deutzia longifolia
Any well-drained soil, full sun or semi-shade, deciduous shrub, grown for flowers, height 2m (6 ft), spread 3m (10 ft).

Elaeagnus x *ebbingei*
Any well-drained soil, full sun, evergreen, grown for foliage and flowers, height and spread 5m (15 ft).

Euonymus
(evergreen varieties)
Any well-drained soil, full sun or semi-shade, grown for foliage, autumn colour, and fruits, many species.

Ilex **Holly**
Any well-drained soil, semi to full shade, deciduous or evergreen, grown for foliage and berries, many species.

Kerria japonica
Any soil, full sun, deciduous shrub, grown for showy yellow flowers, height and spread 3m (10 ft).

Pachysandra terminalis
Prefers damp soil, full shade, evergreen perennial, grown for tufted foliage, height 10cm (4 in), spread 20cm (8 in).

Philadelphus **Mock orange**
Any well-drained soil, full sun or semi-shade, deciduous shrub, grown for fragrant flowers, height 2.5m (8 ft), spread 1.5m (5 ft).

Potentilla **Cinquefoil**
Any well-drained soil, semi to full shade, perennial or deciduous shrub, grown for flowers, many species.

Sorbus aria **Whitebeam**
Any well-drained soil, full sun or semi-shade, deciduous tree, grown for flowers, fruits, and autumn colour, height 15m (50 ft), spread 10m (30 ft).

Spiraea prunifolia
Well-drained soil, full sun, deciduous shrub, grown for mass of small flowers, height and spread 2m (6 ft).

Tamarix gallica **Tamarisk**
Any well-drained soil, full sun, deciduous shrub, grown for foliage and flowers, height 4m (12 ft), spread 6m (20 ft).

Viburnum lantana
Wayfaring tree
Any soil, but not too dry, full

sun or semi-shade, deciduous shrub, grown for foliage, flowers, and fruits, height 5m (15 ft), spread 4m (12 ft).

Architectural plants

TREES

Acer japonicum
Full moon maple
Well-drained, acid soil, full sun or semi-shade, deciduous, grown for foliage, height and spread 10m (30 ft).

Ailanthus altissima
Tree of heaven
Well-drained soil, full sun or semi-shade, deciduous, grown for foliage, height 25m (80 ft), spread 15m (50 ft).

Catalpa bignonioides 'Aurea'
Indian bean tree
Damp, alkaline soil, full sun or semi-shade, deciduous, grown for foliage and flowers, height and spread 10m (30 ft).

Eucalyptus gunnii
Cider gum
Any well-drained soil, full sun, evergreen, grown for bark, flowers, and aromatic foliage.

Rhus typhina
Stag's horn sumach
Any well-drained soil, full sun or semi-shade, deciduous, grown for foliage and autumn colour, height 5m (16½ ft), spread 6m (20 ft).

SHRUBS

Aralia elata
Japanese angelica tree
Any well-drained soil, full sun, deciduous, grown for bold leaves and flowers, height and spread 10m (30 ft).

Arundinaria palmata
Bamboo
Any soil, semi to full shade, evergreen, grown for foliage.

Clerodendrum trichotomum
Any well-drained soil, full sun, deciduous, grown for showy flowers, height and spread 3m (10 ft).

Cordyline australis
Cabbage tree
Any well-drained soil, full sun or semi-shade, half hardy, evergreen, height 15m (50 ft), spread 5m (16½ ft).

Decaisnea fargesii
Well-drained but not dry soil, full sun, deciduous, grown for foliage, flowers, and fruits, height and spread 6m (20 ft).

Fatsia japonica
Japanese aralia
Any well-drained soil, full sun or semi-shade, evergreen, grown for foliage, flowers, and fruits, height and spread 3m (10 ft).

Magnolia grandiflora
Bull bay
Prefers damp soil, full sun, evergreen, grown for showy, fragrant flowers, height and spread 10m (30 ft).

Mahonia japonica
Any well-drained soil, full sun or semi-shade, evergreen, grown for foliage and flowers, height 2m (6½ ft), spread 3m (10 ft).

Paeonia lutea ludlowii
Tree peony
Prefers alkaline soil, full sun, deciduous, grown for large, bright green leaves as much as for flowers, height and spread up to 2.5m (8 ft).

Viburnum rhytidophyllum
Any soil, semi to full shade, evergreen, grown for foliage,

flowers, and red fruits that mature to black, height and spread 3m (10 ft).

Yucca
Well-drained, alkaline soil, full sun, evergreen, grown for bold, sword-shaped leaves, height up to 1.8m (6 ft).

PERENNIALS

Acanthus mollis
Bear's breeches
Any well-drained soil, full sun or shade, semi-evergreen, grown for large leaves and spikes of flowers, height 1.2m (4 ft), spread 45cm (18 in).

Arum italicum 'Pictum'
Lords and ladies
Well-drained soil, sun or semi-shade, grown for ornamental leaves, height up 25cm (10 in), spread to 30cm (1 ft).

Crambe maritima **Sea kale**
Well-drained soil, full sun, grown for bold leaves and large sprays of white flowers, height and spread 60cm (2 ft).

Eryngium **Sea holly**
Any well-drained soil, full sun, some species evergreen, grown for foliage and flowers.

Euphorbia characias wulfenii
Any soil, full sun to full shade, evergreen, grown for spikes of yellow-green blooms, height 1m (3 ft), spread 80cm (32 in).

Gunnera
Prefers moist soil, full sun, grown for foliage, height and spread to 1.5m (5 ft).

Helleborus lividus corsicus
Corsican hellebore
Prefers damp soil, accepts shade, evergreen, grown for winter flowers, height and spread 45cm (18 in).

Hosta
Plantain lily
Prefers damp soil, accepts shade, grown for decorative foliage, height to 1m (3 ft).

Iris foetidissima
Stinking iris
Any soil, thrives in bog or water garden, full sun to full shade, evergreen, rhizomatous, grown for flowers, height to 1m (3 ft), spread indefinite.

Libertia
Any well-drained soil, full sun to full shade, rhizomatous, grown for foliage, decorative seed pods, and flowers, height and spread 60cm (2 ft).

Onopordum acanthium
Cotton thistle
Well-drained soil, full sun, biennial, grown for foliage and spectacular overall appearance, height 1.8m (6 ft), spread 1m (3 ft).

Peltiphyllum peltatum
Umbrella plant
Prefers moist soil, full sun to full shade, grown for unusual foliage, height to 1.2m (4 ft), spread 60cm (2 ft).

Phormium tenax
New Zealand flax
Well-drained, alkaline soil, full sun, evergreen, grown for bold, sword-shaped leaves, height 3m (10 ft), spread 1–2m (3–6½ ft).

Rodgersia
Prefers moist soil, full sun or semi-shade, rhizomatous, height to 1.2m (4 ft), spread 75cm (2½ ft).

Romneya
Californian poppy
Well-drained, alkaline soil, full sun, perennial, grown for its large white flowers, height and spread 2m (6½ ft).

Sedum **Stonecrop**
Any well-drained soil, full sun to full shade, most species evergreen, grown for rosettes of fleshy leaves.

Silybum **Holy thistle**
Well-drained soil, full sun, biennial, grown for spectacular foliage, height 1.2m (4 ft), spread 60cm (2 ft).

Stipa gigantea
Golden oats
Well-drained soil, full sun to full shade, evergreen, height 2.5m (8 ft), spread 1m (3 ft).

Scented plants

Buddleia davidii
Butterfly bush
Any well-drained soil, full sun, deciduous, mostly hardy, fragrant flowers mid-summer to autumn, height and spread 5m (15 ft).

Chimonanthus praecox
Wintersweet
Well-drained, alkaline soil, full sun, deciduous, fragrant yellow flowers in winter, height 2.5m (8 ft), spread 3m (10 ft).

Convallaria majalis
Lily-of-the-valley
Prefers moist soil, semi-shade, rhizomatous perennial, fully hardy, flowers spring, height to 30cm (1 ft).

Jasminum officinale
Common white jasmine
Any well-drained soil, full sun, semi-evergreen or deciduous, twining climber, flowers summer to autumn, height to 12m (40 ft).

Lathyrus odoratus
Sweet pea
Any well-drained soil, full sun, annual climber, fully hardy, scented flowers summer to early autumn, height to 3m (10 ft).

Lilium regale **Regal lily**
Any well-drained soil, full sun, summer-flowering bulb, height to 2m (6½ ft).

Lonicera periclymenum
Common honeysuckle
Any well-drained soil, full sun or semi-shade, deciduous, twining climber, fully hardy, flowers mid to late summer, height to 7m (22 ft).

Magnolia sinensis
Prefers neutral to acid soil, full sun or semi-shade, deciduous, fully hardy, flowers late spring and early summer, height 6m (20 ft), spread 8m (25 ft).

Nicotiana alata
Tobacco plant
Any well-drained soil, full sun, grown as an annual, half hardy, flowers late summer to autumn, height 60cm (2 ft), spread 30cm (1 ft).

Prunus x *yedoensis*
Japanese flowering cherry
Any well-drained soil, full sun, deciduous, fully hardy, flowers early spring, height to 9m (27 ft), spread to 10m (30 ft).

Reseda odorata **Mignonette**
Any well-drained soil, full sun, annual, fully hardy, flowers attract bees, height to 60cm (2 ft), spread to 30cm (1 ft).

Syringa x *chinensis*
Rouen lilac
Well-drained, alkaline soil, full sun, deciduous, fully hardy, lilac-purple flowers late spring, height and spread 4m (12 ft).

Viburnum x *burkwoodii*
Prefers moist soil, full sun or semi-shade, semi-evergreen, fully hardy, flowers spring, height and spread 2.5m (8 ft).

Water plants

BOG AND WATERSIDE

Acorus calamus
Sweet flag
Open, sunny position in up to
25cm (10 in) depth of water,
semi-evergreen, perennial,
marginal water plant, height
75cm (30 in), spread
60cm (2 ft).

Aponogeton distachyos
Water hawthorn
Open sunny position in deep
water, deciduous, perennial,
grown for floating leaves and
fragrant white flowers, spread
1.2m (4 ft).

Butomus umbellatus
Flowering rush
Open, sunny position in up to
25cm (10 in) depth of water,
deciduous, perennial, rush-
like, marginal water plant,
grown for flowers, height 1m
(3 ft), spread 45cm (18 in).

Calla palustris **Bog arum**
Sunny position in mud or up to
25cm (10 in) depth of water,
semi-evergreen, perennial,
spreading marginal water
plant, grown for its foliage and
showy spathes surrounding
flower clusters, fully hardy,
height 25cm (10 in), spread
30cm (1 ft).

Caltha palustris
Marsh marigold
Open, sunny position,
deciduous, perennial, marginal
water plant, grown for
flowers, height and spread
25cm (10 in).

Juncus effusus f. *spiralis*
Corkscrew rush
Open, sunny position.
evergreen, perennial rush,
grown for twisting stems,
height 1m (3 ft), spread
60cm (2 ft).

Myosotis palustris
Water forget-me-not
Sun or semi-shade in mud or
very shallow water,
deciduous, perennial, marginal
water plant, grown for
flowers, height 15cm (6 in),
spread 30cm (1 ft).

Sagittaria sagittifolia
Common arrowhead
Open, sunny position in up to
23cm (9 in) depth of water,
deciduous, perennial, marginal
water plant, grown for foliage
and flowers, fully hardy, height
45 cm (18 in), spread
30cm (1 ft).

FLOATING AQUATICS

Azolla caroliniana
Fairy moss
Sun or shade, deciduous,
perennial, floating water fern,
grown for decorative foliage
and to control algae by
reducing light beneath water,
spread indefinite.

Eichhornia crassipes
Water hyacinth
Open, sunny position in warm
water, evergreen or semi-
evergreen, perennial, floating
water plant, spread 23cm (9 in).

Nymphaea **Water lily**
Open, sunny position in still
water, deciduous, summer-
flowering, perennial water
plant, grown for floating leaves
and flowers, many varieties.

SUBMERGED AQUATICS

Elodea densa
Canadian pondweed
Sunny position, semi-
evergreen, perennial,
spreading, submerged water
plant, grown for oxygenating
water and to provide a

depository for fish spawn.
Small white flowers in
summer. Spread indefinite.

Hottonia palustris
Water violet
Sun, clear, cool water,
deciduous, perennial,
submerged water plant, grown
for handsome foliage and
flowers, spread indefinite.

Myriophyllum aquaticum
Parrot's feather
Full sun, deciduous, perennial,
submerged water plant, grown
for foliage and to provide
depository for fish spawn,
spread indefinite.

Potamogeton crispus
Curled pondweed
Full sun, prefers cool water,
deciduous, perennial,
submerged water plant, grown
for foliage, spread indefinite.

Plants for rapid growth

Buddleia davidii
Butterfly bush
Any well-drained soil, full sun,
deciduous, grown for fragrant
flowers, grows up to 3m
(10 ft) in a season, mostly
hardy, height and spread 5m
(15 ft).

Calendula officinalis
Pot marigold
Any well-drained soil, full sun,
fast growing annual, grown for
flowers, height and spread
60cm (2 ft).

Cytisus x *praecox*
Warminster broom
Prefers well-drained but not
over-rich soil, full sun,
deciduous, grown for abundant
flowers, height 1m (3 ft),
spread 1.5m (5 ft).

Digitalis purpurea **Foxglove**
Prefers well-drained soil and semi-shade, biennial or perennial, grown for flower spikes, height to 1.5m (5 ft), spread 60cm (2 ft).

Helianthus annuus
Sunflower
Well-drained soil, full sun, fully hardy, annual, grown for large daisy-like flower heads 30cm (1 ft) or more across, height to 3m (10 ft), spread 30cm (1 ft).

Impatiens walleriana
Busy Lizzie
Moist or damp soil, full sun or semi-shade, evergreen, grown as an annual, grown for flowers, height and spread to 60cm (2 ft).

Matthiola incana
Brompton stock
Well-drained, alkaline soil, full sun or semi-shade, grown as an annual for fragrant flowers, fully hardy to frost tender, height to 60cm (2 ft), spread 30cm (1 ft).

Nemesia strumosa
Well-drained soil, full sun, annual, half hardy, grown for summer bedding, height to 45cm (18 in), spread 15cm (6 in).

Nicotiana alata
Tobacco plant
Well-drained soil, full sun, grown as an annual for fragrant flowers, height 60cm (2 ft), spread 30cm (1 ft).

Passiflora caerulea
Passion flower
Well-drained soil, full sun or semi-shade, evergreen or almost evergreen, grown for unique flowers, height 10m (30 ft).

Polygonum baldschuanicum
Russian vine
Prefers damp soil, full sun to full shade, deciduous twining climber, fully to half hardy, grows up to 3m (10 ft) in a season, height 12m (40 ft).

Tropaeolum majus
Nasturtium
Prefers poor soil, full sun, fast-growing annual, fully hardy, height 20cm (18 in), spread 30cm (1 ft).

Unusual plants for containers

BAMBOOS AND GRASSES

Arundinaria viridistriata
Bamboo
Well-drained soil, full sun, evergreen, grown for foliage and purple stems, height 1.5m (5 ft).

Carex morrowii
Japanese sedge grass
Well-drained soil, full sun, evergreen perennial sedge, grown for foliage, height and spread 20cm (18 in).

Cortaderia selloana
Pampas grass
Well-drained soil, full sun, evergreen, stately perennial grass, grown for silvery, plume-like panicles, height to 2.5m (8 ft), spread 1.2m (4 ft).

Deschampsia caespitosa
Tufted hair grass
Tolerates sun or shade, evergreen, perennial grass, grown for dainty panicles of spikelets, height to 1m (3 ft), spread to 30cm (1 ft).

Festuca glauca
Blue fescue
Any well-drained soil, full sun, evergreen perennial, grown for blue-green leaves, height and spread to 10cm (4 in).

Hakonechloa macra 'Aureola'
Well-drained soil, full sun, herbaceous rhizomatous grass, grown for green-striped yellow leaves and autumn colour, height 40cm (16 in), spread to 60cm (2 ft).

Miscanthus sacchariflorus
Amur silver grass
Well-drained soil, full sun, herbaceous rhizomatous perennial, grown for foliage, height 3m (10 ft), spread indefinite.

Molinia caerulea 'Variegata'
Variegated purple moor grass
Prefers acid soil, full sun, herbaceous perennial grass, grown for foliage and flowers, height 60cm (2 ft).

Spartina pectinata 'Aureo Marginata'
Cord grass
Moist soil, full sun, herbaceous rhizomatous grass, grown for foliage, height to 2m (6½ ft).

Stipa gigantea
Golden oats
Well-drained soil, full sun to full shade, evergreen perennial grass, grown for silvery spikelets, height 2.5m (8 ft), spread 1m (3 ft).

FERNS

Blechnum penna-marina
Moist, neutral to acid soil, semi-shade, evergreen or semi-evergreen fern, grown for foliage, height to 30cm (1 ft), spread to 45cm (18 in).

Dryopteris goldiana
Giant wood fern
Moist soil, semi to full shade, deciduous fern, grown for foliage, height 1m (3 ft), spread 60cm (2 ft).

Matteuccia struthiopteris
Ostrich feather fern
Prefers wet soil, semi-shade, deciduous rhizomatous fern, grown for foliage, height 1m (3 ft), spread 45cm (18 in).

Osmunda regalis **Royal fern**
Very wet conditions, full sun or semi-shade, deciduous fern, grown for foliage and flower spikes, height 2m (6½ ft), spread 1m (3 ft).

Phyllitis scolopendrium
Hart's tongue fern
Moist, well-drained, alkaline soil, semi-shade, evergreen fern, grown for leathery fronds, height to 75cm (30 in), spread to 45cm (18 in).

Polypodium vulgare
Common polypody
Moist, but well-drained soil, semi-shade, evergreen, creeping fern, grown for sculptural fronds, height and spread to 30cm (1 ft).

Polystichum setiferum
Soft shield fern
Moist, but well-drained soil, semi-shade, evergreen or semi-evergreen, grown for textured fronds, height 60cm (2 ft), spread 45cm (18 in).

Country garden plants

WOODY MATERIAL (SHRUBS)

Buddleia davidii
Butterfly bush
Any well-drained soil, full sun, deciduous, vigorous, arching shrub, grown for clusters of violet-purple fragrant flowers that attract bees and butterflies, height and spread 5m (15 ft).

Cistus laurifolius
Rock rose
Well-drained, alkaline soil, full sun, evergreen, grown for showy flowers and fragrant foliage, height and spread 2m (6½ ft).

Cornus alba
Red-barked dogwood
Any soil, semi to total shade, deciduous, grown for winter stems, foliage, flowers, and fruits, height and spread 3m (10 ft).

Crataegus monogyna
Common hawthorn
Prefers damp soil, full sun or semi-shade, deciduous, grown for flowers and fruits, height 10m (30 ft), spread 8m (25 ft).

Cytisus scoparius
Common broom
Any well-drained soil, full sun, deciduous, grown for abundant pea-like flowers, height 3m (10 ft), spread 1.5m (5 ft).

Daphne odora
Well-drained, alkaline soil, full sun or semi-shade, evergreen, grown for fragrant flowers, height and spread 1.5m (5 ft).

Hippophäe rhamnoides
Sea buckthorn
Any soil, full sun, deciduous, grown for foliage and showy fruit, height and spread 6m (20 ft).

Lavandula angustifolia
Lavender
Well-drained, alkaline soil, full sun, evergreen, grown for aromatic foliage and flowers, height and spread 60cm (2½ ft).

Lippia citriodora
Lemon verbena
Well-drained soil, full sun, deciduous, grown for aromatic foliage and sprays of tiny flowers, height and spread 3m (10 ft).

Lonicera periclymenum
Common honeysuckle
Any well-drained soil, full sun or semi-shade, deciduous twining climber, grown for fragrant flowers, height to 7m (22 ft).

Rosa **Shrub rose**
Any soil, full sun or semi-shade, many varieties.

Rosmarinus officinalis
Rosemary
Well-drained, alkaline soil, full sun, evergreen, grown for flowers and aromatic foliage, height and spread 2m (6½ ft).

Salvia officinalis **Sage**
Well-drained soil, full sun, evergreen or semi-evergreen shrub, grown for aromatic foliage, height 60cm (2 ft), spread 1m (3 ft).

Syringa **Lilac**
Any well-drained soil, full sun, deciduous, grown for fragrant flowers, height and spread 4m (12 ft).

ANNUALS AND PERENNIALS

Achillea millefolium **Yarrow**
Any well-drained soil, full sun, perennial, grown for flowers, height and spread 60cm (2 ft).

Alcea rosea **Hollyhock**
Well-drained soil, full sun, biennial, grown for tall spikes of flowers, height 60cm (2 ft), spread to 30cm (1 ft).

Anchusa azurea
Well-drained soil, full sun, perennial, grown for flowers, height 50cm (20 in), spread 60cm (2 ft).

Aster **Michaelmas daisy**
Any well-drained soil, full sun, perennial, grown for daisy-like

flowers that appear in late summer, many species and cultivars.

Cardamine pratensis
Cuckooflower
Moist soil, full sun or semi-shade, perennial, grown for flowers, height 45cm (18 in), spread 30cm (1 ft).

Centaurea cyanus
Cornflower
Any well-drained, even poor soil, full sun, annual, grown for flowers, height to 1m (3 ft), spread 30cm (1 ft).

Cheiranthus cheiri
Wallflower
Well-drained, alkaline soil, open position, full sun, evergreen perennial, grown for flowers, many cultivars, height to 60cm (2 ft), spread to 38cm (15 in).

Cosmos atrosanguineus
Chocolate cosmos
Moist, well-drained soil, full sun, tuberous perennial, grown for chocolate-scented flowers, height 60cm (2 ft), spread 45cm (18 in).

Delphinium **Larkspur**
Well-drained soil, open, sunny position, perennial or annual, grown for spikes of flowers, many cultivars.

Dianthus
Carnation, Pink
Any well-drained soil, full sun, perennial or annual, grown for mass of flowers, often scented, excellent for cutting, many species.

Digitalis purpurea
Foxglove
Well-drained soil, semi-shade, but will tolerate most conditions, biennial or perennial, grown for flower spikes, height to 1.5m (5 ft), spread 60cm (2 ft).

Echinops **Globe thistle**
Any soil, full sun, perennial, grown for globe-like flowers, height 1.2m (4 ft), spread 1m (3 ft).

Fragaria vesca
Wild strawberry
Well-drained soil, sun or semi-shade, perennial, grown for fruits, height to 30cm (1 ft).

Godetia
Well-drained but not rich soil, full sun, annual, grown for flowers, height to 60cm (2 ft), spread 30cm (1 ft).

Helianthus annuus
Sunflower
Well-drained soil, full sun, annual, grown for large daisy-like flower heads 30cm (1 ft) or more across, height to 3m (10 ft), spread 30cm (1 ft).

Iberis sempervirens
Candytuft
Well-drained soil, full sun, evergreen, grown for flowers, height to 30cm (1 ft), spread to 60cm (2 ft).

Lathyrus latifolius
Everlasting pea
Well-drained soil, full light, herbaceous climber, grown for flowers, height 2m (6½ ft).

Lunaria annua **Honesty**
Well-drained soil, semi-shade, biennial, grown for flowers and silvery seed pods, height 75cm (2½ ft), spread 30cm (1 ft).

Lupinus 'Thundercloud'
Lupin
Well-drained, alkaline soil, full sun, perennial, grown for flowers, height to 1.2m (4 ft), spread 45cm (18 in).

Lychnis 'Abbotswood Rose'
Well-drained soil, full sun, perennial, grown for pink flowers, height to 38cm (15 in), spread 23cm (9 in).

Lythrum salicaria
Purple loosestrife
Moist or wet soil, full sun or semi-shade, perennial, grown for flowers, height 75cm (30 in), spread 45cm (18 in).

Nepeta grandiflora **Catmint**
Moist, well-drained soil, full sun, perennial, grown as edging plant, height to 80cm (32 in), spread to 60cm (2 ft).

Nicotiana alata
Tobacco plant
Any well-drained soil, full sun, grown as an annual for fragrant flowers, height 60cm (2 ft), spread 30cm (1 ft).

Oenothera perennis
Evening primrose
Well-drained soil, full sun, perennial, grown for profuse flowers, height to 60cm (2 ft), spread 30cm (1 ft).

Phlox caespitosa
Moist, well-drained soil, full sun, evergreen perennial, grown for flowers, height 8cm (3 in), spread 12cm (5 in).

Plantago nivalis
Well-drained soil, full sun, evergreen perennial, grown for foliage and form, height in leaf 2.5cm (1 in), spread 5cm (2 in).

Primula veris **Cowslip**
Moist, well-drained soil, full sun or semi-shade, perennial, grown for flowers, height and spread 20cm (8 in).

Pulmonaria angustifolia
Lungwort
Moist, well-drained soil, semi to full shade, perennial, grown for flowers, height 23cm (9 in), spread to 30cm (1 ft).

Ranunculus ficaria
Lesser celandine
Moist, well-drained soil, sun or shade, tuberous perennial,

grown for heart-shaped leaves and flowers, height 5cm (2 in), spread to 20cm (8 in).

Reseda odorata
Mignonette
Any well-drained soil, full sun, annual, grown for flowers, which attract bees, height to 60cm (2 ft), spread 30cm (1 ft).

Saponaria officinalis
Soapwort
Well-drained soil, full sun, perennial, grown for flowers, height to 1m (3 ft), spread 30cm (1 ft).

Scabiosa atropurpurea
Sweet scabious
Well-drained, alkaline soil, full sun, annual, grown for flowers, height to 1m (3 ft), spread to 30cm (1 ft).

Solidago virgaurea
Golden rod
Well-drained soil, full sun to full shade, perennial, grown for foliage and flowers, height and spread 10cm (4 in).

Thymus praecox **Thyme**
Moist, well-drained soil, full sun, perennial, grown for aromatic leaves, height 1cm (½ in), spread indefinite.

Trifolium repens
White clover
Well-drained soil, full sun, semi-evergreen perennial, grown for foliage, height 12cm (5 in), spread 30cm (1 ft).

Valeriana officinalis
Valerian
Well-drained soil, full sun, perennial, grown for flowers, attracts cats, height to 1.2m (4 ft), spread 1m (3 ft).

Verbascum nigrum
Dark mullein
Well-drained soil, sunny, open site, but tolerates shade, perennial, grown for yellow

flowers that shoot up on narrow spikes, height 1m (3 ft), spread 60cm (2 ft).

Viola odorata **Sweet violet**
Well-drained soil, full sun to full shade, semi-evergreen perennial, grown for distinctive flowers, height 7cm (3 in), spread 15cm (6 in).

Wild flowers

Achillea millefolium
Yarrow
Hedgerow, well-drained soil, full sun, vigorous perennial, feathery leaves and flat heads of rich red flowers, height 10cm (4 in), spread 23cm (9 in).

Anthyllis vulneraria
Kidney vetch
Coastal, well-drained soil, full sun, bushy perennial, flowers usually yellow, variable species.

Campanula rotundifolia
Harebell
Hedgerow and coastal, any soil, full sun to full shade, perennial, flowers blue or violet, variable species.

Digitalis purpurea
Foxglove
Hedgerow and woodland, well-drained, moist soil, semi-shade, perennial, tall spikes of tubular flowers to 1.5m (5 ft).

Dipsacus fullonum
Teasel
Likes damp sites, biennial, prickly, height to 2m (6½ ft).

Galium verum
Lady's bedstraw
Coastal, any well-drained soil, full sun to semi-shade, perennial, golden-yellow fragrant flowers, height to 1.2m (4 ft).

Lotus corniculatus
Common bird's foot trefoil
Coastal, well-drained soil, full sun, perennial, yellow flowers, height to 50cm (20 in).

Lychnis flos-cuculi
Ragged Robin
Woodland, prefers damp soil, marshy areas, perennial, pink flowers, height to 1m (3 ft).

Myosotis arvensis
Field forget-me-not
Coastal, hedgerow, and woodland, well-drained soil, sand dunes, perennial, bright blue flowers, height to 60cm (2 ft).

Plantago lanceolata
Ribwort plantain
Well-drained soil, full sun, grassy and waste places, flowering stems to 50cm (20 in).

Sanguisorba minor
Salad burnet
Moist soil, full sun, perennial, bottle brush-like flower spikes to 1m (3 ft).

Silene alba **White campion**
Hedgerow and woodland, well-drained soil, full sun, perennial, height to 1m (3 ft).

Stachys sylvatica
Hedge woundwort
Hedgerow and woodland, poor soil, semi-shade, perennial, reddish-purple flowers, height to 1.2m (4 ft).

Broad-leaved trees

LARGE TREES (height to over 18m/60 ft)

Acer platanoides
Norway maple
Well-drained, alkaline soil, full sun or semi-shade, deciduous.

Acer pseudoplatanus
Sycamore
Any soil, full sun or semi-shade, deciduous.

Aesculus
Horse chestnut
Any well-drained soil, full sun or semi-shade, provides dense shade, deciduous.

Ailanthus altissima
Tree of heaven
Well-drained soil, full sun or semi-shade, deciduous.

Alnus **Alder**
Prefers damp soil, full sun or semi-shade, deciduous.

Carpinus
Hornbeam
Prefers damp soil, full sun or semi-shade, deciduous.

Fagus **Beech**
Well-drained, alkaline soil, full sun or semi-shade, provides dense shade, deciduous.

Fraxinus **Ash**
Any well-drained soil, full sun or semi-shade, deciduous.

Juglans regia **Walnut**
Well-drained, alkaline soil, full sun or semi-shade, provides dense shade, deciduous.

Liriodendron tulipifera
Tulip tree
Any well-drained soil, full sun or semi-shade, deciduous.

Platanus **Plane**
Any soil, full sun or semi-shade, provides dense shade, deciduous.

Populus **Poplar**
Any soil, full sun or semi-shade, deciduous.

Quercus **Oak**
Prefers damp soil, full sun or semi-shade, provides dense shade, deciduous.

Salix **Willow**
Prefers damp soil, full sun or partial shade, deciduous.

Tilia **Lime**
Any soil, full sun or semi-shade, provides dense shade, deciduous.

Ulmus **Elm**
Any soil, full sun or semi-shade, provides dense shade, deciduous.

MEDIUM-SIZED TREES (height up to 18m/60 ft)

Acer campestre **Field maple**
Any well-drained soil, full sun or semi-shade, deciduous.

Acer negundo **Box elder**
Any well-drained soil, full sun or semi-shade, deciduous.

Betula **Birch**
Any well-drained soil, full sun or semi-shade, deciduous.

Catalpa bignonioides
Indian bean tree
Damp, alkaline soil, full sun or semi-shade, provides dense shade, deciduous.

Crataegus **Hawthorn**
Prefers damp soil, full sun or semi-shade, deciduous.

Eucalyptus gunnii **Cider gum**
Any well-drained soil, full sun, evergreen.

Gleditsia
Any well-drained soil, full sun or partial shade, deciduous.

Laburnum
Golden rain
Well-drained, alkaline soil, full sun, deciduous.

Magnolia kobus
Any soil, full sun or semi-shade, deciduous.

Prunus cerasifera
Cherry plum
Any well-drained soil, full sun or semi-shade, deciduous.

Pyrus **Pear**
Acid or alkaline soil, full sun or partial shade, deciduous.

Robinia
Well-drained, alkaline soil, full sun or semi-shade, deciduous.

Sorbus aria **Whitebeam**
Any well-drained soil, full sun or semi-shade, deciduous.

SMALL TREES (height up to 10m/30 ft)

Koelreuteria paniculata
Pride of India
Well-drained, alkaline soil, full sun or semi-shade, deciduous.

Parrotia persica
Persian ironwood
Prefers alkaline soil, full sun or semi-shade, deciduous.

Prunus dulcis **Almond**
Any well-drained soil, full sun or semi-shade, deciduous.

Prunus persica **Peach**
Any well-drained soil, full sun or semi-shade, deciduous.

Prunus serrulata
Japanese cherry
Any well-drained soil, full sun or semi-shade, deciduous.

Rhus typhina
Stag's horn sumach
Any well-drained soil, full sun or semi-shade, good form, grown for foliage, autumn colour, and, in some species, fruit clusters.

Sorbus aucuparia
Mountain ash
Any well-drained soil, full sun or semi-shade, deciduous.

CONIFERS

Abies **Silver fir**
Any damp soil, full sun or semi-shade, height to over 18m (60 ft).

Cedrus **Cedar**
Any soil, full sun or semi-shade, height over 18m (60 ft).

Chamaecyparis **False cypress**
Any soil, full sun or semi-shade, height over 18m (60 ft).

Cupressus **Cypress**
Any well-drained soil, full sun or semi-shade, height up to 18m (60 ft).

Ginkgo biloba
Maidenhair tree
Any well-drained soil, prefers semi-shade, deciduous, height to over 18m (60 ft).

Juniperus **Juniper**
Any well-drained soil, full sun or semi-shade, height up to 18m (60 ft).

Metasequoia
Dawn redwood
Prefers damp soil, full sun or semi-shade, deciduous, height to over 18m (60 ft).

Picea **Spruce**
Prefers damp soil, full sun or semi-shade, height to over 18m (60 ft).

Taxodium distichum
Swamp cypress
Prefers damp soil, full sun or semi-shade, height to over 18m (60 ft).

Taxus baccata **Yew**
Any well-drained soil, full sun to total shade, height to 15m (50 ft).

Thuja plicata
Western red cedar
Any soil, full sun or semi-shade, height to 18m (60 ft).

Hedges

Berberis **Barberry**
Any well-drained soil, full sun or semi-shade, some species grow to over 3m (10 ft), evergreen and deciduous.

Carpinus **Hornbeam**
Prefers damp soil, full sun or semi-shade, height to over 3m (10 ft), deciduous.

Cotoneaster
Any soil, full sun to full shade, some species grow to over 3m (10 ft), evergreen and deciduous.

Escallonia
Well-drained soil, full sun, height to 3m (10 ft), generally evergreen.

Fagus **Beech**
Well-drained, alkaline soil, full sun or semi-shade, height to over 3m (10 ft), deciduous.

Griselinia
Well-drained, alkaline soil, full sun or semi-shade, height to over 3m (10 ft), evergreen, tender.

Hebe **Veronica**
Well-drained, alkaline soil, full sun or semi-shade, height up to 3m (10 ft), evergreen, slightly tender.

Ilex **Holly**
Any well-drained soil, semi to full shade, height to over 3m (10 ft), evergreen, tender.

Ligustrum **Privet**
Any soil, full sun to full shade, some species grow to over 3m (10 ft), evergreen or semi-evergreen, fast growing.

Olearia **Daisy bush**
Any well-drained soil, full sun or semi-shade, height up to 3m (10 ft), evergreen, tender.

Pittosporum
Any well-drained soil, full sun or semi-shade, height to over 3m (10 ft), evergreen.

Potentilla **Cinquefoil**
Any well-drained soil, semi or full shade, some species grow to over 3m (10 ft), deciduous.

Prunus lusitanica
Portuguese laurel
Any soil, semi or full shade, some species grow to over 3m (10 ft), evergreen.

Pyracantha **Firethorn**
Any well-drained soil, full sun to full shade, height to over 3m (10 ft), evergreen.

Rosmarinus officinalis
Rosemary
Well-drained, alkaline soil, full sun, some species grow to over 3m (10 ft), evergreen.

Plants for topiary

Buxus sempervirens
Common box
Any soil, full sun or semi-shade, evergreen, height and spread 5m (15 ft).

Carpinus betulus
Common hornbeam
Prefers damp soil, full sun or semi-shade, deciduous, height 25m (80 ft), spread 20m (70 ft).

Crataegus monogyna
Common hawthorn
Prefers damp soil, full sun or semi-shade, deciduous, height 10m (30 ft), spread 8m (25 ft).

Ilex aquifolium
Common holly
Any soil, semi to full shade, evergreen, grown for foliage and berries, height 8m (25 ft), spread 3.5m (12 ft).

Ligustrum ovalifolium
Privet
Any soil, full sun to full shade, evergreen or semi-evergreen, height 4m (13 ft), spread 3m (10 ft).

Lonicera nitida
Honeysuckle
Any well-drained soil, full sun or semi-shade, evergreen, height 2m (6 ft), spread 3m (10 ft).

Pyracantha **Firethorn**
Any well-drained soil, full sun to full shade, evergreen, height and spread to 3.5m (12 ft).

Rosmarinus officinalis
Rosemary
Well-drained, alkaline soil, full sun, evergreen, height and spread 1.8m (6 ft).

Taxus baccata **Yew**
Any well-drained soil, full sun to total shade, height to 15m (50 ft), spread to 10m (30 ft).

Shrubs

LARGE SHRUBS (height to over 3m/10ft, although the genus may include smaller species)

Acacia dealbata **Mimosa**
Well-drained, acid soil, full sun, good form, tender, grown for foliage and flowers.

Aralia elata
Japanese angelica tree
Any well-drained soil, full sun, strong form, slightly tender, grown for bold leaves and profuse flowers.

Arbutus
Strawberry tree
Prefers alkaline soil, full sun or semi-shade, good form, grown for foliage, flowers, and fruits.

Arundinaria **Bamboo**
Any soil, semi to full shade, good form, grown for foliage.

Aucuba japonica
Well-drained, alkaline soil, full sun to full shade, good form, grown for foliage and fruits.

Berberis **Barberry**
Any well-drained soil, full sun or semi-shade, grown for flowers and fruits.

Buddleia **Butterfly bush**
Any well-drained soil, full sun or semi-shade, grown for fragrant flowers.

Camellia japonica
Prefers damp, acid soil, semi to full shade, strong form, hardy, grown for flowers and foliage.

Ceanothus **Californian lilac**
Well-drained, alkaline soil, full sun, grown for flowers.

Chaenomeles
Flowering quince
Any well-drained soil, full sun to semi-shade, very hardy, grown for fragrant flowers and showy fruits.

Cordyline australis
Cabbage tree
Any well-drained soil, full sun or semi-shade, strong form, half hardy, grown for foliage.

Cotinus **Smoke tree**
Well-drained, alkaline soil, full sun or semi-shade, good form, grown for foliage, flower heads and autumn colour.

Cotoneaster
Any soil, full to total shade, grown for foliage, flowers, and fruits.

Cytisus **Broom**
Any well-drained soil, full sun, good form, grown for abundant flowers.

Elaeagnus
Any well-drained soil, full sun, very hardy, grown for foliage, fragrant flowers, and ornamental fruits.

Escallonia
Well-drained soil, full sun, grown for glossy foliage and profuse flowers.

Eucryphia x *nymansensis*
Prefers damp, acid soil, semi-shade, grown for foliage and fragrant flowers.

Euonymus
Any well-drained soil, full sun or semi-shade, strong form, grown for foliage, autumn colour, and fruits.

Garrya elliptica
Silk-tassel bush
Any soil, full sun or semi-shade, good form, grown for winter and spring catkins.

Genista **Broom**
Any well-drained soil, full sun, grown for flowers.

Griselinia littoralis
Well-drained, alkaline soil, full sun or semi-shade, strong form, slightly tender, grown for foliage.

Hamamelis **Witch hazel**
Prefers acid soil, full sun or semi-shade, good form, grown for autumn colour and fragrant flowers.

Helichrysum
Well-drained, alkaline soil, full sun, flowers grown for drying.

Hibiscus
Tree mallow
Well-drained, alkaline soil, full sun, grown for flowers.

Hippophäe
Any soil, full sun, good form, grown for foliage and showy fruits.

Ilex **Holly**
Any soil, semi to full shade, good form, grown for foliage and berries.

Ligustrum **Privet**
Any soil, full sun to full shade, grown for foliage and, in some species, flowers.

Magnolia
Prefers damp soil, full sun, good form, grown for fragrant flowers.

Pittosporum
Any well-drained soil, full sun or semi-shade, good form, grown for ornamental foliage and fragrant flowers.

Pyracantha **Firethorn**
Any well-drained soil, full sun to full shade, grown for foliage, flowers, and fruits.

Rhamnus alaternus
Italian buckthorn
Any soil, full sun to full shade, good form, grown for foliage and fruits.

Rhododendron
Prefers damp, neutral to acid soil, semi to full shade, some tolerate full sun, grown for species.

MEDIUM-SIZED SHRUBS (height up to 3m/10 ft)

Abelia chinensis
Prefers well-drained soil, full sun, grown for foliage and flowers.

Artemisia **Wormwood**
Well-drained, alkaline soil, full sun, grown for fern-like, silvery foliage.

Caryopteris **Blue spiraea**
Well-drained, alkaline soil, full sun to semi-shade, grown for foliage and flowers.

Choisya ternata
Mexican orange blossom
Any well-drained soil, full sun to full shade, good form, grown for foliage and flowers.

Cistus **Rock rose**
Well-drained, alkaline soil, full sun, half hardy, grown for flowers.

Cortaderia selloana
Pampas grass
Any soil, semi to full shade, grown for plume-like silvery panicles.

Deutzia
Any well-drained soil, full sun or semi-shade, grown for profuse flowers.

Fatsia japonica
Japanese aralia
Any well-drained soil, full sun or semi-shade, grown for foliage, flowers, and fruits.

Hydrangea
Prefers damp soil, semi to full shade, grown for flowers.

Hypericum
St. John's wort
Any soil, semi to full shade, grown for flowers.

Kerria japonica
Any soil, full sun, grown for showy flowers.

Laurus nobilis
Sweet bay
Any well-drained soil, full sun, good form, grown for foliage.

Lonicera **Honeysuckle**
Any well-drained soil, full sun or semi-shade, grown for fragrant flowers and climbing habit.

Mahonia
Any well-drained soil, full sun or semi-shade, good form, grown for foliage, flowers, and, in some species, bark.

Myrtus communis **Myrtle**
Well-drained, alkaline soil, full sun, half hardy, grown for flowers, fruits, and aromatic foliage.

Olearia **Daisy bush**
Any well-drained soil, full sun or semi-shade, strong form, grown for foliage and daisy-like flowers.

Paeonia **Tree peony**
Prefers alkaline soil, full sun, grown for bold foliage and showy blooms.

Philadelphus **Mock orange**
Any well-drained soil, full sun or semi-shade, grown for fragrant flowers.

Phormium tenax
New Zealand flax
Well-drained, alkaline soil, full sun, good form, grown for bold leaves.

Pieris
Prefers damp soil, semi-shade, grown for foliage and unusual flowers.

Potentilla **Cinquefoil**
Any well-drained soil, semi to full shade, grown for foliage and flowers.

Romneya
Californian poppy
Well-drained, alkaline soil, full sun, good form, grown for flowers.

Rosa **Shrub rose**
Any soil, full sun or semi-shade, grown for flowers.

Rosmarinus officinalis
Rosemary
Well-drained, alkaline soil, full sun, strong form, grown for flowers, and aromatic foliage.

Rubus
Ornamental bramble
Prefers fertile, well-drained

soil, full sun to full shade, grown for foliage, flowers, or ornamental stems.

Santolina **Cotton lavender**
Well-drained, alkaline soil, full sun, half hardy, grown for aromatic foliage and flowers.

Senecio
Any well-drained soil, full sun, good form, grown for foliage and daisy-like flowers.

Spartium junceum
Spanish broom
Any well-drained soil, full sun, good form, grown for green shoots and showy flowers.

Syringa **Lilac**
Any well-drained soil, full sun, grown for fragrant flowers.

Ulex europaeus **Gorse**
Well-drained, alkaline soil, full sun or semi-shade, grown for spring flowers.

Viburnum
Any soil, semi to full shade, grown for flowers and foliage.

Weigela
Any well-drained soil, full sun or semi-shade, grown for showy flowers.

Yucca
Well-drained, alkaline soil, full sun, good form, grown for bold, sword-shaped leaves.

SMALL SHRUBS (height up to 1.5m/5 ft)

Ceratostigma
Well-drained, alkaline soil, full sun, grown for flowers and autumn colour.

Chimonanthus **Wintersweet**
Well-drained, alkaline soil, full sun, slightly tender when young, grown for flowers.

Convolvulus cneorum
Well-drained, alkaline soil, full sun, good form, grown for flowers.

Daphne
Well-drained, alkaline soil, full sun or semi-shade, grown for fragrant flowers and, in some species, foliage or fruits.

Lavandula **Lavender**
Well-drained, alkaline soil, full sun, grown for aromatic foliage and flowers.

Nandina domestica
Sacred bamboo
Well-drained, alkaline soil, full sun, good form, half hardy, grown for foliage and flowers.

Pachysandra terminalis
Prefers damp soil, full shade, grown for tufted foliage.

Pernettya mucronata
Prefers acid soil, full shade, good form, grown for showy fruits.

Perovskia
Well-drained, alkaline soil, full sun, strong form, grown for aromatic foliage and flowers.

Phlomis fruticosa
Well-drained, alkaline soil, strong form, grown for foliage and flowers.

Sarcococca humilis
Sweet box
Any well-drained soil, full sun to full shade, grown for foliage, fragrant winter flowers, and spherical nuts.

Skimmia japonica
Well-drained, moist soil, full sun to full shade, good form, grown for flowers, foliage, and fruits.

Teucrium fruticans
Shrubby germander
Well-drained, alkaline soil, full sun, grown for deep blue flowers and grey-green, sometimes aromatic foliage.

Bulbs

Allium beesianum
Any soil, full sun, flowers late summer, height to 30cm (1 ft), spread to 10cm (4 in).

Anemone blanda
Windflower
Any soil, full sun or semi-shade, flowers early spring, height to 10cm (4 in), spread to 15cm (6 in).

Chionodoxa sardensis
Glory of the snow
Any soil, full sun or semi-shade, flowers winter to early spring, height to 20cm (8 in), spread to 5cm (2 in).

Colchicum autumnale
Autumn crocus
Any well-drained soil, full sun, flowers autumn, height and spread to 15cm (6 in).

Crinum bulbispermum
Well-drained, acid soil, full sun or semi-shade, bears pink flowers with dark red stripes in summer, height to 1m (3 ft), spread 60cm (2 ft).

Crocus
Any soil, full sun or semi-shade, flowers spring or autumn, many species.

Eranthis hyemalis
Winter aconite
Any soil, full sun, flowers early spring, height and spread to 10cm (4 in).

Fritillaria meleagris
Snake's head fritillary
Any soil, full sun or semi-shade, flowers spring, height to 30cm (1 ft), spread to 8cm (3 in).

Galanthus nivalis
Common snowdrop
Alkaline soil, full sun or semi-shade, flowers winter to early spring, height to 15cm (6 in), spread to 8cm (3 in).

Galtonia candicans
Summer hyacinth
Any well-drained soil, full sun, flowers summer, height to 1.2m (4 ft), spread to 23cm (9 in).

Hyacinthus orientalis
Hyacinth
Any well-drained soil, full sun or semi-shade, flowers spring, height to 20cm (8 in), spread to 10cm (4 in).

Leucojum roseum
Snowflake
Any well-drained soil, full sun, flowers early autumn, height to 10cm (4 in), spread to 5cm (2 in).

Lilium candidum
Madonna lily
Any well-drained soil, full sun, flowers summer, strongly scented, height to 2m (6½ ft).

Muscari comosum
Tassel grape hyacinth
Any well-drained soil, full sun or semi-shade, flowers late spring, height to 30cm (1 ft), spread 12cm (5 in).

Narcissus **Daffodil**
Any well-drained soil, full sun or semi-shade, flowers spring, many species.

Nerine masonorum
Any well-drained soil, semi-shade, flowers late summer, mostly tender, height to 20cm (8 in), spread to 10cm (4 in).

Scilla non-scripta **Bluebell**
Well-drained, alkaline soil, full sun or semi-shade, flowers spring, height to 40cm (16 in), spread to 10cm (4 in).

Perennials

Acanthus venustum
Bear's breeches
Any well-drained soil, full sun or shade, strong form, grown for leaves and spikes of flowers, height and spread 10cm (4 in).

Achillea millefolium **Yarrow**
Any well-drained soil, full sun, strong form, grown for plate-like flower heads, height and spread 60cm (2 ft).

Agapanthus africanus
African lily
Any well-drained soil, full sun, needs frost protection, strong form, grown for flowers, height 1m (3 ft), spread 50cm (20 in).

Alchemilla mollis
Lady's mantle
Prefers damp soil, accepts shade, strong form, grown for foliage and greenish-yellow flowers, height and spread 50cm (20 in).

Anemone japonica
Japanese anemone
Any well-drained soil, full sun or shade, good form, grown for flowers, height 1.5m (5 ft), spread 60cm (2 ft).

Aster sedifolius
Michaelmas daisy
Any well-drained soil, full sun, grown for daisy-like flower heads, height 1m (3 ft), spread 60cm (2 ft).

Bergenia cordifolia
Elephant's ears
Any well-drained soil, accepts shade, grown for flowers, height 45cm (18 in), spread 60cm (2 ft).

Brunnera macrophylla
Siberian bugloss
Any well-drained soil, full sun,

grown for flowers, height 45cm (18 in), spread 60cm (2 ft).

Campanula persicifolia
Bellflower
Prefers damp soil, full sun to full shade, grown for bell-shaped flowers, height 1m (3 ft), spread 30cm (1 ft).

Chrysanthemum
Any well-drained soil, full sun, grown for flowers, many species and cultivars.

Dianthus **Carnation, Pink**
Any well-drained soil, full sun, grown for flowers, often scented, many species and cultivars.

Dierama pumilum
Angel's fishing rod
Prefers damp soil, full sun, strong form, half hardy, height 75cm (30 in), spread 30cm (1 ft).

Digitalis purpurea **Foxglove**
Any well-drained soil, semi-shade, grown for summer flower spikes, height to 1.5m (5 ft), spread 60cm (2 ft).

Echinops 'Taplow Blue'
Globe thistle
Any soil, full sun, strong form, grown for globe-like, spiky flower heads, height 1.2m (4 ft), spread 1m (3 ft).

Euphorbia **Spurge**
Any soil, full sun to full shade, good form, grown for flowers and foliage, many species.

Gaillardia pulchella
Any well-drained soil, full sun, hardy, grown for flowers, height 45cm (18 in), spread 30cm (1 ft).

Geranium **Cranesbill**
Any soil, full sun or semi-shade, grown for foliage and attractive flowers, many species.

Helenium 'Bressingham Gold'
Sneezewort
Any soil, full sun, grown for
sprays of daisy-like flower
heads, height 1m (3 ft), spread
60cm (2 ft).

Helleborus lividus
Christmas rose
Prefers damp soil, accepts
shade, good form, grown for
winter and spring flowers,
height and spread 45cm (18 in).

Hemerocallis fulva
Tawny daylily
Any soil, accepts shade,
grown for flowers, height 1m
(3 ft), spread 75cm (2½ ft).

Hosta **Plantain lily**
Prefers damp soil, accepts
shade, good form, grown for
decorative foliage, many
species.

Iris
Any soil, full sun to full shade,
good form, grown for
distinctive and colourful
flowers, many species.

Libertia ixioides
Any well-drained soil, full sun
to full shade, strong form,
grown for foliage, decorative
seed pods, and flowers, height
and spread 60cm (2 ft).

Macleaya cordata
Plume poppy
Any well-drained soil, full sun
to full shade, strong form,
grown for overall appearance,
height 1.5m (5 ft), spread
60cm (2 ft).

Oenothera perennis
Evening primrose
Well-drained soil, full sun,
grown for profuse flowers,
height to 60cm (2 ft), spread
30cm (1 ft).

Paeonia **Peony rose**
Prefers damp soil, full sun to
full shade, good form, grown

for bold foliage, showy blooms
and colourful seed pods, many
species.

Papaver orientale
Oriental poppy
Any well-drained soil, full sun,
grown for cup-shaped flowers,
height 1m (3 ft), spread to
1m (3 ft).

Phlox maculata
Prefers damp soil, accepts
shade, grown for flowers,
height 1m (3 ft), spread
45cm (18 in).

Rheum palmatum
Ornamental rhubarb
Well-drained soil, full sun to
full shade, strong form, grown
for foliage and striking overall
appearance, height and spread
2m (6½ ft).

Rudbeckia fulgida
Coneflower
Any well-drained soil, full sun
to full shade, grown for flower
heads, excellent for cutting,
height 1m (3 ft), spread
60cm (2 ft).

Sedum **Stonecrop**
Any well-drained soil, full sun
to full shade, good form,
grown for fleshy foliage and
flowers, many species.

Sisyrinchium striatum
Any well-drained soil, full sun,
good form, grown for foliage
and flowers, height to 60cm
(2 ft), spread to 30cm (1 ft).

Stachys lanata **Lamb's ears**
Any well-drained soil, full sun
to full shade, good form,
grown for woolly leaves,
height 15cm (6 in), spread
60cm (2 ft).

Veronica cinerea **Speedwell**
Any soil, full sun to full shade,
grown for flowers, height
15cm (6 in), spread
30cm (1 ft).

Zantedeschia aethiopica
Arum lily
Prefers damp soil, full sun to
full shade, good form, grown
for foliage and yellow spadix
produced in white spathe,
height to 40cm (16 in), spread
30cm (1 ft).

Annuals

Ageratum **Floss flower**
Prefers damp soil, full sun, half
hardy, grown for flowers,
height and spread to 30cm (1 ft).

Alyssum maritimum
Any well-drained soil, full sun,
half hardy, grown for flowers,
height to 15cm (6 in), spread
to 30cm (1 ft).

Antirrhinum **Snapdragon**
Any well-drained soil, full sun,
half hardy, grown for flowers,
height to 1m (3 ft), spread to
45cm (18 in).

Cheiranthus cheiri
Wallflower
Well-drained, alkaline soil, full
sun, hardy, grown for flowers,
height to 60cm (2 ft), spread
to 38cm (15 in).

Chrysanthemum
Any well-drained soil, full sun,
grown for flowers, many
species and cultivars.

Dianthus **Carnation, Pink**
Any well-drained soil, full sun,
grown for flowers, often
scented, many species.

Dimorphotheca annua
Cape marigold
Any well-drained soil, full sun,
hardy, grown for flowers,
height to 30cm (1 ft), spread
15cm (6 in).

Eschscholzia caespitosa
Poppy
Any well-drained soil, full sun,

hardy, grown for poppy-like flowers, height and spread 15cm (6 in).

Helianthus annuus
Sunflower
Well-drained soil, full sun, hardy, grown for large flower heads, height to 3m (10 ft), spread to 30cm (1 ft).

Iberis umbellata
Candytuft
Any well-drained soil, full sun, or semi-shade, hardy, grown for flowers, height to 30cm (1 ft), spread 20cm (8 in).

Limnanthes douglasii
Meadow foam
Any well-drained soil, full sun, hardy, grown as edging plants, height 15cm (6 in), spread 10cm (4 in).

Lunaria annua
Honesty
Any soil, semi-shade, biennial, grown for flowers and silvery seed pods, height 75cm (2½ ft), spread 30cm (1 ft).

Mesembryanthemum criniflorum **Ice plant**
Any well-drained soil, full sun, half hardy, grown for flowers, height 15cm (6 in), spread 30cm (1 ft).

Moluccella laevis
Shell flower
Any soil, full sun, grown for flowers for drying, height 60cm (2 ft), spread 20cm (8 in).

Pelargonium
Geranium
Any soil, semi-shade, over-winter indoors for following year, grown for colourful flowers, many species.

Reseda odorata
Mignonette
Any well-drained soil, alkaline soil, full sun, perennial in mildest areas, grown for

fragrant flowers that attract bees, height to 60cm (2 ft), spread 30cm (1 ft).

Silybum marianum
St. Mary's thistle
Any well-drained soil, full sun, hardy biennial, grown for spectacular foliage, height 1.2m (4 ft), spread 60cm (2 ft).

Tropaeolum majus
Nasturtium
Prefers poor soil, full sun, hardy, grown for brightly coloured flowers, height 20cm (8 in), spread 30cm (1 ft).

Herbs

Allium schoenoprasum
Chives
Moist, well-drained soil, full sun or semi-shade, hardy perennial, cut leaves for re-growth, height to 25cm (10 in), spread to 10cm (4 in).

Anethum graveolens **Dill**
Well-drained soil, full sun, protect from wind, hardy annual, gather leaves when young, height to 1.5m (5 ft).

Anthemis nobilis
Perennial chamomile
Light, well-drained soil, full sun, hardy evergreen perennial, gather leaves as needed, height to 30cm (1 ft).

Carum carvi **Caraway**
Rich loam, full sun, hardy biennial, gather leaves when young, seed heads in late summer, height to 20cm (8 in) first year, 60cm (2 ft) second year.

Hyssopus officinalis **Hyssop**
Light, well-drained, alkaline soil, full sun, hardy, semi-evergreen shrub, pick flowers as they appear, pick leaves as needed, height to 1.2m (4 ft).

Melissa officinalis
Lemon balm
Moist soil, full sun with midday shade, hardy herbaceous perennial, pick leaves as needed, especially as flowers begin to open, height to 1m (3 ft).

Monarda didyma
Bergamot
Moist soil, sun or semi-shade, hardy herbaceous perennial, collect leaves in spring or summer when flowers form, height to 1m (3 ft).

Ocimum basilicum **Basil**
Moist, well-drained soil, warm sun, midday shade, tender annual, pick leaves when young, height to 45cm (18 in).

Origanum majorana
Sweet marjoram
Well-drained, alkaline soil, full sun, midday shade, half-hardy perennial, pick young leaves as needed, height to 60cm (2 ft).

Rosmarinus officinalis
Rosemary
Well-drained soil, sunny position, hardy evergreen shrub, pick leaves all year round, height to 2m (6½ ft).

Salvia officinalis **Sage**
Well-drained soil, full sun, hardy evergreen shrub, pick leaves just before flowers appear, height to 60cm (2 ft).

Symphytum officinale
Comfrey
Neutral soil, rich in nitrogen, full sun, hardy, herbaceous perennial, pick leaves in midsummer, height to 1.2m (4 ft).

Tanacetum vulgare **Tansy**
Any soil, but not too wet, full sun or semi-shade, hardy, herbaceous perennial, pick leaves as needed, height to 1.5m (5 ft).

INDEX

Figures in italics refer to illustrations.

ACKNOWLEDGMENTS

Designers: Paul Cooper, Steve Wilson, Marie Chung
Editor: Jane Rollason
Typesetter: Goodfellow & Egan, Cambridge
Reproduction: Colourscan, Singapore

Dorling Kindersley
Managing editor: Jemima Dunne
Managing art editor: Philip Lord
Editor: Victoria Sorzano
Production: Helen Creeke

Photographic credits
(t=top, b=bottom, c=centre, l=left, r=right)
Boys Syndication pp. 22t, 26, 56; John Brookes pp. 7, 20, 63, 117, 156, 178, 196;
Camera Press pp. 30, 35b, 62, 92, 135; Eric Crichton pp. 146tl, 152br, 154tc, 155l, 157tc,
157bl, 157br, 159tl, 159bc, 163tr, 165tl, 167l, 167c, 170tl, 170tr, 179tc, 179bl, 179br,
181c, 186bl, 189l, 189r; Geoff Dann pp. 12, 14, 21, 28, 32t, 32b, 36, 82, 83, 84tl, 84tr,
85tl, 85tr, 85c, 85b, 99, 100, 106, 111, 113, 119, 132cr, 132bl, 136, 143c, 143b, 144, 145,
164, 184br; John Glover pp. 146bc, 152br, 154bl, 154br, 157tr, 159br, 179tl, 179tr;
Pamela J. Harper pp. 16, 24, 40; Jerry Harpur pp. 146tr, 146bl, 146br, 149tl, 149tc, 149bl,
149bc, 152bl, 154tl, 154tr, 155c, 155tr, 157tl, 157bc, 159tr, 159bl, 163tl, 163bc, 165tc,
165tr, 165bl, 167r, 170tc, 170bl, 170bc, 170br, 179bc, 181l, 181r, 184tl, 184tc, 184tr,
184bl, 184bc, 186bc, 186br; Neil Holmes Photography pp. 54, 152bl, 154bc, 165br;
Jacqui Hurst pp. 15b, 107, 133, 153; Impact Photos pp. 15t, 140, 175; Dave King p. 189c;
Andrew Lawson p. 163bl; Georges Leveque p. 73;
Michael McKinley p. 71; Tania Midgley (Vision International) pp. 19c, 19r;
Ivan Ruperti p. 50; Harry Smith Collection pp. 177, 190;
Pamela Toler pp. 38, 48, 134; Elizabeth Whiting & Associates pp. 19l, 22bl, 22br, 42, 43,
44, 46, 64, 69, 86, 95r, 95l, 96, 115, 124, 126, 127 128, 129, 161, 167tr;
Steven Wooster pp. 77, 103, 123, 148bl, 148br, 162;
George Wright p. 139